*A Soldier's Wife*
# WELLINGTON'S MARRIAGE

Joan Wilson

WEIDENFELD AND NICOLSON · LONDON

Copyright © by Joan Wilson 1987

First published in Great Britain by
George Weidenfeld & Nicolson Limited
91 Clapham High Street
London SW4 7TA

All rights reserved. No part of this publication
may be reproduced, stored in a retrieval system,
or transmitted, in any form or by any means,
electronic, mechanical, photocopying, recording
or otherwise, without the prior permission of
the copyright holder.

ISBN 0 297 791 710

Printed in Great Britain at The Bath Press, Avon

# Contents

List of Illustrations vii
Preface ix
Acknowledgements xi
Introduction by Elizabeth Longford xiii

1 Patrimony and Politics 1
2 Lord Longford's 'Determination' 10
3 The Storm 16
4 Rebellion 23
5 Letter to India 41
6 Matrimonial Dilemma 51
7 'Chance of her Favour ...' 58
8 Business at Home 64
9 Five Dublin Days 79
10 An Enemy's Country 89
11 The House in the Park 100
12 'Till my Husband Returns' 116
13 The Public Gaze 130
14 Homecoming 144

Maps: Eighteenth-century Dublin 3
       Ireland in 1806 24

Appendix 1 Relationships 163
Appendix 2 Family Trees 168
Appendix 3 Wellington's Career (Summary) 173
Manuscript and Published Sources 175
Index 181

# *Illustrations*

Elizabeth, Countess of Longford (Duke of Wellington, Stratfield Saye)
Edward, 2nd Baron Longford (Duke of Wellington, Stratfield Saye)
The Edgeworth family (by kind permission of Mrs M. A. E. Butler)
The Hon. Arthur Wellesley (Duke of Wellington, Stratfield Saye)
Catherine (Kitty) Pakenham, Viscountess Wellington (Duke of Wellington, Stratfield Saye)
Pakenham Hall (by kind permission of Mr Thomas Pakenham)
Edward Pakenham
Hercules Pakenham (Duke of Wellington, Stratfield Saye)
The Upper Court, Dublin Castle
Lady Olivia Sparrow
General Sir Galbraith Lowry Cole
The Irish Packet off Liverpool
A bill from Robert Birchall's 'Musical Circulating Library' (Duke of Wellington, Stratfield Saye)
Arthur (Douro) and Charles Wellesley (Duke of Wellington, Stratfield Saye)
The Pantiles, Tunbridge Wells (by kind permission of Tunbridge Wells Borough Council)
Spoof letter written by Kitty to Margaret Packer (Duke of Wellington, Stratfield Saye)
Arthur, Marquis Wellington (Duke of Wellington, Stratfield Saye)
Catherine, Duchess of Wellington (Duke of Wellington, Stratfield Saye)
Water-colour of spring flowers by Kitty (Duke of Wellington, Stratfield Saye)

# *Preface*

The career of Arthur Wellesley, 1st Duke of Wellington, has been so often brilliantly discussed, analysed and chronicled that it might be thought there is nothing more to say on the subject. But there is. One vital aspect of his life has been underplayed or dismissed with a few perfunctory lines – his marriage. What is known of Wellington's wife, apart from the received opinion that she was not a success and he had been 'forced' into marriage through the machinations of an interfering go-between?

This explanation of how Kitty Pakenham became his wife is not borne out by the letters he wrote over a period of years to Kitty's friend Olivia Sparrow, from India. Nor is it in keeping with his character. He was little concerned with public opinion; did not easily submit to pressure from friend or foe. He was essentially his own man, his decisions the result of a careful weighing of the facts and probabilities.

In examining from the surviving evidence the circumstances that led to Wellington's marriage, it is clear that his courtship of Kitty Pakenham, and his initial rejection by the Longford family, was a goad that changed him from a happy-go-lucky ADC to a soldier dedicated to efficiency and success. Without this goad, what would he have been? What would have been the history of Europe in the nineteenth century?

It is ironical that this 'failure' in his youth was the motive behind his gruelling dedication to work over many years in India. When military and financial success was eventually achieved and he returned to England 'for one purpose only' (to marry Kitty), the achievement of this purpose, so long postponed, was a personal disaster for them both.

Yet, once more, failure in private life stimulated him to further military success. Would his years in the Peninsula, without a single period of leave in England, have proved so dedicated to victory if he had been happily married?

This is a study of Wellington and his wife; why they married and why the marriage began to disintegrate from the very beginning. It is the reverse of the public image of the Great Duke: a private view of small events, not scandalous or disgraceful, but sad, that shaped the lives of two people over the eventful years of 1790 to 1814. Courage and the power to endure are the attributes of a soldier – here they can be applied to the soldier's wife.

# Acknowledgements

In collecting information on the courtship and marriage of Arthur Wellesley and Kitty Pakenham, I have been fortunate to have access to letters and family records in the archives at Stratfield Saye, recorded and in some cases collected by Gerald, 7th Duke of Wellington. The present and 8th Duke has maintained this family interest and added to the historic collection as opportunity occurred. I am most grateful to him for permission to study the personal papers of the 1st Duke and his wife.

The most recent and definitive biography of the Great Duke is by Elizabeth Longford and I have quoted extensively from her absorbing books, *Wellington. The Years of the Sword* and *Wellington. Pillar of State*. I am also personally indebted to the author for encouragement and advice in commencing this work, intimately concerned with an ancestor of the Longford family.

I would like to thank Thomas Pakenham for his patient introduction to the complexities of Pakenham family relationships and for suggesting sources of relevant unpublished material in the National Library of Ireland and the Public Record Office, Northern Ireland. The staff of both these institutions have been unfailing in their help with my inquiries, as have the staff of the London Library and of the Manuscripts Department, British Library.

I recall with gratitude a visit to the residence of the United States Ambassador in Phoenix Park, Dublin, formerly Secretary's Lodge; and in particular Mrs Elizabeth Shannon's kindness in sharing her knowledge of her home with me.

I am grateful to Lord Bathurst for information on the Bathurst Papers and to Desmond Guinness and Sir John Ainsworth for their assistance.

## *Acknowledgements*

In the early stages of the work, the Hon. Georgina Stonor provided essential information and encouragement. Suggestions and ideas on presentation from the Marchioness of Douro, Kitty's great-great-great-granddaughter (by marriage), gave the final impetus to complete the project.

To assist the reader, additional punctuation has been added where required in quotations from original documents.

Stratfield Saye,
September 1986

# Introduction by Elizabeth Longford

This is the story of a marriage. Not a successful one but one of unusual interest. Arthur and Kitty Wellington led the life of a married couple for twenty-five years, from their curious wedding day in a Dublin drawing-room on 10 April 1806 to Kitty's death at Apsley House, 'No 1 London', on 24 April 1831. But, as the author makes clear in her stimulating Preface, the story begins in 1790 when the foundations of the marriage were laid – though 'foundations' is perhaps too solid a word for me to use of such a flimsy structure – and concludes when Wellington came home after five solid years' absence – that was solid, at any rate – in the Peninsula. There were other not inconsiderable absences, also, during the first eight years of their 'married' life. By 1814 the marriage, argues Joan Wilson, was virtually over.

Joan Wilson feels that justice has not been done to Kitty Pakenham, as the 1st Duchess of Wellington was born. Indeed, Kitty's part in the marriage has hitherto formed just one aspect of her famous husband's numerous biographies. Through more extensive use of Kitty's diary than any previous biographer, Joan Wilson has succeeded in 'isolating' the viruses at work in this marriage and in studying them scientifically during the make-or-mar period. Working as Archivist on the Wellington family papers through fruitful years, she has produced new material in the shape of unpublished documents, and new insights into the central problem. Above all, her close connection with the family has enabled her to write about both Arthur and Kitty without prejudice and, as it were, as a friend.

For instance, she is loth to debit Arthur with a piece of notorious insensitivity. When he saw Kitty again – to marry her – for the first time after their forced parting twelve years earlier, he whispered to his brother the Revd Gerald Wellesley (the officiating clergyman), 'She's grown ugly, by Jove!' (I hope she will forgive me for believing the story. After all, it can have emanated only from the Revd Gerald, who was to become Prebendary of Durham.)

What went wrong with the marriage? Arthur's first two proposals to Kitty were turned down by her family on the grounds of his financial and other inadequacies. Joan Wilson then shows that, owing to the excessively long parting of the lovers, Kitty and Arthur built up an exaggerated memory of each other's virtues over the years. And because they never met again until they married, they were unable to appreciate the different people they had respectively become: Arthur dedicated to the public service instead of to her; Kitty no longer the strong character she had seemed when the toast of Dublin Castle in its heyday, before the crushing blow of the Union.

Arthur's consequent disappointment in and neglect of Kitty was balanced by Kitty's neglect of her household duties, sometimes carried as far as falsifying the accounts and resulting in one misappropriation for which he never forgave her. Where Arthur was unkind to Kitty, she in turn was uncharitable about his friends.

Because of his neglect of her during the Peninsula War, writing few letters and never returning on leave, she was afraid to mix in society. For in so doing she would expose her ignorance of his position and lack of newsy letters. This withdrawal was to become a habit. Conversely, when she did meet his special young friend Lord Burghersh, we find her calling him 'an insignificant, chattering blockhead'.

Yet despite all this, Joan Wilson discovers a positive gain in the situation, at least for Arthur. His first proposals to Kitty having been vetoed by her family, he was 'goaded' into a military career. As for Kitty, she loved him to the end. And loving has its own way of making people happy.

Kitty has long deserved a biography of her own. This graceful study of a hero's wife, though never underplaying the sombre issues, is always handled with a light touch. I am glad that it should be the work of a scholarly and perceptive woman.

# CHAPTER 1

# *Patrimony and Politics*

Kitty Pakenham, the Hon. Catherine Dorothea Sarah Pakenham, was born in January 1772, in Ireland, the second of nine children, at Pakenham Hall (now known as Tullynally Castle), seat of the Longford family for three hundred years, near the small town of Castlepollard some sixty miles west of Dublin.

Her father, Edward Michael, 2nd Baron Longford, was a bluff, good-tempered, enlightened landowner and Post Captain in the Royal Navy. Her mother, also named Catherine, was the daughter of the Rt Hon. Hercules Langford Rowley (the similarity of the names, Langford and Longford, on different sides of the family, could be confusing). She was a woman of deep religious belief, in the Anglo-Irish Protestant tradition; strong-willed, intolerant, with a quick temper; yet she enjoyed the devotion of her large family and was a popular hostess in County Westmeath and at their town house in Dublin.

Little is known of Kitty Pakenham's early years – the family records having been destroyed in a fire at Langford Lodge, a property on the banks of Lough Neagh, some years ago. The household was a large and happy one, providing a home not only for the immediate family but for other relatives. Kitty's upbringing and education were greatly influenced by her paternal grandmother, Elizabeth, Countess of Longford in her own right, daughter and sole heiress of Michael Cuffe MP, who spent her long widowhood at Pakenham Hall. Elizabeth not only brought a fortune to her husband's family on their marriage but also a fine library, which she augmented and cared for throughout her long life. This charming and cultivated woman made a favourite of her little grandchild Kitty, encouraging her love of reading, as she had done for other young people in the neighbourhood. Her most notable success was with her young relative Richard Lovell Edgeworth, inventor and man of science, who admitted that without her influence he might have devoted his life to 'sport and frivolity' instead of academic achievement.[1] He fathered a large family. The unfortunate demise of one spouse after another did not deter the widower from replacing each helpmate, after a decent interval, with another admirable lady, who would take up the housekeeping duties, frequent pregnancies and motherly responsibilities for numerous stepchildren, some little younger than she, with uncomplaining efficiency. His eldest daughter, Maria, achieved international fame as an author and authority on education; Sir Walter Scott paid tribute to the influence of her character-sketches on his work. Maria had great affection for the Pakenham family and was a frequent visitor to the house which she called 'the seat of hospitality and the resort of refined society'.[2]

Kitty was Maria's particular favourite, although some four years her junior; the younger girl's high spirits, slim figure, expressive grey eyes, unruly curls and flawless complexion contrasting with Maria's dark hair and skin and her somewhat staid and solid appearance. Both were short, but Kitty's lack of height was appealing – her slightly imperious manner, dogmatic statements and intolerance, of which the rather heavy jaw-line and Pakenham chin might have given warning, would have been less acceptable in a taller woman. Coming from this charming miniature, her faults could not be taken seriously; so much spirit from so small a person could only be admired.

They both shared a quick intelligence but Kitty lacked the power of concentration, of detached, analytical thought and expression which distinguished Maria's conversation and writings. Both enjoyed a joke and could laugh at human weakness. Both were gossips, but whereas Kitty could never keep a secret, Maria's indiscretions were often deliberate, while she observed and recorded the result. Kitty's unthinking revelations were a danger to her friends, although without malice and regretted as soon as uttered. Yet she could converse with great seriousness on moral issues, enjoyed reading sermons and discourses on religious matters nearly as much as the latest romance. She professed high and romantic standards of behaviour, condemned deception and fearlessly exposed weakness of principle in others, for their own good. Her impulsive generosity was a byword among the needy and the rogues.

In those happy days, after her presentation at the Viceregal Court at one of the Dublin Castle Drawing-rooms, she was the toast of Dublin – Lady Longford's Lily (a name derived from the pale perfection of her skin) had a host of admirers, among them a young ADC to the Viceroy, Arthur

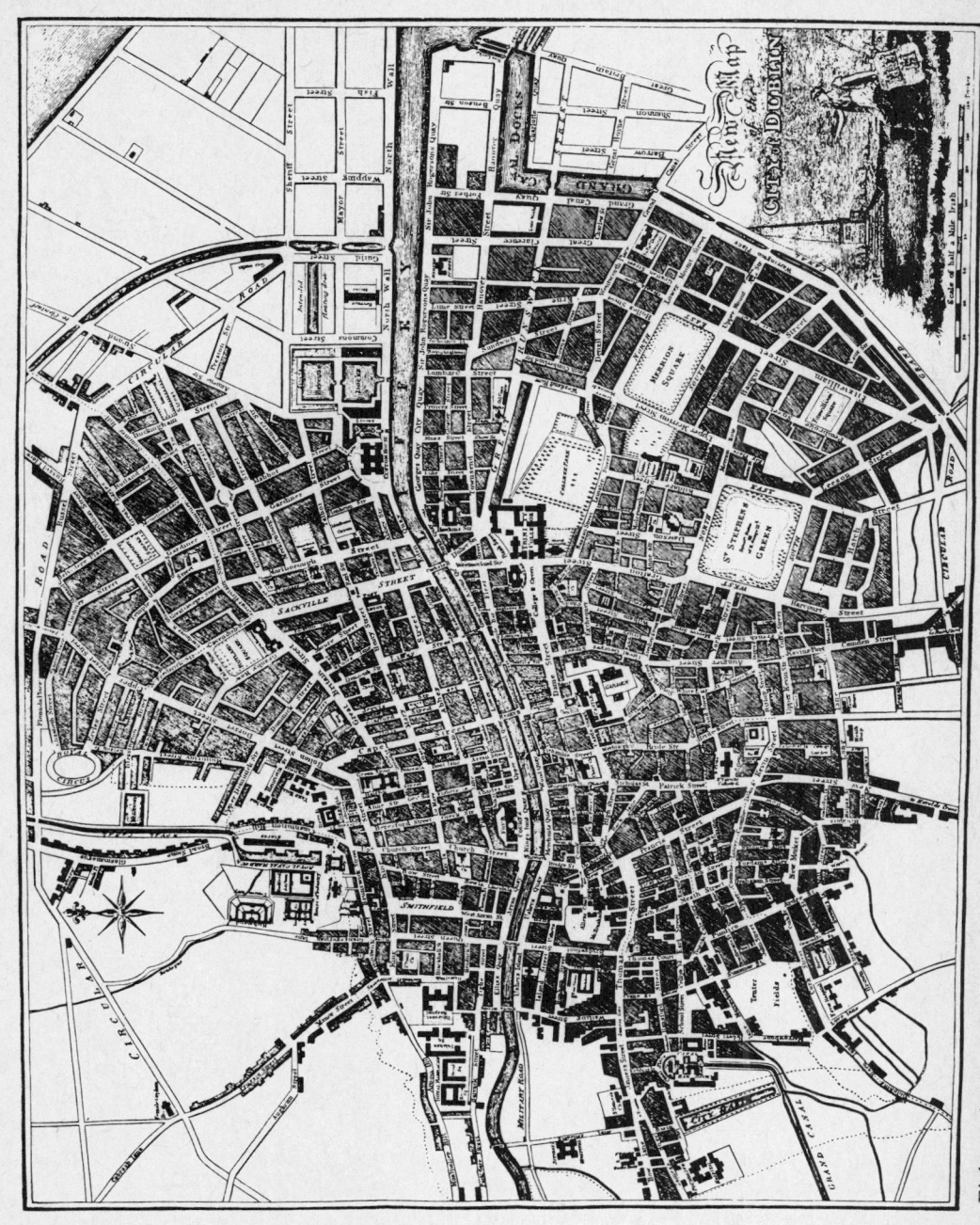

Eighteenth-century Dublin

Wesley (not yet Wellesley), third and undistinguished son of the Earl and Countess of Mornington, whose seat was Dangan Castle, County Meath, between Dublin and Pakenham Hall. They were remotely connected by marriage, as was often the case with the old Irish Protestant 'Ascendancy' families, who had intermarried for generations since settling in Ireland with no noticeable deterioration in the quality of the stock. In some ways, these Anglo-Irish men and women seemed to produce proportionally more beauty, wit and talent in their offspring than similar families across the Irish Sea. Dublin, in the last quarter of the eighteenth century, had developed into one of the most elegant and sophisticated capitals in Europe, where music and art flourished; wide streets, great houses and fine buildings housed the leaders of social and political life. Citizens with less affluence and wealth could also participate in the classic revival. Monuments and parks, squares, streets, crescents and terraces of more modest dwellings combined to give noble vistas that lifted the heart, however low the money in the pocket. Dubliners could walk the streets of their city with pride, whether Protestant, Catholic or nothing at all.

The Morningtons had a town house in Upper Merrion Street, the Pakenhams in Rutland Square. The young ADC, now twenty-one, enjoyed every aspect of Dublin life: balls and entertainments in the great houses, gambling, flirtations, picnics in the country with the daughters and sisters of brother officers and, when funds permitted, the less innocent pleasures of the Dublin brothels.

Arthur Wesley had always had a serious interest in music. His father had been Professor of Music at Trinity College, a composer of note and patron to visiting musicians, organizing concerts for charity where new works could be performed. Unfortunately, his social life absorbed most of the family fortune. Arthur was twelve in 1781 and about to enter Eton when his father died and three years later, with debts mounting and creditors pressing, the widowed Countess was forced to depart for Brussels, taking Arthur with her. She placed her 'ugly son' at the School of Equitation at Angers in France, and for a happy year (1786) Arthur attended the military academy, learnt to speak excellent French, learnt the courtly manners of a French gentleman, learnt the art of riding and the rudiments of warfare, kept a little terrier as a pet and played the violin. He was seventeen.

Returning to England, he was gazetted lieutenant in the 76th Regiment, transferred to the 41st and with the help of his brother Richard, now Lord Mornington, was appointed ADC to the Lord Lieutenant of Ireland, Lord Buckingham, soon to be succeeded by Lord Westmorland. On the way to Ireland, travelling with his eccentric grandmother, Lady

Dungannon, whose family (Hill-Trevor) had property at Brynkinalt, Denbighshire, they visited two of her old friends in Wales, known as the Ladies of Llangollen. One of them, Eleanor Butler, described her visitor as a 'charming young man' – handsome, tall (in fact he was only about five foot six) and elegant.[3]

No doubt he was glad to be going home, to the friends, the sporting and social life he loved. He took for granted the darker side of Irish life – the traditional and mindless killings and torture among rival peasant gangs which often originated in land and tenancy disputes, and the equal barbarity from the military in an effort to keep law and order. The division was not necessarily between native Catholics and immigrant Protestants, although political and economic discrimination against Catholics persisted. Both religious sects provided recruits for the Volunteers and their allies, the Society of United Irishmen, whose aims were more distinct than those of the sporadic local disputes – they shouted defiance of colonial rule and had achieved at last recognition of independence for the Irish Parliament under the Crown. Great orators spoke, something was always about to happen – but what? For the young, everything was exciting, wonderful and full of hope. The American adventure had attracted to the New World young men from Ascendancy and Catholic families, irked by the Colonial status of Ireland, and with the help of these young men, had succeeded. George Washington was President of a newly independent country, the United States of America. In France, the Rights of Man had been declared, the Bastille stormed, ancient authority was in ruins. Irishmen were ready to fight, but the cause was not yet clear. Factions formed and dissolved with endless complications and ferment as the new ideas of Liberty, Equality, Fraternity bubbled to the surface. Kitty's and Arthur's friends drank loyal toasts to King George III and the Revolution in France in the same breath and felt none the worse for the indigestible mixture.

In this exhilarating political climate, young Arthur succeeded (in 1790) to the family seat in the Irish Parliament as Member for Trim, County Meath – his brother, William, having left the constituency for a more promising political career in the English House of Commons. Trim, on the River Boyne, some twenty-eight miles from Dublin, had memories for Arthur – he had attended school there for a time and spent many hours looking across the river to the ruined castle on the further shore, picturing the bloody battles round its walls, while his classmates construed their Latin prose.

Richard, Lord Mornington, his eldest brother and head of the family, was struggling with the family finances – not helped by the frivolous behaviour of his grandmother Lady Dungannon, in England, who was briefly imprisoned for debt, until rescued by her daughter and grandson and shipped off to a French Convent, to the delight of the scandalmongers in Dublin. Richard, brilliantly clever, vain and extravagant, paid off the old lady's debts and brought her home in six months. For some time, he had been endeavouring to cut his ties with Ireland by selling his estates and thus some ready money was available to purchase promotion for Arthur, although his younger brother's gambling and indebtedness would not be cured by the increase in army pay, which was minimal.

Both Pakenhams and Wesleys were frequent visitors to Summerhill, home of the Langfords, Kitty's cousins. This rich and splendid estate adjoined that of the Morningtons at Dangan and was a convenient meeting place, halfway between Dublin and Pakenham Hall. It is likely that Arthur and Kitty played together there as children and the gardens of Summerhill may have seen the awakening of first love. In the eyes of the more affluent Ascendancy families, of which the Pakenhams were one, the Wesleys were something of a disaster and although the boys and girls were friends, an alliance with the rather disreputable and impoverished Wesleys would not be contemplated.

Richard had already decided that advancement in public life, which he desperately needed, could only be achieved in England with the help of his friend, Prime Minister Pitt. This desertion of Ireland was another black mark, particularly with families such as the Pakenhams who believed in improving their land and tenanted farms. Arthur Young, on one of his tours of Ireland, recorded his pleasure in meeting Kitty's father, Lord Longford – 'so spirited an improver' – while he had been less pleased with the Dangan estates, where huge sums of money had been spent in creating pleasure gardens and lakes, instead of using the land to grow useful crops.[4]

While Arthur was busy with his duties as ADC and attendance at the Irish Parliament, enlivened by the pleasures and scandals of Dublin life, Kitty followed the usual routine for a young woman in fashionable society. During the Season of spring and summer entertainments, the family would be at their Dublin town house, attending Court functions at Dublin Castle, private balls, concerts and the theatre. The rest of the year would be spent at Pakenham Hall or Langford Lodge on Lough Neagh, or on a round of visits to friends; hunting, shooting, amateur theatricals, musical evenings, poetry readings, both of published works and amateur contributions, in which Kitty excelled.

One of her great friends at this time, apart from Maria Edgeworth, was Grace Staples, some three years her junior and stepsister to Louisa Pakenham, Kitty's aunt, wife of Tom Pakenham of Coolure, a pleasant house on the banks of Lough Derravaragh, within walking distance of Pakenham Hall. In contrast to Kitty's home – a square Georgian house, soon to become a white fairy-tale castle with battlements and turrets, set on a terrace which overlooks valleys and farms to distant hills – Coolure was on the lake shore, where low hills with wooded slopes have green watermeadows at their foot. Small streams flow into the lake, resting in still reflection of the surrounding trees, except where drifts of waterfowl disturb the surface and the clap of their wings breaks the serenity of the air.

Tom Pakenham had married Louisa Anne Staples in 1785. She was the favourite niece of Louisa Conolly, restorer and improver of one of the great houses of Ireland, Castletown, at Celbridge, County Kildare, built by Speaker Conolly in 1722 – the first of the Irish Palladian mansions and one of the most magnificent. Speaker Conolly's son inherited the property and in 1758, at the age of twenty-five, married the fifteen-year-old daughter of the Duke of Richmond, Lady Louisa Lennox from Goodwood Park, Sussex. Her sister, Amelia, Duchess of Leinster, was the mother of the romantic and tragic revolutionary, Lord Edward Fitzgerald, and lived in another glorious house, Carton, not far from Celbridge.

Louisa Conolly spent her life restoring and enriching Castletown House and on her death-bed, in 1821, asked to be carried to the lawn in front of the mansion, so that her eyes could be fixed to the last on the house she had brought to perfection during sixty-three years of loving care. She had no children and left the estate to her niece, Louisa Pakenham of Coolure. Louisa's son, Tom, subsequently changed his name to Conolly to honour the founder of the estate and as a condition of the legacy.

All this was in the future and not envisaged by Kitty and Grace Staples as they walked through the Coolure woods or sat beside the lake in the summer of 1790 – their talk was probably of Kitty's presentation at Dublin Castle and her circle of admirers, or perhaps of the recent death of Sarah, nurse and dearly loved friend of the Staples family, an event which Kitty recorded in a poem, dedicated to 'Miss G. Staples'. The high-flown sentiments and religious feeling of the composition, in neo-Classical style, contrasted pleasantly with the summer afternoon; the rhyming of 'doom' and 'gloom' accentuating the happiness of being alive and young, while poor Sarah was consigned to the 'dread silence of eternity'. The two friends may have wept a little at the depth of feeling so admirably expressed:

> Poor humble Sarah! Be my life's decline
> Blest with such friends, such be my end as thine.

> For thine were friends would make the greatest vain,
> Their smile distinction, so their frown was pain ...

and so on, for many stanzas to the conclusion:

> Let one short word her various worths include,
> Can eloquence say more than 'She was good'.

The poem was probably read again at Pakenham Hall, as part of an evening's entertainment. Arthur, full of admiration, may have been there, the lofty phrases striking no false note when delivered with such sincerity. Kitty kept the poem among her papers to the end of her life.

A less elevated topic of conversation may have been a horrific double murder at neighbouring Edgeworthstown. *Faulkner's Journal* reported in May 1790 that an 'aged and respected couple' had been murdered as they lay in their bed 'in a manner too shocking for description' – they had been battered to death and the house robbed of £150 'in cash'. The *Journal* listed subscribers to a reward of £300 'to any person (the monster who actually perpetrated the murder excepted) who shall discover and prosecute to conviction any villains concerned'. Kitty's father, Lord Longford, subscribed £27 15s 0d; Lord Granard, £31 12s 6d; while her uncle, Thomas Pakenham, and R. L. Edgeworth, Maria's father, each contributed £11 7s 6d.

A straightforward crime of violence for cash against respectable people stimulated a reaction of horror and protest from the *Journal*'s readers. On the other hand, the ineffective yet horrific atrocities of peasant gangs – the White Boys, the Ribbon Men, the Defenders, the Peep-o'-Day Boys, etc. – who waged private wars against each other from sectarian motives linked to vendettas, reprisals or greed for profit from the 'subscriptions' extorted from terrified labourers or tenant farmers, had become commonplace and unremarkable. The local militia and garrison troops matched cruelty with cruelty in the name of law and order, in a manner that sickened the mind.

In the Irish Parliament the pace of protest and agitation for electoral reform was gaining momentum. The year 1790 saw a revival of the Volunteers, a force particularly strong in Belfast, formed originally to replace garrison troops withdrawn to fight in America against rebellious colonists. Since their triumph eight years before in gaining a large measure of self-rule for Ireland, the Volunteers had declined, but the success of the French Revolution, and the rise of local leaders outspoken in their criticism of Dublin Castle and widespread corruption, had stimulated recruitment once more.

Outstanding personalities and allies in the Independence movement were John Keogh, of the Catholic Committee, and the Protestant revolutionary, Wolfe Tone of the Volunteers. A spectacular review of the Volunteers was held in Belfast in 1790, the companies marching through the streets with banners and music, followed by a battery of cannon. Behind this, a huge portrait of Mirabeau, the French revolutionary leader, was followed by a triumphal car carrying a dramatic painting of the opening of the Bastille dungeons, with emaciated prisoners emerging from their cells or hanging in chains. On the reverse of this canvas appeared Hibernia (Ireland) in shackles, with a Volunteer artilleryman holding before her 'the radiant image of Liberty'. In the evening, three hundred patriots, mainly Protestant, sat down to dinner in the Linen Hall and drank toasts to 'the King of Ireland; to General Washington, the ornament of Mankind; to Grattan, Molyneux, Franklin and Mirabeau – these last two 'midst applause that threatened to shake the building to the ground'. The Northern Whig Club, active in this celebration, contained among others Lord Robert Stewart (Arthur's boyhood friend, later Lord Castlereagh) and Sir Hercules Rowley (Kitty's uncle on her mother's side).[5] Castlereagh never repudiated his youthful brief support for the Whig faction in Ireland. An equally surprising and transient member was Wolfe Tone, who wrote his first political pamphlet in 1790 eulogizing Grattan and the Whigs; an allegiance soon to be completely reversed.

Cooperation between the Protestant Volunteers and the Catholic Committee under Keogh was becoming more and more effective. This development alarmed not only the Viceroy, Westmorland, who was personally a fanatical opponent of the Catholic Church, but also Prime Minister Pitt in London. Pitt could not contemplate an independent Ireland so close to Britain, with substantial pro-French sentiments. Such a development would constitute a threat to national security as well as to an economically important source of food supplies for the British Army.

Although these events were earnestly discussed at Pakenham Hall, they were temporarily eclipsed by the tragic death of Kitty's maternal grandmother, Viscountess Langford of Somerhill (Summerhill),[6] at the age of fifty-nine. As some consolation, the year brought good news for the young man most often in Kitty's thoughts – Arthur had been promoted to Captain in the 58th Foot, a promotion he was easily able to combine with attendance at the Irish Parliament as MP for Trim. Kitty must often have wondered anxiously what the future could hold for them. Arthur had few prospects of achieving wealth and position in Dublin politics or in the Army, unless sent abroad on active service.

CHAPTER 2

# Lord Longford's 'Determination'

Arthur and Kitty were now openly in love. He was deeply involved in family business, as well as with his duties at Dublin Castle, but Dublin social life enabled the young couple to be frequently together. Richard, in disposing of his Irish estates, had nominated Arthur his representative in Ireland to work with the family agent, John Page, not only in the selling of land but also as adjudicator in disputes between agent and tenants.

Richard had already sold the Wesley house in Upper Merrion Street and this lost amenity provided Arthur with an excellent pretext for visits to the Pakenhams in Rutland Square. Kitty's father and mother did not appear to be opposed to her friendship with Arthur – but this comparative calm was soon to be broken.

It seems likely that in 1792 Arthur approached Lord Longford to ask for the hand of his daughter. While Kitty's parents had been indulgent in allowing a friendship between young Wesley and Catherine, they had not anticipated such a serious development. Their houses were always full of young people and it was hard to keep track of the changing attachments. Possibly it was only Kitty's grandmother who realized they were deeply in love. She had always taken an interest in the young couple, finding their love of books and music and Arthur's latent intellectual capacity qualities which endeared them to her.

The proposal generated some family disagreement. Kitty's grandmother spoke favourably of young Wesley who, in spite of his slightly dissipated life, read serious books and appreciated her library as much as his own at Dangan Castle. Lord Longford, absorbed in the improvements he was making to his estates, and his lively and intelligent wife both considered young Wesley would not be a good match. His personal reputation and that of his family were against him. None of their daughters was yet married and they considered it premature and undesirable for their beautiful Catherine to be committed to a young man with prospects as poor as those of Arthur Wesley.

Kitty's niece recorded years later that the Duchess of Wellington had told her of this unhappy episode. According to this account, not only was Arthur's proposal refused, but Lord Longford gave him a homily on how a young man should succeed in life, and specifically how he could correct his many faults before embarking on a useful career. He pointed out that Arthur was one of a large family, a younger son with little chance of inheritance, whose energies 'had seldom been displayed, except in gaiety and music'. Quite soon after this painful interview death claimed the 2nd Baron Longford. Could it have been accelerated by arguments between his widowed mother and his uncompromising wife over the affair of Kitty and Arthur?

With Longford's death at the age of forty-nine, his eldest son Thomas became head of the family. Thomas and his mother were highly conscious of the necessity to maintain the family's reputation, which would eventually be enhanced by his elevation to an earldom on the death of his grandmother Elizabeth, Countess of Longford.

Kitty's brother, eighteen years old and two years her junior, had absolute moral and financial power to dispose of her hand in a manner he and his mother considered best for her future. Should their wishes be ignored, not only would the couple experience social ostracism but no financial support could be expected from Pakenham Hall. To a young man with Arthur's poor prospects, this would be a very serious matter and entail real hardship for his wife. It was also unthinkable, in a closely knit and loving family, to create a rift between mother and daughter, which would cause great pain and conflict with the moral principles on which Kitty had been brought up.

It was vital, if all was not to be lost, that Arthur should build up his fortune and reputation. One avenue might be through his parliamentary activities. Until now, he had been a passive member of the Irish Parliament, content to sit in silence at debates and follow obediently in the steps of the Ascendancy leaders. He had listened unmoved to the sarcasm of Grattan and Wolfe Tone, who had called young men like himself from pocket boroughs 'the common prostitutes of the Treasury Bench'.[1] All this would have to change. Arthur Wesley began to speak in Parliament. In January 1793, he seconded the Address from the Throne, speaking on the depredations of the French, their imprisonment of Louis XVI and the Terror that the revolutionaries had imposed on France. He also supported the British Government's more liberal attitude towards the Irish Catholics and, in short, made a competent speech[2] which could be discussed in favourable terms at the Pakenham table, although his moderate approach to the Catholic question might not find favour with Longford.

Arthur also turned to his eldest brother for help. As Dangan Castle had now been sold and one of the greatest libraries in Ireland dispersed for ever, it was possible to borrow money from Richard to purchase two promotions in the year 1793: first to the rank of major in the 33rd Regiment of Foot and then to lieutenant-colonel in the same regiment.

Nothing more could be done. While Kitty would have shared in the general rejoicing at the marriage that year of her eldest sister Bess to Henry Stewart of Trycallen, county Donegal, a rising young lawyer and agent for the Pakenham estates, she must have felt a sharp contrast between that happy state and her own.

World events were now to play a part in the development of this Irish love affair. After the execution of Louis XVI in February 1793, France declared war on Britain and Holland. The Terror was at its height in Paris and Europe was plunging into chaos. Declarations of war must be good news for an ambitious soldier and it seems likely that the young man who dined with Jonah Barrington after an evening in Parliament was moderately optimistic about his future.

Barrington, the distinguished lawyer, wit and man-about-town in Dublin society, described his guest as 'frank, open-hearted and popular', but juvenile in appearance and unpolished in his address. Arthur brought with him to the dinner-party a fellow MP, Robert Stewart, later Lord Castlereagh, who had been elected MP in the same year as Arthur and was described as a 'not very moderate patriot'.[3]

Meanwhile, the year was bringing great changes to Pakenham Hall. The new owner had decided to restore and remodel part of the house in spite of the boisterous and destructive behaviour of his younger brothers and their friends. In his notes expressing admiration for the furniture and pictures at Inveraray Castle, he commented that in his house 'they would have been smashed to bits within a week'.[4] The work was being planned under the guidance of a fashionable Dublin architect, Francis Johnston, and although Kitty's brother found inspiration in the romanticism of the Gothic revival, there was an underlying practicality in turning the house into a stronghold. Local disturbances were becoming more frequent, and although the attacks were usually directed against small landlords or tenants who had failed to contribute to one gang or another, yet there was a ground-swell of unrest which was to erupt in the Rebellion of 1798, when over 30,000 people were to die in the space of five months, six times the number killed in the American War of Independence in five years.⁵

Support for the French Revolution was widespread and included men like Lord Edward Fitzgerald. Lord Edward, related by marriage to Kitty's aunt at Coolure, was described in 1793 as having turned 'a complete Frenchman, crops his hair, despises his title, walks the streets instead of riding and thence says he feels more pride in being on a level with his fellow citizens'. Lord Edward had married a beautiful Frenchwoman, Pamela de Genlis, and because of his extreme opinions felt somewhat isolated in Dublin society. He was to become, after his violent death in 1798, one of the tragically romantic figures of Irish folklore.

The shock of her father's death, following so closely on his refusal of Arthur's offer for her hand, marked the beginning of the end of Catherine's carefree youth. Her twenty-first birthday fell in the year which brought the happiness of her sister's wedding, but also the terrible news from Europe of the execution not only of the King of France, but of the beautiful and misguided Marie Antoinette, an old woman at thirty-eight, who went bravely to the guillotine in the autumn of 1793.

Kitty was glad to be able to resume her friendship with her neighbour Maria Edgeworth and with her brilliant but eccentric father, who had recently returned from England; but this could not offset the nagging worry of her suspended relationship with Arthur Wesley.

In the new year, Kitty was to suffer a further loss. Her beloved grandmother Elizabeth, Countess of Longford, presiding genius of the library, died in January 1794 aged seventy-three. Kitty's brother succeeded to his grandmother's title and now became the 2nd Earl. With this elevation in the Irish peerage, Kitty's hopes of marriage with Arthur became even more remote.

Arthur had gone to England in the autumn to complete the sale of the Dangan Castle estates and returned to Ireland to command his regiment, the 33rd, as lieutenant-colonel at the age of twenty-four. His rapid promotion was not unusual, given sufficient funds to purchase advancement. Kitty's brother Edward became a major at the age of seventeen and Lowry Cole, a family friend and son of the Earl of Enniskillen, commanded a regiment at the age of twenty-two.

This was a crucial period for the young soldier. His rebuff from the Pakenhams and the straight talk he had had with Kitty's father had sunk home. He made a conscious decision to put away his frivolous youth and to concentrate on his military career. It was probably at this crisis that he made a rule to study for some hours every day, which he continued, as circumstances permitted, all his life.⁶

Kitty's niece Catherine Hamilton, recalling Kitty's account of this period in their courtship, says that Arthur realized that music was a distraction from his profession and decided to give up playing the violin. He did not 'dash his favourite instrument to pieces' (or burn it), but gave it to a friend, binding himself by a voluntary and deliberate engagement never more to spend his time in an indulgence, which 'til then had proved his bane'.

The spring of 1794 passed quietly in Dublin, while news from Europe told of the horrors of the French Revolution continuing its progress through blood and terror. Arthur's regiment was moved to Cork to await orders for active services and at last, in June, these arrived.

It was probably from Cork that Arthur made his final effort to persuade the Pakenham family that he should marry Kitty. Records of his second proposal and his rejection do not survive, but a last, undated letter, written before he sailed, revealed his disappointment and intention not to give up the struggle. The letter is headed 'Barracks, Tuesday' and addressed to the 'Hon. C.D.S. Pakenham':

> If this letter should reach you I hope you will impute my troubling you this second time to the fear I have that my first letter may have offended. It never was intended to offend, and if any expression it contained could at all tend to give offence, I hope that the determination I have just received is, in your eyes, a sufficient punishment for a crime of much greater magnitude.
>
> As Lord Longford's determination is founded upon prudential motives and may be changed should my situation be altered before I return to Ireland, I hope you will believe that should anything occur which may induce you and him to change your minds, my mind will remain the same.
>
> In the meantime, with best wishes for your happiness, believe me, your most obedient servant,
>
> A. Wesley

This letter was of vital importance in determining the future pattern of their relationship. Arthur had made up his mind; Kitty Pakenham was the only woman he wanted to marry and he carried the memory of his first love and their frustrated courtship through long years of active service.

The troops from Ireland, including Arthur's regiment, sailed to join the army of the Duke of York in Flanders. The aimless proceedings of this royal general in Europe have been for ever encapsulated in the nursery rhyme: 'He marched them up to the top of the hill and he marched them down again.' In fact, there were few hills in Flanders and little to do except find ways to combat the winter cold, and later the horrors of starvation, as organization crumbled and retreat turned into disaster and death; an experience which left an indelible memory of needless waste and suffering in the mind of young Wesley.

## Lord Longford's 'Determination'

In Dublin, Kitty's friends were talking of the wonderful entertainment at the Marchioness of Antrim's 'most superb rout, ball and supper' held at her ladyship's house in Merrion Square on a spring evening in 1794. The Dublin papers reported 'a most brilliant and extremely numerous assemblage of the first rank and fashion. His Excellency, the Lord Lieutenant and most of the nobility of the town were present. . . . The following ladies with universal and unbounded applause performed a Scots ballet . . .'. The fourteen performers included the Countess of Antrim and Lady Isabella Beresford, who danced in uniform dresses of white muslin, trimmed with blue ribbons, 'the sachets and petticoats trimmed with silver fringe . . .'. Their head-dresses were white turbans with blue feathers spangled in silver. Music, 'all in the Scots style, was compiled for the occasion'. The ballet excited so much admiration that the whole company came crowding into the ballroom, which 'scarcely left the charming performers room to move. By the polite and persuasive interference of the noble Marchioness, the room was tolerably well cleared and the press of the company restrained by barriers of ribbon held by noblemen'. Dancing started at eleven o'clock and at one 'the company was summoned to the supper room, where elegance and plenty seemed to vie in the decoration of the festive board . . . while wit, beauty and all the gaiety and splendour of fashion enlivened the enchanting scene'. Dancing was resumed after supper and the company separated 'with reluctance' at six o'clock in the morning.

The year closed with news of the marriage of Arthur's brother Richard to his French mistress, Hyacinthe Roland, by whom he already had five children. The scandals attaching to Richard's private life and the strange behaviour of their grandmother, Lady Dungannon, did not improve Arthur's chances with Kitty and her family.

Kitty told her niece many years later that her mother and brother had strictly forbidden any communication with Arthur Wesley. Long, empty years stretched ahead in which the only news she received of him would be secondhand. She had given her promise not to break the embargo and she kept her word. Such a prohibition was not unusual in the circumstances. Sons and daughters were expected to obey their parents' wishes to the letter and, as Arthur remarked after many years of separation, her behaviour had been completely correct in every aspect of their relationship. He admired her strength of will in putting duty to her family and obedience to their wishes before her own inclinations.

# CHAPTER 3

# *The Storm*

At Dublin Castle, Lord Westmorland's term of office as Viceroy was ended at last. He had come to Ireland at a most critical period of her history, a young man of not much over thirty with courage and considerable charm. He and his wife entertained lavishly and were staunch friends of the Protestant Ascendancy. He watched with scepticism and disapproval the growing alliance between Presbyterians, mainly of Scottish descent in the north, and the Catholic Committee. For this reason he clung to office even after the death of his wife in 1793, which brought a sudden end to their happy round of progresses and parties, hoping to see the inevitable schism which would sever what he considered to be an unnatural and dangerous cooperation between Protestants and Catholics.

In this hope he was out of step with the British Government. Pitt, alarmed by the progress of the revolutionary forces in Europe and by Britain's isolation, wanted to promote further agreement with the Irish Catholic population and considered that more concessions were required to win the sympathies and loyalty of the majority of the people. At last Lord Westmorland could stand Pitt's 'weakness' no longer and resigned, to be replaced by a man who would carry out Pitt's conciliatory policy towards the Catholics, a policy approved by the leader of the Independence movement, the Irish Protestant MP, Grattan. Accordingly, Pitt appointed Lord Fitzwilliam as Viceroy in December 1794. In the new year he and his wife, a daughter of the Earl of Bessborough, appeared in Dublin.

Supporters of Catholic emancipation had great hopes that the new Viceroy, a man of noble birth, intelligent and rich, would be able to fight the Castle bureaucracy and maintain his independence of the

'Undertakers', the small but powerful group of Ascendancy politicians who manipulated the Irish Government, and thus avoid their sticky web of patronage and corruption, which had enmeshed and strangulated so many of his predecessors.

He made a spectacular start. Within his first few days of office he dismissed Beresford, Commissioner of Customs and the spider at the centre of much of the Castle intrigue; Toler, Attorney-General (later Lord Norbury); Wolfe, the Solicitor-General; and Cooke, Military Secretary. The reformers were jubilant and the Castle clique panic-stricken. But the Castle rallied its forces. Beresford made a direct appeal to Pitt and to King George III. Within a few days the tables were turned. Pitt ordered that the dismissed officers should be reinstated and the noble Viceroy was left to contemplate the bitter truth that in politics instructions to carry out reforms should not be taken too seriously. He was not a man to accept compromise. On 25 March 1795, he left the country to the accompaniment of an extraordinary demonstration of sorrow and anger, unique in the history of Ireland.

Dublin proclaimed his departure a day of humiliation; shops were closed and hung with black and the citizens lined the streets to bid him farewell. Grattan, never failing to rise to a great occasion, made a bitter speech expressing the general sorrow and denouncing the treachery of Pitt, who had given him assurances that Fitzwilliam would adopt a policy favourable to the Catholics, leading eventually to that much desired goal when Catholics would be eligible for election to the Irish Parliament – a goal the far-sighted Protestant Grattan believed essential for peace in Ireland.

Beresford, although an arch-manipulator of Irish politics, was also responsible for many improvements in Dublin, not least as a member of the Wide Streets Commission. His efforts to beautify the city included the erection of the magnificent Custom House, which still dominates the banks of the Liffey.

But on the day of the Viceroy's departure all his good works were of no avail. The mob attacked Beresford's house and even stoned the Custom House itself, as a symbol of his hated domination. The Lord Chancellor, Fitzgibbon, Earl of Clare, was also a target for mob violence. His sister described how, when he was returning from Dublin Castle after 'swearing in' Lord Camden, the new Viceroy, 'a ferocious mob of no less than 6,000 men and several hundred women assembled together in College Green ... armed with pistols, cutlasses, sledges [hammers] saws and crowbars ... and the women were all of them armed, with their aprons full of paving stones'.

The mob began to throw showers of stones into the Chancellor's coach and he would have been stoned to death if he had not held his 'great square official purse before him ...'. His sister had disguised herself in her kitchen-maid's dress and had her apron full of stones, so that she could mingle with the mob and save her brother. She set up a cry that the soldiers were coming and so rescued him from being hung from the lamp-post outside his own front door.[1]

Arthur was now on his way home from the abortive Flanders campaign, his first military action behind him, fought with some distinction at Boxtel in September 1794. On his return he had an interview with the newly appointed Viceroy, Camden, in London before leaving for Ireland in March 1795. He spent April in Dublin, trying to persuade the Viceroy to open the doors of patronage for him, using his brother Richard's influence in an effort to gain position and money enough to renew his offer for Kitty's hand.

In April, he spoke in the Irish Parliament, gallantly accepting a challenge from the formidable Grattan, who, in attacking Arthur's old master, Lord Westmorland, had scornfully stated that 'no veteran of the Army nor any old officer had ventured to defend him'. Arthur did venture: he rose to speak and made a solid contribution of common sense in the sea of oratory with which Grattan could so easily swamp the Chamber.[2]

At Pakenham Hall and Edgeworthstown the talk was not all of the extraordinary happenings in Dublin. There was discussion of the protracted sale of Dangan Castle library – 10,000 books dispersed for ever – the end of an epoch for the Wesleys.

There was disturbing news of further outbreaks of violence in the neighbouring county of Longford. In April, Maria Edgeworth had written to her aunt, saying her father had been busy 'committing robbers to gaol' and that the raising of the militia, the local volunteer force, had brought more trouble to the county. She reported that Lord Granard's carriage had been 'pelted' at Athlone and that the people of Edgeworthstown were robbed every night.

With the ending of parliamentary business in June, Arthur had returned to his constituency, lodging at Fosterstown. From there he made fresh efforts to interest the Viceroy in his future, desperately trying to further his career and prove his worth. He asked for appointments with the Revenue or the Treasury Boards, mentioning his brother's name and ready to turn his back on a military career, even to sell his commission. Kitty would have heard of his efforts through mutual friends, the family prohibition against any form of direct communication being still in force.

## The Storm

It must have been a wretchedly frustrating time for both the young people – not so young now; Arthur was twenty-six and Kitty twenty-three and nothing had been achieved.

Richard was becoming exasperated at his brother's predicament and constant requests for assistance. Did he deliberately suggest Arthur's name, without his knowledge, for the post of Surveyor-General of the Ordnance, already held by Kitty's uncle, Captain Thomas Pakenham of Coolure? Arthur had been a frequent guest at Coolure in the happier days of their courtship and it is inconceivable that he would willingly have given offence to Kitty's uncle, who had shown him considerable kindness. Nevertheless, the suggestion was made and received favourably by Camden but with indignation by Tom Pakenham who, when he heard of it, blamed a 'deep-laid scheme of Lord Mornington's'.[3] The young couple must have been in despair when news of this gaffe reached Pakenham Hall and family loyalty rallied against the Wesleys and their plots and pretensions.

It was now late summer and Arthur had decided to return to his regiment at Southampton. Hope of a happy conclusion to their romance was at its lowest ebb. He was about to sail with the 33rd, under orders for the West Indies, and the chances of survival in those deceptively beautiful but unhealthy islands were poor. Depression gave place to actual illness and while waiting to sail he had an attack of fever, possibly a legacy from the appalling campaign in the Netherlands at the beginning of the year.

At Pakenham Hall, Kitty dutifully tried to follow her mother's and brother's instructions to forget Arthur Wesley. She should concentrate on other friends more suited to her position; go out more, visit her sister in Donegal and her relations at Bective Castle and Summerhill. Dear Maria and her father were coming over from Edgeworthstown for a literary evening – poetry-reading and a little music. She must have the harp re-strung and play for the company as she used to do. In the meantime, she could finish the flower studies in watercolour she had started months before.... Her family watched poor Kitty anxiously for signs of a decline to which young women were prone when under the stress of an unhappy love affair.

They had not long to wait. Depression at the end of an abortive engagement was deepened by anxiety for the safety of the man she loved. Arthur had sailed for Barbados in November 1795, but the first night out from Southampton the fleet was hit by a tremendous gale. Seven ships were wrecked on Chesil Beach and five hundred soldiers perished there. The rest, including Arthur's transport, returned to Portsmouth and waited again for sailing orders. In December, in the face of gale-force winds, the fleet sailed once more and the Dublin papers recorded with suitable horror the terrible saga of events. One transport was blown to the Spanish coast; a hundred more were not accounted for but eventually turned up, one by one, in the West Indies. The remaining thirty ships, after seven terrible weeks of storms and winter weather, were driven back to the Solent and eventually to the peace of Poole harbour, where Arthur was lucky to find himself alive in February 1796.

During that sad autumn Kitty had been making a brave attempt to live and enjoy a normal life. To cheer her, kind Richard Edgeworth had written a humorous poem in which he represented Kitty as a slave of extreme ugliness with characteristics the antithesis of 'Lady Longford's Lily'. His little joke would have gone down well when read in Richard's best dramatic style and probably succeeded in bringing that illusive smile to Kitty's face which had been her greatest charm.

> Since nature made my form so coarse,
> My skin so brown, my voice so hoarse,
> My teeth so black, my lips so white,
> My heels so heavy and my head so light ....

The poem was kept among her papers to remind her, after years of exile, of that evening with family and friends in the drawing-room at Pakenham Hall, the long windows curtained against the cold, her brothers sprawled in front of the fire, her sisters with their embroidery pausing to applaud the poem. All of them laughing and talking with that intimate informality and instant understanding of old, remembered jests which is the essence of family life. Candle flames moved slightly in the warm air, their light reflected on porcelain and silver, on softly glowing mahogany, on the folds of satin and lace and on the well-loved faces. Permeating the memory, the never-forgotten bitter-sweet smell of burning turfs.

On the reverse of the manuscript can still be seen faint pencil sketches for a necklace of cameos, similar to one still at Stratfield Saye, worn by the little duchess, and very faintly the outline of a man's head with a slightly prominent nose ....

The family had gathered together for Christmas, but in spite of their gentle care and encouragement, incessant worry for Arthur's safety preyed on Kitty's mind. Not long after the Edgeworths' visit she became seriously ill. During that bleak season there would have been no news of Arthur's ship; only the knowledge that most of the West Indies fleet were scattered or lost. Those not blown far out across the Atlantic were battling against terrible weather off the dangerous Brittany coast. In such a prolonged series of gales, the chances for survival of heavily laden sailing vessels were small.

It is not known how long her illness lasted, but on 9 January 1796 she was able to compose a poem, 'while lying in extreme weakness on a sick bed'. Some days later her friend, Miss Fanshawe, called to see her and kindly copied the poem in pencil while seated on Kitty's bed. The seriousness of her illness is reflected in the opening lines:

> Returning from the gates of death
> Within whose awful porch I lay,
> Again to draw the vital breath
> And view the cheerful day:
>
> The soul on poised wings that hung
> Ready to flit in viewless air,
> The pallid lips and faltering tongue,
> Oh what shall they declare?

The poem continues for many verses and ends on a more cheerful note:

> Rescued from sorrow, pain and death;
> Their terrors sealed, withdrawn their sting.
> Let me, as long as I have breath,
> Sing praises of my King.

Here she is not only giving thanks for recovery from 'pain and death', but she has also been 'rescued from sorrow', perhaps by the news that her mourning for Arthur was premature and he had made a safe return to port.

Her illness seems to have been one of high fever and partial unconsciousness. Had it been smallpox, the disease malicious gossips in later years claimed to have marred her appearance, there would have been a reference in the poem to disfigurement and a prayer for strength not to grieve over loss of beauty, etc. Her niece Catherine, who was brought up at Stratfield Saye, firmly rejected the story that Kitty had ever suffered from smallpox.

In the spring, to Kitty's joy, Arthur returned to Ireland to convalesce from another attack of fever. Plans for his regiment had been changed and they were now under orders to embark for India. In April they sailed, but Arthur was not with them. He intended to make good his recovery and follow the transports in a fast cruiser, which would allow him to catch up with the convoy before it reached its destination.

April found him in Dublin, making final arrangements for the care of his constituency at Trim, which had been offered by Richard to his cousin, Sir Chichester Fortescue, Ulster King of Arms. Other business included the settlement of some of his debts and arrangements to service the rest while he was abroad.

There is no record of any meeting or even a letter passing between the young people, but something continually drew Arthur back to Ireland during this period, while Richard and the rest of the family were doing their best to sever connections with their Irish background. It seems certain that Arthur's intention to marry Kitty remained unchanged and that she, in spite of family pressure, still hoped that fate would treat them both more kindly in the future.

Early in May, Arthur was promoted colonel and in June was back in London, lodging at 3 Savile Row[4] and buying a number of reference books on the Orient – dictionaries of Indian dialects, accounts of campaigns in India, histories of the various regions and government reports on the sub-continent and the activities of the East India Company. Included in his travelling library were twenty-four volumes of Swift's works and Adam Smith's *Wealth of Nations*. Swift was probably chosen not only for enjoyment of his sardonic commentary on Irish affairs, but also because Laracor Church, a living of the famous dean for many years, was on the Dangan estates and stories of the talented and eccentric author were well known to Arthur.

By the end of the month preparations were complete and he was at Portsmouth, boarding a cruiser for the new era in his life. A six months' voyage should not be wasted – he would use the time to learn everything he could about his future field of action. The India Station for a young soldier was full of opportunity and Arthur had already determined that 'should my situation be altered before I return to Ireland' it would be for the better and the Pakenhams would be forced to change their opinion of him.

Kitty was also finding distraction in serious reading. Her copy of the memoirs of George III, published in 1796, is heavily annotated in her hand, with dates inserted in the margin to produce a time-scale of the more important events. Did she hope the vague promises of the Viceroy, Lord Camden, on possible political appointments and patronage made to his departing ADC, would one day result in Arthur resuming his career in Irish affairs? Whatever her motive for the study of recent history, it was once again the theme of books and learning that was common to them both.

# CHAPTER 4

# *Rebellion*

Arthur had sailed for India. At twenty-seven he had escaped at last from the problems of Ireland, and in the summer of 1796 was making a fast voyage along the coast of Africa to the Cape. After four months' sailing he rejoined his regiment in Capetown, where the transports were collecting new supplies. With Dublin, Dangan Castle and Pakenham Hall well below the horizon he began to enjoy life again, flirting at garrison parties with Henrietta Smith, aged seventeen, who was travelling to India with her sister. George Elers, a relation of the Edgeworths and a captain in the 12th Foot, writing his memoirs of Capetown at this time, remarked that Henrietta had 'a pretty little figure' and Arthur Wesley was 'all life and spirits', remarkably clean in his person, with clear blue eyes, a large acquiline nose and a quickness of speech reflecting the quick intelligence of his mind. Capetown was a happy interlude in a boring journey, relieved by his India studies. The journey was resumed in November and the transports arrived in Calcutta halfway through February 1797.[1]

The situation he had left behind was far from happy. Everywhere the century was closing in the grip of violent forces, with anarchy replacing the spirit of reason and enlightenment which had been nourished in the eighteenth century and hailed in the salons of Europe as a new dawn of civilization. The rise of Napoleon Bonaparte had begun with his defeat of the Austrians at Lodi in May 1796. August saw an alliance between France and Spain and in October Spain added a declaration of war against Britain.

Arthur and Kitty's story pauses at this point and political events in Ireland and elsewhere dominate the scene. Irish history is of extraordinary complexity and the few years between 1796 and 1801 produced upheavals

Ireland in 1806

Ostell's General Atlas (Ireland), 1806.

## LOCATIONS

1. Pakenham Hall
2. Dangan Castle
3. Summerhill
4. Langford Lodge
5. Florence Court
6. Brown Hall
7. Killala
8. Castlebar
9. Trycallen
10. Edgeworthstown
11. Bantry Bay
12. Lough Swilly

## Rebellion

with repercussions continuing to this day. Reference to these events is necessary to explain how a young woman living in Ireland at this time had no chance to vegetate – she was at the centre of momentous crises and great tragedies which touched every section of the community and could only be endured with courage, fortitude and great spiritual strength.

In these years a suitor for Kitty's hand presented himself, Galbraith Lowry Cole, a son of Lord Enniskillen and an old friend of the family. Meanwhile, the Irish death-wish erupted once more on the pages of history, this time invoking the help of Napoleon – Britain's, and Europe's, greatest danger.

In the last days of 1796 an invasion fleet sailed from France, avoiding the British naval blockade at Brest. By 21 December thirty-five heavily armed ships, with 12,000 French soldiers on board, were lying off the south-west coast of Ireland at Bantry Bay.[2] On the flagship was a young man who was to become a legend, Wolfe Tone – a slightly built, handsome Irish barrister of thirty-three, son of a Protestant coach maker in Dublin, a founder member of the United Irishmen, hater of England and dedicated admirer of French revolutionary ideas. The object of his bi-partisan force was to reform the Irish Parliament, preferably with independence from British rule, so that Catholics could become MPs and hold public office – a reform not yet achieved, although considerable concessions had been made to the Catholic population. The French, in return for their support, would be granted bases in Ireland for the invasion of England.

Suspicion of the Independence movement was growing rapidly in Britain and had intensified the suppression and persecution of its members with the outbreak of war with France. Those who supported the 'United Irishmen' were regarded by the British Government as traitors who were willing to submit friends and foes alike to the domination of Napoleon. Many were caught and imprisoned and Wolfe Tone had been expelled to America in 1795. As so often in Irish history, persecution intensified opposition and the leaders of the underground movement decided closer collaboration with France was their only hope. They believed their supporters were ready for revolution so long as France could be persuaded to mount an invasion. Wolfe Tone was chosen as ambassador to Napoleon and left America for France, confident of persuading the French Directory that the Irish countryside would rise to support a French expeditionary force. Amazingly, his eloquence was successful and the rulers of France appointed Lazare Hoche, one of the great revolutionary generals, to command a force whose task was to invade Ireland and from there to make a conquest of England.

Tone was appointed an adjutant-general in the French Army, and wearing his French uniform he paced the deck of the flagship of the invasion fleet, impatient to set foot on Irish soil and lead the way to Cork and to a victory that would topple the power of England for ever. 'I hate the very name of England . . .', he wrote in his journal, 'and I will hate her always.'

On that December day conditions in Bantry Bay were favourable for a landing. All that was needed was to order the troops into the boats and establish a beach-head under the protective guns of the French fleet. But the order could not be given. General Hoche had not arrived; his frigate had become separated from the main fleet after leaving Brest, and so the ships stood on and off the shore to wait in the icy cold for his arrival. As the days passed the easterly wind increased and when at last Hoche arrived and they could attempt the landing, the wind was against them. To the astonishment of the inhabitants of Bantry, the transports dropped anchor in the bay to await better conditions. Two more days passed and the wind reached gale force with blasts of snow to blind and confuse, so that one captain after another, to avoid the perils of that bleak coast, cut their cables and made for the open sea. By 27 December the storm had risen to hurricane force and the few remaining ships, of which Wolfe Tone's was one, were forced to run for France.

The effect on Ireland of this attempted invasion was not at all as anticipated by Tone. When the alarming news reached General Dalrymple, in command of the Cork garrison, he moved at once towards Bantry with what troops he had, receiving every support from the Irish peasant farmers, who helped to dig his transports out of the snow drifts and 'behaved charmingly', sharing their meagre supplies with his men and giving them shelter from the bitter weather.

Before his forces reached the coast, the last of the French fleet had left Irish waters and in England the Cabinet congratulated itself on repelling an invasion without firing a shot. Lord Camden wrote: 'We have had an escape which . . . I wish had not been owing so entirely to the winds . . . .' He warned that a 'universal discontent prevails here that a hostile fleet should have presumed to insult our coast for three weeks'.

At Pakenham Hall the new year brought invitations to two weddings. In March, Olivia Acheson, one of Kitty's most treasured friends, married Bernard Sparrow, a soldier with a distinguished military career, who was comfortably situated with a castle in Armagh and a house in Huntingdonshire. From the north came news of Lowry Cole's sister's engagement to Blayney Balfour of Townley Hall, Drogheda; Florence Cole was also a dear friend of Kitty's and the Enniskillen family were frequent visitors to Dublin and neighbouring country houses.

Lowry was probably already well known to Kitty, although he had spent considerable time abroad. They were the same age and although he was a second son, his career prospects were good, having entered the Army at fifteen as a cornet in the 12th Light Dragoons and then studied 'the art of war' for two years at the University of Stuttgart – there were no military colleges in Britain. Promotion was rapid. As soon as he returned from Germany his father arranged a captaincy for him in the 70th Foot. After a pleasurable period travelling in Europe with his brother, the outbreak of war with France brought him home. He was gazetted major at the age of twenty-one and joined the 86th Foot for service in the West Indies, taking part in the capture of Martinique and Guadeloupe.[3] Soon promotion came again – to lieutenant-colonel in the Coldstream Guards.

With the escalation of unrest in the previous year, 1796, his father and their neighbours Lord Tyrone and the Marquis of Abercorn were already raising armed bodies of yeomanry, which they paid from their own pockets and officered with their sons. These volunteers were used against the rebels in Ulster and Leinster and also in Waterford, where sporadic outbreaks of violence induced further cooperation for defence between great and small landowners.

Lowry Cole was now on the staff of the Commander-in-Chief, Lord Carhampton, as ADC and was available to attend his sister's wedding and renew old friendships at Pakenham Hall. He was twenty-five, and with three of his sisters married, it would be surprising if they did not plot among themselves to find a suitable bride for 'dear Lowry'. Florence would immediately have thought of her childhood friend, sweet Kitty Pakenham, who had had such an unfortunate love affair with Arthur Wesley.

Thoughout the fearful summer of 1797, General Lake carried out a ruthless disarming of Ulster, where rebellion had again come to the surface. At the same time a romance was growing between Kitty and Lowry Cole. Her family and friends all urged her to encourage him, but at the same time news was arriving from India of a rise in the fortunes of the Wesley brothers – the name would soon be changed to 'Wellesley' at Richard's instigation, an ancient style and, in his opinion, more distinguished. Richard had been appointed Governor-General of India in October 1797, by a stroke of good fortune. The tragedy unfolding in Ireland had alarmed the British Government to such an extent that Lord Cornwallis, designated Governor-General, was switched to Ireland as Commander-in-Chief and Richard appointed to India in his place.

Although the mails from India were lamentably slow, a letter taking six months or even a year to reach home, Kitty would have heard of Arthur's safe arrival in Calcutta and possibly of his popularity there, both as a commander and off-duty among his military 'family' and their wives. She was facing a terrible dilemma. On the one hand was Lowry Cole, a charming and devoted young soldier, eager to offer his hand and much approved by her mother and brother. On the other was her deep-seated first love, her memory of Arthur Wellesley, a man with whom she had shared years of frustrated hope and to whom she had committed herself as far as she could in the face of her family's opposition.

The turmoil in Ireland echoed her conflicting emotions. The situation was growing steadily worse. In May, a plan was discovered to assassinate Lord Carhampton who, next to Chancellor Fitzgibbon (Lord Clare), was the most hated man in Ireland.[4] With the mutinies of the British Navy at Spithead and the Nore during April and June and with increased infiltration by rebels into the garrison forces in Ireland, the authorities realized the dangers of the situation and that a further French invasion attempt was imminent. Fear increased the ferocity with which they tried to suppress dissident groups, loosely allied under the banner of the United Irishmen.

After the horrors of his disarming of Ulster, Lake moved against the rebels in the south with equal ferocity. Feeling against the Irish rebels and their traitorous alliance with the hated French was further exacerbated when it was discovered that the grievances of the mutineers at Spithead and the Nore had been inflamed by members of the United Irishmen. One of the leaders of the mutiny, Lee, had come straight from the United Irish headquarters in Dublin to enlist in the Navy only a few months before the insurrection. Half the sailors and petty officers at that time were Irish Catholics. Wolfe Tone, in a published address, had invited the Irish sailors to make themselves masters of their ships, with freedom to plunder English commerce as a reward. It was later discovered by a committee of the House of Commons that crews had been sworn to be true to Ireland, to erect a Catholic government there and to be 'faithful to their brethren who were fighting their cause against tyrants and oppression'.[5] There had been plans to sail various ships into Irish harbours, kill the officers and hoist the green flag of Liberty, and afterwards to kill the Protestant residents and destroy their homes.

It is not necessary here to recount the horrors of 1798. It has been done in that most moving and exciting account of the Rebellion by Thomas Pakenham in *The Year of Liberty*. The impact of these events on the Pakenham family and their friends changed their society as inevitably as some great natural disaster. For years they had lived with the rumblings of an impending earthquake, and when at last disaster struck the pattern of their lives was on the point of change. For Kitty, brought up in the simple faith that God was merciful and ordered everything according to His will, the reality of the appalling cruelties by Irishmen against Irishmen during the Rebellion, uniquely barbarous by any standards – and yet not out of step with the recurring theme of violence in Irish history – destroyed her youth.

Already her life had known its full share of personal tragedy. Now, at the age of twenty-six, she was confronted every day with eye-witness accounts of rebels cut down in battle, flogged or hanged; the death of friends and the burning of houses where she had spent many happy hours; appalling atrocities committed by both sides, often against innocent and kindly people she had known as friends or servants. Fears for the safety of households of women and children dear to her and fear for the safety of Pakenham Hall itself haunted every minute of the day. Tenants and labourers known to her since childhood were caught in a tragedy not of their choosing and might be forced to raise the dreaded pikes of the rebels against her home.

The situation was complex. In Ulster, revolutionary Protestant Dissenters, mainly of Scottish origin and particularly active in Belfast, Wolfe Tone's former stronghold, had been weakened by Lake's cruel initiative under martial law in 1797. For Tone, the aim of the Rebellion had hardened into independence for Ireland through revolution on the French pattern, combined with the defeat of Britain by Napoleon. According to MacDermot,[6] Tone, in France, failed to realize that many of his most influential supporters, the majority non-Catholic like himself, had begun to hate and fear Napoleon and were not prepared to plunge Ireland into civil war for such an alliance. To his disappointment, only a handful of northern rebels joined a diverse group of Gaelic and Catholic Irish in the south, under the green flag of the United Irishmen. The last notable event before the rising was the capture in May, through treachery, of Lord Edward Fitzgerald, Tone's Commander-in-Chief and a relative of Louisa Pakenham. He was fatally wounded while resisting arrest in Dublin after killing one of his captors.

As sporadic violence broke out across the country in the summer of 1798, the Rebellion degenerated without Fitzgerald's leadership into a desperate rising of scattered groups of Irishmen, whose immediate aim was to abolish tithes and rents and to take a bitter revenge for the excesses of Lake's army, now active in the south. In some areas the rebels were encouraged and led into an unprecedented explosion of religious and racial hatred by a few fanatical priests. These clerics presided at forced conversions of Protestants to Catholicism on pain of death, and were merciless towards loyalists or anyone not in active support of the Rebellion.

Against the rebels was an equally diverse group representing the British Crown – garrison troops recruited in England, Scotland and Ireland from all denominations, combined with the local Irish units of militia, yeomanry and volunteers. Tone had counted on these Irish units to join the rebels, but they did not. The loyalist defenders were in many places ill-prepared, undisciplined and licentious, although generally superior in weapons and training to the pike-carrying rebels. As the Rebellion of '98 spread, erupting where least expected and where village communities had least protection, thirty thousand died in five months. As in all civil strife, whatever the aims of the instigators, many innocent people suffered cruelly.

Cornwallis, at the height of the Rebellion, said he found himself in a scene of horror 'the like of which I had never witnessed in America, India or anywhere'. His pity was for the rebels. 'The deluded wretches are still wandering about in considerable bodies and are committing still greater cruelties than they themselves suffer', he wrote to Portland in June 1798.[7]

Kitty's uncle from Coolure had helped to organize the defence of Dublin Castle, while her friend and suitor Lieutenant-Colonel Galbraith Lowry Cole had been ordered to Tara Hill, Bective, near to her aunt's house at Summerhill and to Arthur's old home, where 8,000 rebels were assembled. On a day in May, the rebels on the summit of the hill watched Lowry Cole's yeomanry climb towards them with a field gun. As evening approached, battle was joined and for some time the issue was in doubt. At dusk, the troops made a desperate charge and their gun was nearly captured, but as the rebels swarmed over their defences, thinking victory was theirs, the cannon opened fire, cutting great gaps through their lines and putting the rest to flight.

In the morning, 350 rebels lay dead on Tara Hill and an enormous number of pikes and other weapons were captured, for the loss to the yeomanry of thirteen killed and a score wounded.

In England, the extraordinary power of the Irish question to excite violence was demonstrated when Pitt, under mounting pressure from all sides and fear of imminent French invasion, rounded on an Irish Foxite, Tierney, during a Commons debate and accused him of wishing to obstruct the defence of the country for his own ends. Tierney objected to the Speaker, but Pitt refused to withdraw. The result was a challenge and a duel. Both fired twice and missed and honour was satisfied.

Events in the south of Ireland were moving to a climax. Rebels, led by Catholic priests with the cry 'Death to Protestants', had begun the Wexford Rising. The horrors that followed are well known and Camden's appeals to England for help became more and more urgent. The successful insurgents, gaining in numbers as they went, captured Enniscorthy and then Wexford itself, hauling down the English flag and flying the Irish Harp, on its green ground, above the barracks. The first Irish Republic was proclaimed and a rebel army of 15,000 men roamed the city.[8]

The principal organizer, Father John Murphy, established a strongpoint outside Wexford town at a well-known landmark, Vinegar Hill, concentrating most of his rebel forces there. Meanwhile, the loyalists in the town were being systematically massacred, and on midsummer's day, 1798, ninety-seven Protestant men were piked to death on Wexford Bridge after a summary 'trial' where, if nothing convincing was said in favour of the accused, execution was immediate. The prisoner was made to kneel on the bridge with two pikemen in front and two behind. At a given signal the pikemen speared the man, raised him, still piked, above their heads and threw the body into the river. This slaughter was stopped by the initiative of General Moore, later to die so tragically at Corunna, who was part of the force sent to quell the Rebellion. Ignoring his commander's order to delay an advance on the city, he sent a detachment of regular troops into the town to arrange a surrender.

At Vinegar Hill the main rebel force was defeated and during this engagement Lowry Cole was wounded. Although hundreds of rebels were killed, a large part of the force escaped to re-form in other parts of Ireland. Wexford, Wicklow and the midland counties were overspread with detached parties of banditti, who appeared as 'cruel robbers, housebreakers and murderers' and the atrocities committed at Wexford were repeated on a smaller scale. The houses of Protestants were fired, the men piked or shot, the women and children sometimes burned alive. The rebels, when caught, were slaughtered in revenge.[9]

At least one person benefited from the action at Vinegar Hill. Lowry Cole was one of the very few casualties on the government side and was suitably lionized by his family and friends, not least the Pakenhams. He was elected MP for County Fermanagh later in the year and his valour and success probably impressed not only his old friend Longford but also Kitty. She may have allowed him to pay serious court to her at this time and many of their friends expected them to announce an engagement.

The rebellion in Ireland had been a signal for Wolfe Tone and his French supporters to renew their efforts to persuade Napoleon that a second invasion attempt would bring about the downfall of England. France decided to send immediate assistance to the rebels and General Humbert was appointed to lead an expedition, which would sail in two parts, one from La Rochelle and the second from Brest.

In spite of the wild impatience of the Irish contingent, only Humbert's force of 1,100 men was ready in August and Tone's younger brother Mathew, with Barclay Teeling as Irish adviser, sailed for the chosen invasion point – a remote and unlikely landing place at Killala, County Mayo, on the north-east coast.

Extraordinary events followed the landing of this tiny force. Humbert soon realized that he would not receive reinforcement from France and that Irish support would be minimal unless he could achieve a spectacular victory as soon as possible. He made a forced march from Killala to Castlebar, twenty-six miles to the south, where 3,500 loyalists troops were concentrated to attack him.

Everything depended on surprise, but as they approached the town the alarm was given and the tiny French force with a contingent of Irish recruits was fired on from prepared positions in the early morning mists and victory seemed certain for the defenders. Humbert was in a desperate situation. At the first round of fire his Irish supporters fled. The French veterans continued their advance and, as they came in sight of the Irish militia defending the town, the troops confronting them suddenly panicked, throwing down their arms and bolting to the rear, forcing the regular soldiers into confusion. The French could hardly believe their luck as they pressed on into the town – the inhabitants, the garrison troops and the militia fleeing in all directions before them and not stopping until they had put thirty miles between themselves and the invaders. The French were too tired to pursue but the race from Castlebar needed no encouragement from them – some of the deserters pressing on beyond Tuam in County Galway as far as Athlone, some sixty-three miles away, in twenty-seven hours.[10] This extraordinary event was meat and drink for Irish humour from that day onward and the stories of the 'Castlebar Races' are still sure of a hilarious reception in convivial company.

The French victory at Castlebar had the hoped-for effect. Humbert was assured of local risings in counties that had been little touched by the Rebellion so far, particularly in Longford and Westmeath. Maria Edgeworth described the confused situation: 'We, who are so near the scene of action, cannot by any means discover what number of French actually landed: some say eight hundred, some one thousand eight hundred, some eighteen thousand. The troops marched and counter-marched as they say themselves, without knowing where they were going or for what ...'.

Maria's own strength of mind was soon to be tested. On 4 September reports started to come in that groups of armed men were collecting on the borders of Longford and Westmeath, several hundred having formed a camp at Fruen Hill, near Mullingar. At Edgeworthstown men with green boughs in their hats, and carrying the long pikes which were the main armament of the insurgents, marched along the roads, inflamed by rumours of an impending massacre of Catholics by Protestants. No troops were available to defend Edgeworthstown; the threat of French attack had drained every garrison for Cornwallis's army and Lovell Edgeworth's own yeomanry had marched to Longford to collect their arms.

In this emergency all Protestant families were ordered to leave the town and on 7 September the numerous Edgeworths filled the two family chaises, with Maria, her stepmother and aunt on horseback. At this moment an ammunition cart with six soldiers was passing the house on its way to Longford. The officer offered to escort the family but the Edgeworths were not ready and the cart proceeded without them. Shortly afterwards the house was rocked by a tremendous explosion. A spark from an overheated axle had fired the gunpowder and men and horses had been blown to pieces.

Later in the day Maria and her family fled the house, as three hundred pikemen were within a mile of them. She rode beside her mother and aunt and as they passed the remains of the cart they saw 'the trunk of a dead man, bloody limbs of horses and two dead horses' at the side of the road. The rebels sacked every house in Edgeworthstown except theirs – the reason for their escape being that their housekeeper, who had remained behind, had once lent a small sum to the rebel leader, for which kindness he ordered his men not to touch the house.[11]

In the middle of all this confusion news reached Longford that the French were close and Richard Edgeworth stood-to all night with a handful of yeomanry in the forlorn hope of defending the town. The next day, 8 September, a dragoon rode into Longford and announced that the French had been defeated by General Lake at Ballinamuck, a village some ten miles to the north.

How had their neighbours fared at Pakenham Hall? The rising of the rebel contingents in the midlands round Mullingar on 4 September had encouraged Humbert to drive towards Longford and Westmeath, hoping to join forces with the insurgents there before Lake could attack or Cornwallis cut the road to Dublin. By 7 September the French had reached Cloone and completed nearly half their journey to Dublin with astonishing speed. The news encouraged the pikemen to emerge in increasing numbers and nearly 7,000 rebels were encamped near Multyfarnham at Wilson's Hospital, a Protestant institution some fifteen miles by road from Castlepollard and Pakenham Hall, although much nearer across the narrow arm of Lough Derravaragh which lies in between.

The situation was extremely dangerous. Not only were the rebels present in strength at Wilson's Hospital, but a further 6,000 had risen and attacked Granard, some twenty miles to the north. The Mullingar garrison, hopelessly outnumbered, offered no resistance.

At Pakenham Hall, the young Lord Longford, now aged twenty-four, was made of sterner stuff. He recruited a force of about 100 men from his estate and marched across the newly harvested fields to the rebel camp. As he neared the grounds of Wilson's Hospital, he was informed that not only had the rebels seized a quantity of arms but also a quantity of liquor.[12] Prudently, he decided to halt and send for reinforcements to the Cavan garrison whose commander, a Scot, had begun a march towards the insurgents with 100 Scottish troops and about 250 local yeomanry. When this force advanced on the rebel camp they found many of the United Irishmen ready to surrender and thousands more already on the run for their homes.

The rest were caught between the Cavan forces and Longford's volunteers and before darkness fell more than 200 had been sabred or shot, the remnants escaping across the fields in the gloom, some to drown in Lough Derravaragh, where Kitty and Arthur had spent many tranquil, happy hours only six years before. Now the water was stained with blood and the wildfowl scattered in terror as drowning men flung up their hands in the last agony of death.

It is unlikely that Kitty had the resilience of her friend Maria when faced with the horrors of war. Pakenham Hall welcomed back her brothers after their splendid stand on various fronts against so vast an army of rebels, while the women prayed for their safety. Thomas had distinguished himself, leading his volunteers in defence of his home, while Kitty's uncle had been with Lake at Ballinamuck where the tiny French force was finally defeated. Humbert, arrogant to the last, reported to the Directory that, after obtaining great successes in Ireland, 'I have been obliged to submit to a superior force of 30,000 men'.[13]

The French prisoners were treated with great consideration by Lake and Cornwallis but the rebels were pursued with Lake's usual relentless efficiency 'to teach them a lesson'. It is to the credit of Captain Pakenham that he rode up to the rebel lines to warn the peasants, shouting, 'Run away, boys, otherwise you'll all be cut down.' But this isolated example of humanitarianism did little to stop the slaughter and by the end of the day hundreds of rebels lay dead at Ballinamuck, the number exciting the amazement but not the pity of the loyalists. Among those captured was Mathew Tone (Wolfe's brother) who was immediately hanged.

The next day Pakenham Hall became a temporary headquarters for Lord Cornwallis and his Staff, which included Lowry Cole. Thomas presided at this gathering of military leaders. The family was well represented – by two uncles holding staff appointments and his twenty-year-old brother, now Major Edward Pakenham. In the morning General John Moore joined the party and while plans were discussed for disposing of the Franco-Irish garrisons still encamped at Castlebar and Killala, news was received that Wolfe Tone and part of the French fleet had sailed from Brest for Ireland.

Once more Tone's presence on a French battleship was linked with disaster. He had sailed on the *Hoche*, in company with two other ships, and at last reached the northern Ireland coast near Lough Swilly. There, Sir John Warren caught up with the invasion force and, while the French frigates escaped, the *Hoche* put up a fight which lasted six hours against four British ships of the line as large as herself. At last, in sinking condition, the *Hoche* surrendered on 10 October and Tone, disdaining any attempt to avoid recognition, was captured.

He was determined to be treated as a prisoner of war and not a common felon, but in spite of his objections he was taken to a Dublin prison to await death by hanging. To avoid this ignominious end he attempted suicide by cutting his throat with a pen-knife, partly severing the windpipe. Although he survived this attempt for the time being, his prolonged death agony eventually cheated the hangman and he died in his prison bed on a black November day in 1798. So ended one of the most famous Irish patriots, a Protestant revolutionary who led the United Irishmen with gallantry, eloquence, charm and fanaticism and, inevitably, to tragedy and disaster. Disaster not only for himself but for countless fellow countrymen who, without his charisma and megalomania to mislead them, might have lived to make a constructive contribution to a happier future for Ireland.

The pacification of Ireland after the Rebellion was now crucial to the security of Britain as a whole. The threat of French invasion had not receded and discussion at Pakenham Hall and throughout Ireland on the possibility of Union with England was now of absorbing interest. Kitty would have listened with particular attention, knowing that the Wellesleys had already cut their economic ties with Ireland. Only William Wellesley-Pole, Arthur's elder brother, still owned land in Queen's County and maintained an interest in Irish affairs and Dublin Castle. He had been presented with a sword by the Viceroy in recognition of his part in suppressing the Rebellion of '98.

The first attempt by the administration to have the Act of Union passed by the Irish Parliament failed in January 1799. Castlereagh, as Chief

Secretary, went to work with his usual efficiency from the house he had rented in Upper Merrion Street – Mornington House, Arthur's old Dublin home. Opposition to the Union arose not only from owners of rotten boroughs, but also from Orangemen, fearing that Union would be a prelude to complete Catholic emancipation and the eclipse of the Protestant Ascendancy in Ireland. In addition, there was genuine patriotic feeling from those with no axe to grind that Union would mean the decline of Ireland. Substituting London for Dublin as the seat of power and decision making would entail the departure for England of those with initiative and direct responsibility for the economy, particularly the landowners and improvers. The importance and attraction of Dublin as a cultural and economic centre would be hit hard by the abolition of its Parliament.

All these interests had to be appeased or swamped to obtain a majority for the Union and supporters were won with the offer of fifteen new peerages, with a similar number of promotions for Members of the Irish House of Lords, together with numerous prizes of pensions and public appointments, all carefully engineered by Castlereagh, with the approval of the Viceroy and the British Government.

Perhaps not so well recorded is the disgust Castlereagh and Cornwallis felt for the part they had to play. Cornwallis found his life as Viceroy at this time his 'idea of perfect misery'. 'I long', he wrote, 'to kick those whom my public duty obliges me to court. My occupation is to negotiate and job with the most corrupt people under Heaven. I despise and hate myself every hour for engaging in such dirty work and am supported only by the reflection that without the Union the British Empire must be dissolved. Nothing but a conviction that a Union is absolutely necessary could make me endure the shocking task which is imposed upon me.'[14]

Although Dublin politics produced one sensation after another, domestic life at Pakenham Hall had its own small upheavals. Kitty's younger sister Helen married James Hamilton of Brown Hall, County Donegal. Now both her married sisters were living in the north and journeys to visit them could conveniently be broken at Florence Court, the home of Lowry Cole and his sister Lady Florence Balfour. Kitty was now twenty-seven and the excitement of another wedding in the family must have caused speculation among her friends as to when Kitty, who could still command the admiration of eligible men in her circle, not least that of Lowry Cole, would decide to abandon her attachment for Arthur Wellesley. She could not have failed to hear from friends that the young colonel of the 33rd was a popular member of Calcutta's social round, enjoying the many parties and lavish dinners given by the large British community there. William Hickey, the portrait painter, working in India at this time, recorded that the entertainments given by the officers of the 33rd were notorious for hard drinking and joviality.[15]

From letters between the Wellesley brothers during this period, it is clear that Arthur was determined to make not only a successful military career but also a fortune. An officer's financial position was determined by the amount of active service he could achieve and an expedition on active service could free him from his Irish debts. To be given chief command 'Would make my fortune ...'. This obsession with financial gain had not been a feature of Arthur's character in his younger days. His new motivation had been the blow to his self-esteem at the hands of the Pakenham family, when lack of money and prospects frustrated his plans to marry Kitty Pakenham.

During his early days in India, in spite of his social and military successes, he was lonely and complained that he had not received a single letter from home in over a year. With the arrival of his two brothers and increased responsibility there was less time for nostalgia. Yet in contrast to the heat and discomfort of life in India, memories of home and spring days with his friends in the Irish countryside and of sweet Kitty Pakenham, for ever young and elusive, would be renewed in talk with his military family, many of whom were from Ireland. As the claret flowed at the mess dinner-table and the great fans moved slowly back and forth above their heads, stirring the hot air, talk would be of Ireland and wonderful days with horses and hounds or walking the countryside to shoot or fish; of splendid evenings in the great Dublin houses where the most beautiful women in the world moved through the high, bright rooms alive with music and dancing. As the heat of the day gradually diminished, the sentimental songs of Thomas Moore would silence the tropical night:

> With thee were the dreams of my earliest love;
> Every thought of my reason was thine;
> In my last humble prayer to the Spirit above
> Thy name shall be mingled with mine![16]

or again:

> As slow our ship her foamy track
> Against the wind was cleaving
> Her trembling pennant still looked back
> to that dear isle 'twas leaving ....
>
> So loath we part from all we love,
> From all the links that bind us;
> So turn our hearts as on we rove,
> To those we left behind us.[17]

The pleasant life in the Calcutta drawing-rooms was soon to give way to action. In May 1799, Arthur and his regiment were part of the campaign for the invasion of Mysore, culminating in the storming of Seringapatam and the dramatic death of Tipoo Sultan, his body found beneath a heap of corpses at one of the gates to his city. The death of this warrior king, whose wealth had been obtained by ruthless attacks against neighbouring rulers and the terrorizing of peasants and farmers, opened the way to the pacification of Mysore and a period of peace and safety for the population.

The prize-money from the victory at Seringapatam had been considerable. Harris, the commanding general, had received £150,000, while further down the scale the colonel of the 33rd was richer by £4,000 and at last able to settle his debts. The Governor-General, Richard, Lord Mornington, was raised in the Irish Peerage to become Marquis Wellesley. In his vanity, he resented this Irish promotion as a second-rate honour and a slur on his achievements in India for the British Government.

Because of the six months' interval between the despatch of news from India and its arrival in England by sailing ship, these exciting events were not yet known in Ireland as 1799 drew to its close. The slow death of the Irish Parliament continued, some still hoping for a miracle to revive the corpse. But Castlereagh was doing his work too well; rewards for the 'Ayes' and eclipse for the 'Noes' gained a majority of forty-three votes, after an epic debate on 6 February 1800. The King's recommendation for a legislative Union as being 'In the common interest of both his Kingdoms' was accepted.

Among the majority vote was that of Lowry Cole, the new Member for County Fermanagh and now an acknowledged suitor for Kitty's hand. His 'love affair' with Kitty[18] must have reached its zenith at this time. He was shortly to be posted to Egypt and by the end of April 1801 had sailed for the Mediterranean. Family letters show that his romance with Kitty was broken off at her instigation, some time before 1802. His brother wrote in that year: 'Since that love affair with Kitty Pakenham he [Lowry] seems like a burnt child to fear the fire and not to have any wish to hazard his happiness' by paying attention to any other eligible ladies of his acquaintance.

The century closed with the passing of the Act of Union. As had been feared by many objectors to the measure, transfer of power from Dublin to London had a cataclysmic effect on the social and economic life of the country. Immediately after the Union there was a disastrous fall in property values. 'All the men of fortune are going or gone to England', wrote Lady Enniskillen, Lowry's mother, in 1802. 'I hear most of those who voted for the Union are now sorry for it.' Mornington House,

## Rebellion

Arthur's former home in Dublin, had been sold by Richard to Lord Cloncurry in 1791 for £8,000, then leased to various people, including Lord Castlereagh, and sold again in 1802 for £2,500.[19]

Although in the view of some of the old Ascendancy families the future of Dublin society and of Ireland was in eclipse, not all abandoned hope. It was a brave gesture that prompted Longford to accelerate in 1801 his plans for further substantial alterations to Pakenham Hall. Over the next few years Francis Johnston's 'Gothic' materialized round the walls of the old house in towers and crenulations.[20]

Kitty's much loved younger brother Edward, now aged twenty-two, was in Dublin and about to join his regiment in England. Writing to his mother in March 1800, he tells her he is impatient to be off. 'I get into the chaise this moment . . . . I set out with greater satisfaction to join than ever any other dog did, who left so much behind.'[21] By May he was settled in barracks at Chelmsford and seeing something of his younger brother Hercules while in London and dining with Army friends. As lieutenant-colonel of the 64th Regiment of Foot, he was full of enthusiasm for the career before him. 'I now am but beginning the world,' he wrote to his mother. 'The worst of it is I find more is expected than I fear I shall come up to, but 'tis easy to know the reason. Give me your good wishes and in return I give you all my love.'

In February, the future general sailed with his Regiment from Spithead, in the transport *Coverdale*, for the West Indies via Nova Scotia.

> My dearest mother, the wind is a good one. The fleet is in the act of weighing. I am more than pleased with the idea that I shall find all exactly as I could wish on return. I have a steady trust that I shall be able to get through my duty to the credit of your family and son and that you will be assured of my content and happiness and be not uneasy on my account. Tom will find out where I am going to before I shall know myself; he will inform you how to direct. Almighty bless you – no words can carry my affection. Ever yours, dearest mother, E. M. Pakenham.[22]

In Ireland, Lord Cornwallis had at last laid down his heavy burden of duty. Tired and disgusted with the failure of his efforts to secure Catholic emancipation as a corollary to the Act of Union, which he believed was the only policy to save Ireland from self-destruction, he resigned in February 1801, leaving Ireland for good, to die in India four years later.

Pitt had been displaced by Addington and Lord Hardwicke appointed to Dublin Castle as Lord Lieutenant. In spite of stagnation in trade and increasing poverty among the people, the Hardwickes did their best to heal the rifts in society caused by the Union. Lady Hardwicke was an indefatigable party-giver and cultivated every section of Dublin society, including the social climbers who had largely replaced the old establishment families at the viceregal Court since the Union. In spite of the political stagnation there was still beauty and talent in Dublin. As Lady Enniskillen remarked: 'Dublin was uncommonly gay this spring. All the Unionists strove to prevent people from going to live in England by giving balls and masquerades. Lord and Lady Hardwicke were very much liked .... They gave a number of private entertainments to which Henrietta [her daughter] was always asked.'[23] There is little doubt that Kitty was a frequent visitor to the Castle; but for her the new century was to bring momentous happenings beyond the horizon of the capital's fading glory.

# CHAPTER 5

# *Letter to India*

The Wellesley brothers and many of their contemporaries regarded a call to service in India not merely as an avenue to personal advancement but as a patriotic and moral duty. The subversive plans of the French were based on fostering and supporting tribal conflict, endemic in the Indian states, manipulating one war-lord against another to secure their mutual destruction and the breakdown of organized resistance. Under this strategy, India would fall to the domination of France with the minimum loss in French lives and resources. Napoleon's dream of world conquest could then become a practical possibility. In terms of the conflict in Europe, the denial of the Indian sub-continent to the French was of vital importance to the Allied powers.

The brothers were usually at loggerheads with the directors of the East India Company, who regarded their Eastern trading posts in purely economic terms. Military action was only justified, in their opinion, if trading interests were threatened. Tribal slaughter, local corruption or the tyranny and excesses of native rulers were not the concerns of the company, so long as they did not seriously interfere with trade. The ambitions of the French and the long-term pacification of India were subjects treated with equal indifference and ignorance.

The British Government viewed the situation in different terms. The civil administration in India, of which Richard was now the head, had to consider not only the strategic importance of denying the sub-continent to the French, but the longer-term aim of establishing a peaceful regime, based on cooperation with local rulers, which would have the support and approval of the population. This support could only be gained if the new administration proved to be better than anything they had experienced in the past under the oppressive and war-hungry governments of their own princes and officials.

The pacification of India would bring the blessing of security to a peasantry which had only known the terrors of tribal conflict; destruction of crops, starvation, and appalling cruelties inflicted on them by raiders who burnt their villages. The Wellesley policy was to create a system of government that would be just, incorruptible and merciful; to be administered through enlightened native rulers and supervised by a British civil service with the highest Christian, moral and educational standards attainable and holding the ultimate power to remove any native ruler who abused his people. In a letter to the Indian *Dewan* (Prime Minister) of a young Rajah of Mysore, Arthur defined his principles of administration: 'Protect the ryots [peasants] and traders and allow no man, whether vested with authority or otherwise, to oppress them with impunity.'[1] Justice would be done according to native custom and belief, with scrupulous observance of every pledge given and security for life and property of the poorest and those better off, without the necessity for bribes or influence. A noble aim and also a recipe for practical government which, if properly administered, would require the minimum number of supervisors from the ruling power, because it would have the trust and respect of the population. 'Everything depends', Arthur's letter continues, 'on justice, freedom from corruption and unswerving truth to one's word and to every obligation undertaken.'

In addition to his administrative ability, Arthur's bravery in battle became a legend among his men. In one engagement he had a horse shot under him and another piked, while almost every member of his Staff were either killed or wounded or had their horses killed under them. The local war-lords had everything to gain and nothing to lose by the fiercest resistance they could offer to the British and Indian forces against them. One of Arthur's young officers, Colin Campbell, wrote later: 'I never saw a man as collected as he was in the thick of battle.' This coolness was remarked again and again – he became transformed 'like an eagle' when the danger was greatest.

His native troops, which made up the bulk of his command, were provided with regular rations and equipment, instead of being forced to live off the country by theft and looting, which was the usual custom not only of tribal forces, but of armies under French control. Arthur could speak to his native troops 'With that eloquent and correct knowledge of the native language for which he was celebrated,' wrote Sir John Campbell, one of his commanders. His Indian name was 'Wellesley Bahadur' – Wellesley the Invincible.[2] In 1800 Arthur secured a notable success in defeating Dhoondiah Waugh and a vastly superior Mahratta force, for which he received public commendation from General Harris and appointment as Governor of Mysore.

There were plenty of young men who wanted to try their luck in the sub-continent. In 1801, Lowry Cole's youngest brother Arthur sailed for India, arriving in July after a fairly fast voyage of four months. He wrote to his father Lord Enniskillen, telling him how he had presented his letters of introduction to Lord Edward Clive, Governor of Madras (son of the famous Robert), as soon as he arrived and dined with him the same evening. He had also met Josiah Webbe, Chief Secretary to the Indian Government, a man of very great ability and a firm supporter of the Wellesleys. Arthur Wellesley described him in later years as 'One of the ablest men I ever knew, and what is more, one of the most honest'. Webbe told young Cole that there were positive orders for 'Every Madras writer [clerk] to proceed to the College in Calcutta to learn the language, and the sooner I went the better. I asked him if it were possible for me to avoid going but he said the order was so peremptory that Lord Clive could not dare to take it upon himself to allow any young man to remain here'.[3]

This order, of course, had come from Richard, the Governor-General, who soon after arriving in India determined to change the 'indolence and dissipation' of young recruits to the Indian civil service into something more useful to the country. He promptly established Wellesley College in Calcutta as a training school where the appalling ignorance of Indian customs, history, language and economics shown by young men shipped from England to run the country could be corrected.

It was characteristic of the Wellesleys to make detailed preparations for any new appointment to which they were called. As has been seen, Arthur's choice of a library to take to India for use on the voyage contained books on every aspect of Indian life. He became proficient in Indian dialects as part of his intention to equip himself for a career which would not only benefit himself but would enable him to carry out his work efficiently to the benefit of Britain, India and the destruction of the French. Richard had also acquired an unrivalled knowledge of Indian affairs and culture by the time he was appointed Governor-General. Little has been said of Henry, the youngest brother, who acted as private secretary and personal assistant to Richard and provided a useful liaison between the civil and military policies the brothers were formulating.

In spite of the usually close cooperation between the brothers, a rift developed. In 1801 Richard gave Arthur secret orders to assemble an invasion force in Ceylon for an attack on the French island stronghold now called Mauritius. Almost as soon as Arthur reached Ceylon the orders were countermanded and Arthur recalled. He was furious, both at losing command of the invasion force and at his brother's change of mind. He decided, on his own initiative, to take his troops to Bombay. On arrival he found he had been superseded by General Baird, a more senior officer. In an angry letter to Henry, he told him his prospects were ruined and he would quit India for ever. At the same time he developed an irritation of the skin called the Malabar Itch, which added to his misery.[4]

Unknown to him, a letter was on its way from Ireland which was to revive memories of the past and instigate a chain of events of the greatest importance for Arthur's future.

The letter was written at the end of January 1801, a few days after reports reached Ireland of Arthur's success at Seringapatam in 1799 and his more recent victory over Dhoondiah Waugh. The news of these battles caused something of a sensation among Arthur's friends and coincided with a critical period in Kitty's relationship with Lowry Cole. Did this fresh news of Arthur's military and financial success prompt her to refuse Lowry's proposal, although it might be her last chance of marriage with an attractive man of her own age? She was now twenty-nine and her friends may well have been worried that her rejection of Lowry on the strength of a promise made so long ago was building on false hopes. With Lowry awaiting orders for service abroad, there was every possibility that this time her refusal would be irrevocable. Kitty's romantic attachment to Arthur was a subject for endless speculation among her friends, particularly Olivia Acheson, now Olivia Sparrow, a young matron with a rich husband considerably older than herself and time on her hands to play match-maker.

Kitty would never have given Olivia permission to write directly to Arthur to find out if he was still determined to marry her. How could Olivia's curiosity about Arthur's intentions be satisfied? Could she involve a third party as a sounding-board to test Arthur's reactions on the subject of Kitty's unattached state? An instrument presented itself in the form of a mutual friend who owed Arthur a letter – a colleague of old Captain Pakenham's – Colonel M. Beresford, who was also a close ally of Olivia's.

His letter is artfully constructed, beginning with some racy gossip concerning events and personalities in Dublin and how the Union was got through the Irish Parliament with a mixture of threats and bribery. He describes the acrimonious 'debate' between Lord Clare, Irish chancellor, and Pitt in the Cabinet. 'Pitt proposed that Catholics should sit in both Houses of Parliament – the Irish Chancellor vehemently opposed the proposition – if Mr Pitt carries that point this country must undergo a convulsion, the ultimate consequences of which no man can foresee.'

He then gives a scandalous account of Lord Clare's private life, describing his wife's lover, Lord Ormonde, as 'Drunken, nervous, feeble – and his valour is more than questioned ... which made it necessary for him to fight a couple of duels with a brace of Irish blackguards for no cause whatsoever'. He excuses this malicious gossip by saying 'It is really a melancholy story' and that the Chancellor was 'dying of smothered anguish'.

He then changes the subject to an account of a friend's suicide which was caused by a 'fatal complaint', the result of an accident in the hunting field which, had he lived, would have resulted in castration. 'He could not bear the thought', and killed himself.

The letter continues:

> Now for more agreeable subjects than the two last we have gone over – let me congratulate you, which I most heartily do, upon your successes in India. Your military career has been most fortunate – I hope your circumstances have been equally so – well-knowing what has been done in that line is all that it should be. I don't know what your objects at home may be, but I am certain that you will not take amiss what I say. I know not if Miss Pakenham is an object to you or not – she looks as well as ever – no person whatsoever has paid her any particular attention – so much I say, having heard her name and yours mentioned together. I hear her most highly spoken of by Mrs. Sparrow. She lives so retired that nobody ever sees her. One night, Tom Pakenham [of Coolure] took me to sup to Lady Longford's – I could not avoid looking with all my eyes at the lady and thinking of you and former times. I happened on this just as your letter from the banks of the Nerbadra reached me – but I had not nerves to say anything about you. Enclosed is a letter from Mrs. Sparrow – she is a most charming woman, she talks so handsomely of you that you ought to be flattered. I have seen much of her and for her bear the greatest and highest opinion.

He then continues with more gossip: 'Our friend Cooke has been keeping a common and noted Irish strumpet. This woman receives half the town and parades the streets of Dublin upon one of Cooke's horses with his groom riding after her....'

How welcome such a letter would be, with all its scandalous news of friends and acquaintances – and particularly for the news of Kitty Pakenham. There was more on this subject in the letter enclosed from her most intimate and oldest friend Olivia Sparrow. Arthur's thoughts had already been turning towards home after the disappointment of his abortive mission to Ceylon and he had become somewhat disenchanted with India.

The two letters brought to active life emotions which, he admitted later, had never been fully suppressed during his long service abroad. He had never forgotten Kitty Pakenham or fully recovered from the humiliation of her family's rejection of his proposal.

Why had Olivia brought the matter to Colonel Beresford's attention in January 1801 and prodded him into writing his long overdue reply to Arthur's letter, with her enclosure seeking information on his feelings for Kitty? There is no doubt that Lowry had fallen in love with Kitty and that many people, including her brother Edward, expected them to marry. With his promotion to colonel in January 1801, and the possibility of early service abroad, he seemed set on a lucrative and honourable career and may have insisted that Kitty make a final decision, without further procrastination. Her decision had been to reject him.

Why then did Beresford, who was second-in-command to Tom Pakenham at the Ordnance and knew the family well, carefully make the point in his letter that 'no person whatsoever' had paid her any particular attention, when he and Olivia, of all people, must have been aware of Lowry's 'particular attention' to Kitty? A clue may lie in the gossipy nature of the letter itself; and in Beresford's obvious admiration, if nothing more, for the charms of Mrs Sparrow. Nothing could have been more amusing for these two than to play Cupid for the absent hero in India, at the expense of a supporter of the hated Union at home, Lowry Cole.

Olivia's motive may not have been so much political revenge, as inspired by her compulsive desire to interfere and manipulate the private lives of her friends. She may have wanted to revive the old romance as much for her own satisfaction as for Kitty's. From this point of view it is not surprising that Olivia and Beresford should have been less than truthful in describing Kitty's lack of social life. The picture they wanted to create in Arthur's mind of a woman dedicated to her first love, although partly true, was also nicely calculated to reawaken Arthur's interest. Kitty's rejection of Lowry Cole gave some credence to this picture, but the claim that 'She lives so retired that nobody ever sees her' must have been an inaccurate description of life at Pakenham Hall. Her brother, master of the house, was younger than herself and enjoyed entertaining friends of his own age. Her other brothers, Edward, Hercules and William, were serving abroad, Henry was ordained, two sisters were married and Caroline, the youngest, was popular in Dublin society. The house was still 'the seat of hospitality', as Maria described it, and the family would make frequent visits to the homes of friends. In addition, there was their regular annual programme of visits to their property, Langford Lodge, in Ulster by Lough Neagh and to their Dublin house for the usual round of viceregal functions.

Edward, writing to his mother from St Crois in the West Indies in 1801, remarked that Longford 'Seemed so occupied about P[akenham] Hall and there appears so little idleness among you, its enough to make even a West Indian prick up and to business, but for certain more than enough to make my soul snug. This will hop in when you are seated at the Hall after your northern scamper ... Kitty, I hope, accompanies you – I have praised, it must do for all your family, so of Kit I say nothing'.[5]

Allowing for the usual delays between despatching a letter and its arrival in India, it was probably July 1801 before Arthur read Beresford's communication, and Olivia's enclosure, of the previous January. By that time he was back in Mysore at Lord Edward Clive's personal request. Beresford's letter, with its typically Irish anecdotes and human tragedy as a subject for laughter, must have seemed like a breath of Dublin air – while Olivia's opened old wounds which had never fully healed. In the cool dimness of his house, shuttered against the heat, he sat down to write her a reply. It is undated, but was probably written in August 1801.

> You may recollect a disappointment I met with about eight years ago, in an object in which I was most interested. Notwithstanding my good fortune and the perpetual activity of the life which I have led, that disappointment, the object of it and all the circumstances are fresh in my mind, as if they happened only yesterday. How much more would they bear upon me if I was to return to the inactivity of a home life?
>
> Upon the whole I think that for many reasons referable as well to another person as to me, I am better away, but I acknowledge that I am very anxious to go home and I am not quite certain that I shall not commence my voyage as soon as there is peace.
>
> I have answered your questions candidly and have stated facts which tend rather to my own humiliation. But I do so because I am convinced that you have always been acquainted with the circumstances to which I have alluded; because I wish to shew you the merit of your friend is still felt; and because I know you will not mention them (to more than six full assemblies!).
>
> You are so kind as to enquire after my health. It is excellent. Excepting what I have above mentioned to you, I have reason to be satisfied with everything. Fortune has favoured me upon every occasion and if I could forget that which has borne so heavily upon me for the last eight years, I should have as little care as you appear to have.
>
> When you see your friend, do me the favour to remember me to her in the kindest manner.
>
> You see that I have written you a long letter; I expect a longer answer. You are in the Country where our common friends are, of whom as well as

yourself every intelligence must be interesting. I have nothing to write about excepting yourself and a few lines to answer your enquiries about me. God bless you. Believe me your most faithful servant, Arthur Wellesley.

I'll send this letter to Col. Beresford as I don't know where it would certainly find you.

From this letter it is possible to reconstruct Olivia's questions. When did Arthur think he would come home and did he still have a regard for her friend, Kitty Pakenham? He wanted to come home but there were many reasons, which concerned the 'other person' as well as himself, why he might be better away. He was 'very anxious' to go home and might do so as soon as peace was declared. Talk of peace was much in the air with the change of government in England. Addington, the new Prime Minister, and his adminstration were for appeasement and a preliminary treaty with France was signed in October 1801. Bonaparte had already concluded a series of peace treaties with other European powers and it was only a matter of months before the Peace of Amiens, between Britain and France, was signed in March 1802.

As for his regard for Kitty, the whole tone of his letter emphasizes how great an impact the 'disappointment' of eight years before had had on him. In spite of the 'perpetual activity' of his present life, the object of his disappointment, Kitty, and all the circumstances were still as fresh in his mind as if they had happened yesterday. The affair had 'borne so heavily' on him, that all his successes had not put it out of his mind. His frank letter was to show Olivia that the 'merit' of her friend was still very deeply felt – and from a highly intelligent man, popular and successful, it is clear that no other woman had taken her place over the years as a possible wife. India was not without its quota of attractive and eligible young women, daughters of officers and merchants brought out by their parents to find husbands from the European community. Arthur Wellesley enjoyed their company but his interest apparently centred more on the comely matrons and the domestic comforts of their homes than on their unmarried sisters.

The agonizing slowness of the mails at last brought Arthur's reply. Olivia would have been delighted. Her intervention was proving more successful than she had hoped. It revealed a deeply romantic situation, familiar from the pages of the novels she so much enjoyed. The absent hero, the sweet and faithful creature awaiting his return, the trusted friend, the family reconciliation and – a happy ending! She could not wait to show the letter to Kitty, as Arthur probably guessed she would. Already he might be on his way home. The anticipated peace treaty had been signed. France and Britain were no longer at war.

## Letter to India

In May 1802, Kitty wrote to her friend from Dublin.

God Almighty forbid he should either remain an exile from his country or be unhappy in it. Olivia, you know my heart, at least I believe you do, as well as I know it myself. You know how sincerely I am interested in his happiness and can imagine what gratitude I feel, (indeed much more than can be expressed) for his kind remembrance. My dearest Olivia, you know I can send no message; a kind word from me he might think binding to him and make him think himself obliged to renew a pursuit, which perhaps he might not then wish or my family (at least some of them) take kindly. My first wish, if I was not taking care not to wish about it, would be that he should return and feel himself perfectly free (I do not mean free from regard for those who sincerely regard him, but to act as he pleases) and then – I hardly know what to wish then, for fear of nursing a disappointment for him, for myself, or a vexation for my friends. Yet they all speak of him with kindness, particularly Aunt. I mentioned your having heard from him and Longford expressed pleasure, which I am sure [was] sincere, at his success, saying he deserved all his good fortune.

Perhaps you mentioned him to my mother; in what manner did she speak of him? You see, Olivia, how I trust you. Whatever you say must be from yourself. But do you think he will still be in India as long as till your letter would reach him? His was *nine months* coming. At all events you will write, I dare say. I was in the act of packing up for our journey to town when your letter arrived. It was very odd, but the moment I opened it, before I had read two lines, I knew you had heard from India. Perhaps you will be angry with me when I say I am by no means as certain as you seem to be, as to what his present wish is. He now desires to be kindly remembered, but do you not think he seems to think the business over? In a former letter to you his words were, I believe, 'You cannot say more to her than I feel.' Do you recollect?

Olivia, I am afraid of saying a word ever since your letter arrived for fear it should be his name. So then the sooner I hear from you the better. Pray write soon. I can only tell you we arrived in town yesterday, met mother, who arrived before us, so we have her company to dinner. Believe my love, my true and dear friend, God bless you. Yours affectionately,
C.D.S.Pakenham

It is clear from this letter that Kitty expected Arthur to make an early return from India and that she was still deeply in love with him – though nervous that her friend was making too much of Arthur's kind words. It is also greatly to her credit that the letter speaks clearly of her concern for his happiness rather than her own and that she was trying desperately not to let her hopes of a reunion with the man she wanted to marry eight years before cloud her judgement of his intentions.

It also throws light on the opposition of her family to Arthur's proposal and to Arthur himself. It is her mother's reaction she is most anxious about. She is not at all sure if they would welcome a renewal of his courtship, in spite of his material success in India. It was not merely the harsh words of Kitty's father that blighted the romance, but opposition from her mother and eldest brother to his second proposal before his departure in 1795 for the abortive voyage to the West Indies. It would seem that there was more than economic considerations in their rejection of Arthur as a future son-in-law.

So the matter rested, while the slow ships dipped and rolled across the oceans separating India from home, hazardous messengers between lovers, families and friends.

# CHAPTER 6

# *Matrimonial Dilemma*

The long drawn out crisis in her personal affairs had turned Kitty towards introspection and self-analysis. From her visit to her sister Helen Hamilton at Brown Hall, Lough Eskie, County Donegal, in July 1802, two manuscripts survive in Kitty's hand, written 'On the shores of Lough Eskie', which are pleas for spiritual guidance. The first is a poem in her usual high-flown style, the product of much Bible-reading, sermons, psalms and the hymns of the day. It begins:

> How stands my great account? My soul survey
> The debt Eternal Justice bids me pay
>
> 'Prepare thy house, thy heart in order set,
> Prepare the Judge of Heaven and earth to meet.'
>
> So speaks the warning prophet, awful words
> Which fearfully my troubled soul records.
> Am I prepared and can I meet my doom
> Nor shudder at the dreaded wrath to come?
> Ah no – Great God then snatch me not away;
> In mercy spare me. Grant me time to pray.
>
> Teach me, Oh God, to search and know my heart
> That there no cherished sin may claim a part.
> Let no fond error, loath to quit its place,
> Obstruct within my soul the work of grace.
>
> . . .      . . .      . . .      . . .
>
> Oh never may I wish to build my name
> On the piled ruin of another's fame;

> Or even listen to the insidious lie,
> The low deceit, detested calumny.
> May my firm soul the impious wit detest;
> With scorn discourage the unhallowed jest.
> Teach me to live as born one day to die
> And view the eternal world with constant eye.

There is much more; but beneath the laudable sentiments Kitty is struggling not to fall a prey to illusion, to look objectively at her motives and root out wordly considerations. Her situation was difficult. At the age of thirty she was naturally tempted to build her hopes on marriage with Arthur. She realized her sentimental regard for him, and possibly his for her, might well be a 'fond error' of the heart, 'loath to quit its place'. She had also been distressed by the gossip reaching her from India, through Arthur's returning friends, about his fondness for various ladies, mostly the wives of brother officers – although none of these flirtations amounted to a serious scandal. She begs for help not to listen to the 'insidious lie, The low deceit, detested calumny', but she is only human and although she prays that her 'firm soul' will detest and discourage the 'impious wit' and 'unhallowed jest' of the gossips, she cannot shut her ears. Gossip in the Dublin clubs and round the dinner-tables was scurrilous and spared nobody; succeess for social climbers depended on the ability to blacken reputations and expose to ridicule every facet of human weakness for the amusement of the assembled company.

Not only friends but members of Kitty's family were serving in India. Her young cousin, the son of Tom Pakenham of Coolure, had a post with the East India Company, as did Lowry Cole's young brother. Olivia's brother was in Calcutta in 1804 and 'constantly with the Governor-General' as Arthur informed her. Although the mails were slow and unreliable there was a good deal of coming and going between India and home. Wounded or sick officers sent on leave, families moving back and forth, and the ordinary traffic of commerce kept the lines of communication open and active.

Arthur was conscious that gossip about his life in India had reached Dublin. In a letter to Olivia he reported that Lady William, wife of the Governor of Fort William in Calcutta, had 'lectured him' on how 'the scandalous world' had attacked him again and reports circulated to his disadvantage at home.

In the circumstances, it was not surprising that Kitty prayed for strength to ignore calumnies about Arthur. She was to persist throughout her life in a determination never to believe adverse reports concerning Arthur or anything that he did.

Writing again from the shores of Lough Eskie a few days later she set down another plea for guidance. This time the manuscript concerns a weakness which she recognized in her own character: a propensity to find fault and to criticize her friends and those she loved. It is significant that she kept these papers all her life, finding in them an expression of her emotions which she did not reject as the years passed. In this outpouring, she asks God's help to 'Enlighten the understanding of thy imploring servant. Enable me to distinguish between anxiety for the improvement of those I love and an impulse to indulge my own irritated temper in finding fault.... Let me not express and feel towards others a severity I should find it so painful myself to meet with. Teach me to clear and improve my judgement that I may discern when my interference might be of service and when not; lest by officiously and abruptly offering my opinion, I might give offence when I intended a kindness and increase an evil by lessening the affection of a friend instead of improving it.'

She continues: 'Soften my temper, so that not one word may be spoken with acrimony, impatience or anger.' But she also asks for strength not to shrink from performing 'any of the duties of a friend' although the task may be painful by obliging her to inflict pain. If she has to give advice, she prays her gentleness, sincerity and affection will convince 'That it is only offered in the hope of being of service to a friend. May my wish be ever to amend, never to censure'.

That she had a sharp tongue and a quick temper is indicated in a number of half-joking family references to her 'severity' in letters between her brothers and their mother. Arthur wrote to Olivia that he had observed how she 'stood ... in awe' of Kitty, adding that he believed Olivia would be 'unwilling to tell her anything which could annoy her, or could irritate her against me'. He begged Olivia to keep the nature of their correspondence to herself – a vain hope, in spite of Olivia's assurances of her discretion.

After her visit to Brown Hall in July, Kitty returned home impatient to receive Arthur's reply to Olivia's letter of the previous May. Four months was the minimum transit time for letters from India, but communication via the East-Indiamen was erratic. He could not receive the letter before August or September and a reply could not be expected before the new year. Kitty, already in a state of deep anxiety and depression, convinced herself that Arthur would decide to let the matter drop. Her fears were confirmed when no word from India was received in the spring and summer of 1803.

## A Soldier's Wife

In October, she visited Cheltenham in an effort to improve health and spirits. Her visit coincided with that of her rejected suitor Lowry Cole, who had returned from Malta in January. Was this 'coincidence' an attempt to revive the affair, now she was convinced by his silence that Arthur no longer cared for her? Lowry's brother believed so. 'Kitty is in Cheltenham', he wrote in October 1803. 'I am beginning to think she wishes to bring on the subject again with Lowry, but he fights shy. She will deserve it, as she treated him cruelly.'[1]

Endless questions chased through her mind. Were her secret hopes of a future with Arthur ended for ever? She had lost Lowry's friendship and affection. His coldness towards her at Cheltenham had filled her with remorse for the hurt she had caused. If Arthur should return, how would her family react? Perhaps his silence was due to illness or even death at the head of one of the cavalry charges for which he had become famous. She feared the stories of his involvement with other women might have a basis of truth and that he had formed a serious attachment for one of them.

She was aware her own attractions were fading with the relentlessly advancing years. Her character had also changed. The playful tyranny and youthful enthusiasm for various causes, the charmingly inconsequential repartee which had made her popular in Dublin society had coalesced into the small, thin, anxious woman, somewhat set in her ways, which she saw in the looking-glass each day. She had an uncommon ability to recognize her faults and honestly admitted them with disarming humility. Yet hard times had destroyed her youthful confidence and vitality. In their place was a certain obstinate determination to have the last word. Much of the charm still remained and on good days the old whimsical humour would assert itself. Her loss of weight was only temporary, due to illness and worry, and she could expect to regain the small, plump figure which fashion required. Her friends still loved her for her kindness and consideration; her instinctive generosity, too easily exploited; her ready sympathy. The fluidity of her emotions was still too openly reflected in her face, which could be transformed from a certain dullness in repose to sudden anger, or by an elusive smile, an expressive quality of the eyes, into a countenance which became youthful and endearing. In all her troubles the rock to which she clung was her religion.

Autumn turned to winter and still no word from Arthur. To the misery of uncertainty was added the endless turmoil of building work at Pakenham Hall. Her brother was spending vast sums on changing the old house, a project not to be completed until 1806, when Maria told her father: 'The Castle is now really a mansion fit for a nobleman of his fortune.'

In Dublin, the last spasms of the Rebellion were exhausting themselves.

## Matrimonial Dilemma

Catholic hopes of emancipation had been dashed by the final form of the Act of Union. In 1803, Robert Emmet, a republican visionary, set up a pike factory in Dublin and in July led a mob to attack the Debtors' Prison, killing the guard. By mischance Lord Chief Justice Kilwarden was proceeding along the street in his carriage. The mob dragged him out and killed him. With the arrival of troops the mob dispersed and Emmet was captured – later to be executed.

This brief revival of the Rebellion alienated Pitt's supporters and crushed further efforts towards Catholic emancipation. Anti-Catholic and anti-Irish feeling was further inflamed in Britain by the participation of Pope Pius VII in the coronation of Napoleon the following year.

It was now eighteen months since Olivia had replied to Arthur's letter of August 1801. She had received it in May 1802 and had despatched a reply at once. But it was now January 1804 – three years since she and Beresford had taken the initiative in probing Arthur's sentiments towards her friend. Kitty had long since concluded that hope was surely dead – the dark January landscape mirrored her depression and despair.

Suddenly the gloom lifted. Olivia had received Arthur's reply and an explanation for the terrible delay. His letter was dated the previous year, 7 March 1803. He had replied at once on receiving Olivia's letter of May 1802, which had taken ten months to reach him. A further ten months had elapsed before his answer reached Ireland.

His letter begins:

> I have just received your kind letter of May, 1802. If it had arrived in September last, which is the time it should have reached me, it would have found me disengaged and I should have been in England by this time.
>
> I am at present in command of an army about to advance into the territories of the Mahathras. I think that the service will not last long, but God knows when I shall be able to bring it to a conclusion. At all events I shall return to Europe as soon as I am at liberty. If you could have said more, I wish that you had not been so exceedingly discreet in your letter. But be that as it may, I cannot express how much pleased I am with it and you, or how grateful for your kindness. If I could talk or rather listen to you, I dare say that you could tell me all that I wish to know; but you are too discreet for me now. I only hope that you are even more so in respect to what I have written to you. I am afraid that she could be much offended if she knew that I had entered upon this subject in my letters; and to tell you the truth, if I had not suspected that your own observations had made you acquainted with all the circumstances many years ago; and if I had not observed that you stood in such awe of her ... you would be very unwilling to tell her anything which could annoy her, or could irritate her against me....
>
> If you have been thus discreet and I am not mistaken, I beg you for my sake

to continue ... for some time longer; and when you see her, only do me the favour to remember me to her in the kindest manner.

    I cannot trust myself to write any more about her. Neither shall I tell you all I think about yourself. I am in earnest, however, when I assure you that I consider you as my best friend. I don't recollect in what manner we began this correspondence, but it is certainly in what is called in this country a 'fortunate moment'. Since then you have written to me much more frequently than others from whom I might have expected to hear; and yet I don't believe that you are as fond of scribbling as you are of talking. You have always given me an account of my friend and you have ended at last by a communication of your own observations on a subject in which you know me to be much interested. You may be mistaken, it is true, but I am greatly obliged to you.

    If I have time I will let you know how I get on in my Campaign. At all events I will write to you when anything interesting occurs. I hope it will be short, but I am sure it will be unpleasant. The weather is intolerably hot at this season of the year in India; the thermometer is at 100 in my tent at this moment and at 140 in the sun, so that we are stewing. But I am in good health and equal to any fatigue. God bless you.

              Believe me ever yours most sincerely,
                      Arthur Wellesley

    This letter shows all the anxieties of a man in love. He complains that Olivia is 'too discreet', yet fears a lack of discretion might injure him in Kitty's eyes. He is afraid she would be 'much offended' if she knew he had 'entered upon this subject'.

    It is not difficult to imagine his state of mind, writing in a tent with the temperature at 100 and an 'unpleasant' campaign ahead. He is longing for home and his memories of Kitty and an Irish spring were becoming more real than reality itself, as he read and re-read Olivia's letter.

    A further reminder of home was the arrival of Kitty's cousin, young Tom Pakenham, aged sixteen, son of Admiral Pakenham of Coolure, in whom Arthur was 'particularly interested'.

    On 23 September 1803, the campaign he had anticipated in March culminated in one of his greatest victories in India – the defeat of the Mahratta chief, Scindiah, at Assaye. Yet within five days of this victory he found time to write about young Pakenham to Major Shawe and begins:

> I have received a letter from Mr. T. Pakenham, a writer on the Bengal establishment, respecting whom I am particularly interested. He is the son of Admiral Pakenham, a very old friend of Lord Wellesley and of mine. I believe him to be very young and inexperienced; I therefore most anxiously recommend him to your care and attention. I have also given him a letter of recommendation to my friend, Mr. Ross, whom I have requested to have an eye

upon his conduct and above all things, to prevent him from keeping bad company. Should the College last, of course he will attend that institution. If not, I have desired him to acquire a knowledge of the country languages. I request you to urge him particularly upon this point; and do not allow him to be idle. Desire him to show you the letter I have written him. Do not allow him to run into debt; if he should want money, I have desired him to apply to David Ross or to you. Pray supply his wants if he should require it and apply to David Ross for any sums you may give him.[2]

He then goes on to discuss the destruction of Scindiah's army. The 'College' was Wellesley College which the East India Company was trying to close.

It is significant that Arthur's anxiety for the welfare of young Pakenham was in his mind so soon after a major battle in which, as Colin Campbell describes, 'The General was in the thick of the action the whole time and had a horse killed under him. No man could have shown a better example to his troops than he did. I never saw a man so cool and collected as he was the whole time, though I can assure you 'til our troops got orders to advance, the fate of the day seemed doubtful'.[3] Not only was Arthur's bay horse killed under him during the action, but the beautiful grey Arab, Diomed, the horse left him some years before by Colonel Aston, was also piked.[4] There was little enough he could do in India to show his regard for Kitty, but at least he could keep a fatherly eye on her cousin.

# CHAPTER 7

# *'Chance of her Favour . . .'*

Olivia Sparrow lost no time in replying to Arthur's long-awaited letter of March 1803. It was now January, ten months later. She begins: 'I received your letter this morning. Its chief subject has so entirely engaged my mind that I cannot delay my answer, although I know not whether just now there may be an opportunity of forwarding it.' She assures him that what had already been written 'Is and shall remain a secret to her, unless I receive your permission to the contrary', a piece of bare-faced deception which probably did not deceive Arthur for a minute.

Quite probably he intended that the correspondence should be made known to Kitty, while paying due regard to social delicacy and the fiat of her family against communication, which still demanded that the façade of secrecy and discretion should be maintained.

Olivia's letter is guarded but also encouraging. 'Conjecture was all I could or can hazard and that I will now still more plainly disclose, I think is in your favour . . . .' She tries 'Impartially to consider your mutual situation' and concludes that her first friend must have 'a more than common reason for perseverance in her disengaged state, with frequent and otherwise unobjectionable opportunities for changing it, particularly when interest for a long absent friend is constantly preserved'. Olivia's statement that Kitty had had 'opportunities' for becoming engaged to someone else contradicts Beresford's remark in his original letter that no one had paid Kitty any particular attention.

Olivia ends the letter by wishing him success, not from her own opinion of his merits but from the favourable judgement of others qualified to decide regarding 'The happiness of a friend so dear to me'.

She tells him she has noticed 'An evident increase in good opinion and interest in those friends who, I have heard, were formerly less favourably inclined towards you and whose heads and hearts can only be influenced by real worth and deserved fame. I have written from my heart. Well as you may think you love and esteem the excellence of the person in question, you cannot know her as much as I do and therefore cannot love and admire her as you ought and as (trusting in your deserving her) I could almost say I hope you may have an opportunity to do.'

The letter ends there – unsigned, either from emotion or discretion – but Olivia Sparrow, when an old woman in 1857, added a note: 'Respecting my earliest friend, Kitty Pakenham. Written by me to him ... before his return from India – enquiring of me her sentiments towards him – proving incontestably the total absence of any understanding or engagement between them – and how entirely I had abstained from any communication on which he could ground any engagement from her or through me.' In this note, Olivia intended to refute once and for all a charge frequently brought against her, that she had engineered an engagement between Kitty and Arthur.

Her letter was received in August 1804, and Arthur replied at once from Fort William. He confirmed that his

> Opinion and sentiments respecting the person in question are the same as they have ever been. They were the result of a long and intimate acquaintance, in the course of which I declare I do not recollect one action that I did not approve and that was not consistent with her character and the whole tenor of her life.... If she was consulted respecting a decision which I have never ceased to regret, I have the candour to acknowledge that she acted upon that occasion with the same discretion that has characterized her in every other action of her life.
>
> Every time that I have heard of her since I left Europe has tended to confirm the impression which had been made on my mind by the former knowledge of her and I am convinced that the enthusiasm of an admirer and the partiality of a friend cannot find words to describe all her good qualities.
>
> I certainly think that I did not deserve such a woman and that I was treated exactly as I ought to have been when I proposed myself to her. The question is whether in the opinion of those who, if I should be bold enough to bring this subject forward again will decide, the same reasons against me do not still exist? Will public [service] be allowed as a set-off against the faults imputed to a man's private life by scandal and calumny? Will she, whose penetration nothing can escape, believe in the affection of one against whom the scandalous world has said so much?
>
> These questions which would at all times have made me apprehensive of the consequences of renewing a certain subject, have given me the greatest anxiety lately. As I suspect from a conversation which I had with Lady

William, or rather a lecture she gave me, that the scandalous world had attacked me again and that the reports which they have circulated to my disadvantage, may have reached England. It is not necessary that I should now enter into a discussion regarding the truth or falsehood of the reports, although I by no means allow that they are true. I only say that it is impossible that any report of this kind respecting me for the last 20 months (since I received your letter in 1802) can be true; as I believe it will be admitted that while in the field with the Army I have done no mischief.

I firmly believe that nothing of this kind respecting me shall be circulated again and on this ground I request your good offices to remove the bad impression which will certainly have been made if the reports should have reached your friend. I assure you that if I should ever do anything to forfeit your good opinion, I wish I may at the same time forfeit all chance of her favour.

You will certainly conceive how much pain it has cost me to allude to this subject in a letter to you, but it relieves me from a greater and I have hopes from your exertions. I declare that I should determine never to go near her if I was not sanguine in my expectations that I should have the benefit of your good offices.

I intend to go to England in October or January, if the Government of India should have no occasion for my service. Pray remember me most kindly to Miss Pakenham and to Lord and Lady Longford and your brother.
God bless you and believe me, ever yours most sincerely,
Arthur Wellesley.

Fort William, August 13th, 1804.
I arrived here yesterday and have seen your brother. He is in remarkably good health and looks well although he has had the fever which is common to everybody on their arrival in Calcutta. He was so young when I saw him last and is now so tall that I am not ashamed to own that I should not have known him again. But he resembles you a little. He is constantly with the Governor General and appears to be going on very well.

Arthur's letter makes it abundantly clear that he had never lost interest in Kitty 'since I left Europe'. He bears no resentment against her family for rejecting his proposal: 'I did not deserve such a woman', but had their attitude changed? Obviously he had not lived the life of a recluse in India – there had been gossip which jealousy of the Wellesley brothers was bound to generate. Would his public service and success in the field be sufficient 'as a set-off against the faults imputed to a man's private life by scandal and calumny?' Would Kitty, 'whose penetration nothing can escape', still believe in his affection?

Recent attacks on his reputation had given him great anxiety and although he denies the reports are true, they may still have reached

England and found credibility there. Service in the field had kept him out of mischief during the last twenty months, since receiving her letter in 1802, and he promises that nothing of the kind 'shall be circulated again'. If he does anything to change Olivia's good opinion of him, he would 'forfeit all chance' of Kitty's favour.

He was relying heavily on Olivia's good offices to help his suit and he makes clear his intention to 'bring the subject forward again' when he reaches home. The salient point, as far as Olivia was concerned, was that he still wanted to marry Kitty. His 'Opinion and sentiments ... are the same as they have ever been'. Olivia's campaign for her friend was now on firmer ground.

Arthur did not write to Olivia again from India. Shortly after his last letter had been despatched in 1804 he received the Order of the Bath and was now experiencing a crescendo of public acclaim. His successes against the Mahrattas in the last half of 1803 and his victory at Assaye had become widely known in England and his reputation as a general was established at last.

He now had a sizeable fortune of about £42,000, giving him independence. His rank was major-general, but this appointment had not been confirmed by the Commander-in-Chief, the Duke of York, and therefore only applied to the Madras Staff on the East India Company's strength.[1] He had become somewhat disillusioned with the progress of British interests in India; a disillusionment increased by an action of his brother in repudiating a clause in a treaty, concluded by Arthur with the Indian prince, Scindiah, which Arthur considered a breach of trust. He wrote to General Malcolm on Richard's action: 'I would sacrifice every frontier of India ten times over in order to preserve our credit for scrupulous good faith.'[2]

His health was also suffering after years spent in the killing climate of India, much of the time in tented camps on active service. In February 1805 he decided he had had enough. Writing to John Malcolm, he told him: 'I am anxious to a degree which I can't express, to see my friends again.' By March he was embarked on HMS *Trident* for home.

Had he anything to fear from gossip about his life in India? His name had been linked with several 'married ladies' by Captain George Elers (Maria Edgeworth's cousin), whose character was soured by set-backs in promotion. There is no doubt that Arthur had an affectionate regard for Mrs Freese, wife of Captain John William Freese of the Madras Artillery, sent to Seringapatam in 1801 as commissary of stores. But the vivacious Mrs Freese could not have had very much time for a 'serious' affair with Arthur. She had a large family and the tragic death of her eldest son in

## A Soldier's Wife

India was only mitigated by the birth of a baby boy a few months later. The child was named Arthur, after his godfather Arthur Wellesley. Although some members of Arthur's military 'family' were said to have been shocked by his open admiration for Mrs Freese, it is obvious that her husband did not object, nor could the gossip have had sufficient foundation to cause the future Duchess of Wellington any concern. She generously provided a loving home for Arthur Freese when he was sent to England in 1807, while his parents remained in India.

Arthur Wellesley enjoyed a good party and dancing with pretty women, who were impressed by good looks, impeccable grooming and social graces learned long ago in France. His enjoyment of life was infectious and his ability as a horseman equalled his ability as a dancing partner. Arthur liked the simple pleasures of family life and was fond of children. The Gordon family (Arthur's Paymaster and his wife) had a suite of rooms in his house while their own was being prepared. He expressed quite openly his admiration and affection for Mrs Gordon and the order and domesticity she brought to his establishment. It is not difficult to understand that a pretty women and her children in his house aroused a sentimental regard, helping to offset the harsh realities of death and discomfort on active service.

Mrs Gordon continued to do small errands for the house after they had moved into their own home and pleasantly amusing notes were exchanged between her and Arthur on the 'susceptible youths' on his Staff or about invitations to visit his headquarters 'to enliven us'. He recommended the 'excellent galloping ground' near the camp and told her the floor of his tent was 'in a fine state for dancing and the fiddlers of the Dragoons and 78th and the bagpipes of the 74th play delightfully'.[3]

It all seems innocent enough, but it provided the gossips with sufficient ammunition to shoot at the brilliant young officer, younger brother of a Governor-General whose vanity and extravagance gave valid grounds for dislike and criticism. Many people were willing to take a stick to beat the Wellesley clan, disliked as much for their Irish Protestant background as for their ability and success and above all for their determination to root out corruption.

Before leaving India Arthur made another purchase of books, very different from those he had acquired when setting out nearly nine years before. This time they included a number of romances. Arthur intended to make the best of this voyage as a holiday and period of recuperation from the hardships of his field campaigns. He also purchased a pearl ring – and, thus prepared, set sail in March 1805.

One of his last acts before leaving India was to make provision for the orphan sons of Dhoondiah Waugh, the Mahratta prince he had defeated in 1800 and whose sons he had taken under his protection. He gave instructions that a sum of money should be settled on them to ensure their future security.[4]

CHAPTER 8

# *Business at Home*

Arthur reached England in September 1805, having broken the voyage with a month's stay on the island of St Helena, whose climate he found refreshing and whose remoteness he was to find ideal for another purpose many years later. Although he at once resumed his correspondence with Olivia, he did not, as might have been expected, hasten across the Irish Channel. Almost as soon as he landed, he was summoned to Downing Street for private and confidential discussions with Prime Minister Pitt. Napoleon was now addicted to conquest and the newly crowned Emperor of the French was planning a further campaign in Europe, with an attack on the Prussian and Austrian forces, in his pursuit of world power.

Pitt had a long-standing friendship with Richard and was now greatly impressed with this other Wellesley – with Arthur's ability and experience as a field commander. His refreshing lack of self-interest and his practical common sense were instantly recognized by the Prime Minister. The young General hated party faction and jobbing. His first consideration was whether a course of action would benefit the country and the Crown – a simple, straightforward point of view rarely held by the place-seekers and politically ambitious men who surrounded Pitt.

After eight years in India, his sudden access to the seat of power required strenuous efforts to renew old friendships and, through personal contacts, to learn at first hand the problems facing the Government at home and abroad. Time was short if an effective resistance to Napoleon's armies was to be organized and the few remaining independent countries in Europe were not to fall under his heel.

In addition to official business, Arthur was involved in Richard's personal and political problems. Although they had had their differences in

India, the brothers pulled together in times of crisis. Since his return, the Governor-General had not found a role in British public life which suited his self-esteem. He was also the subject of attacks in Parliament, where efforts were made to impeach him for mismanagement and extravagance in India.

The charges had been brought by his enemies in the East India Company, who had found his insistence on efficiency and clamp-down on corruption little to their liking. Faced with an attack on a member of the family, the Wellesley brothers came to his defence, although his private life, and particularly his treatment of his wife, was a subject for their private criticism and disgust.

It seemed that every hour of every day was occupied in urgent and fascinating public and private affairs; at the same time Arthur had to establish a base for his activities in London. He rented a house at 18 Conduit Street as a temporary headquarters and found time to go shopping – a pleasure anticipated by exiles after a surfeit of native bazaars and importunate merchants abroad.

By a lucky chance, records of his purchases survive in the form of bills made out to Sir Arthur Wellesley and dated within a few days of his landing in England. The first is for 19 September 1805 and is from Robert Birchall's music shop in New Bond Street. Arthur's exuberant happiness at being in London on a crisp September day, his years of exile behind him and a future full of promise with the prospect of marriage at last with the woman he had loved so long ago, is reflected in his choice of music. His eye went at once to the romantic songs: 'Oh Lovely Lady', 'On Stay Sweet and Rest, Lady', 'Lady Beware'. Next he turned to duets and trios for piano and violin from popular light operas – *Proserpina, La Virgine*.... He selected sonatas by Mozart, airs by Beethoven – the list continues for a full page, enough music to assuage the hunger of eight years and to celebrate his bright future.

He strolled down Bond Street, a happy man in his plain, blue coat and immaculate white cravat, which heightened the brownness of his face, the bright blue eyes enjoying every detail of the busy scene. Noting the latest style of carriage, a good pair of horses, catching the glance of some beautiful creature momentarily interested in this elegant stranger whose air of distinction and authority was sharply different from the fashionable and insipid young men who crowded the pavement.

The next day he was out again, this time in Coventry Street, making purchases at Flight and Barr's Worcester China shop for his new home. Here he selected a breakfast and dinner service – with extra muffin plates – all in Worcester's 'Royal Lily' pattern. An obvious choice with his thoughts and memories set on Lady Longford's Lily and happy days in Dublin, soon to be renewed.

Yet still he delayed his visit to Ireland. Was the intrepid soldier nervous about confronting the reality of a dream so long cherished? More likely the reason was the pressure of events, with time galloping away and each day too short for the absorbing work to be done. He was enjoying the freedom of being without official duties yet much in demand at the centre of the nation's affairs.

Olivia had already accused him of 'neglecting' Kitty – in a letter written on 17 September. He did not reply until the twenty-fourth.

> My time has been entirely occupied by business I could not neglect.... I see evidently you imagine that I am unworthy of your friend; I have not vanity enough to feel that I am otherwise. All I can say is that if I could count myself capable of neglecting such a woman, I would endeavour to think of her no more. I hope that you will find that I am not quite so bad as you imagine I am.... What is to become of your friend in the winter? Does she remain in Ireland? Shall I go over to see her? I am very apprehensive that after having come from India for one purpose only, I shall not accomplish it. I think it is not improbable that if troops under orders for embarkation should be sent to the Continent, I shall be ordered to go with them and possibly never see you or her again.

He ends the letter with an account of various gifts he had brought from India and tells her that he would 'Go to Cheltenham, I believe in two or three days, but this house will be my headquarters for some time'.

The Cheltenham visit had two purposes. He had always believed that the spa did wonders for his health and that the fevers and rheumatism contracted years ago were greatly helped by the medicinal waters. At the same time, he could call on his old friend and former Viceroy in Ireland, the Marquis of Buckingham, at Stowe.

His question to Olivia on Kitty's movements in the winter months perhaps arose from hope that the Pakenhams would come to London for a visit. It would have been a conciliatory gesture on their part to arrange for Kitty and Arthur to meet in England, in view of the critical situation and the fact that every army officer was in constant expectation of a sudden call to embark for Europe. An inhibiting factor was that the family was in mourning for the death of Helen's husband, James Hamilton, after seven years of marriage. Helen was in poor health and was only to survive her husband by two years. She was pregnant and already had two small children, John aged six and Edward, two years old. Kitty had been nursing her brother-in-law and he died in her arms at their home, Brown Hall, by

## Business at Home

Lough Eskie, in Donegal. The strain of this bereavement and the care of her sister made it difficult for Kitty to leave Ireland. So the separation continued, this time not by wide oceans but the Irish Channel, as autumn turned to winter and then to spring.

The ingredients for tragedy were slowly and inevitably coming together. Arthur had returned to England to marry in the brief interlude between one period of active service and the next. His vision of domestic happiness had been fixed years before, when he courted Kitty Pakenham in Ireland; eight years in India had enhanced rather than dimmed his early conviction that Kitty was the only woman for him.

As in most love affairs, Kitty and Arthur each had an exaggerated opinion of the good qualities of the other. Such impossible expectations might have been dispelled if they could have had time to know each other again before marriage and reach a tolerant understanding. But Fate was against them. He was caught up in world events and the complications of his brother's indictment. She, in domestic ties and convention. For once in his life Arthur failed to survey the ground before coming to a decision; but even had they met, Arthur's determination was of long standing and his logical mind regarded marriage as no more complicated than any other contract. A wife ran the home and cared for the children; a husband controlled the finances and pursued his career. His experience had not included the emotional conflict and small irritations of living in constant proximity with someone who was not a brother officer or a servant – a person demanding attention and affection, when he had more important things to attend to.

Kitty may have had a better understanding of the difficulties they faced, but she wrongly attributed his single-minded intention to marry her to a romantic love which had persisted through nine years of separation. She wanted to believe her dream of the married state, product of much reading of romantic novels and the sentimentality of the time, in which the wife was the cherished companion of a loving husband, prepared to put her happiness above more mundane considerations. Her circle did not include men of outstanding ability, involved in world events, nor the sophisticated women who complemented their careers. The families she knew included devoted husbands who followed a routine of work and pleasure which gave little cause for domestic conflict. Could not she and Arthur do the same? Could they not attend to their religious and secular duties in a loving relationship which would sustain them till they died, mourned by their dutiful and devoted children?

It is obvious that Arthur never envisaged living for long periods in his ideal home. His plans, even at the height of his domestic fantasy, were all concerned with military service, in which he found the most complete satisfaction. They both realized that time was not on their side. Death was everywhere – for the soldier, the next battle could be the last. For those at home, life expectancy was short. Many illnesses, not fatal in themselves, and childbirth, brought death from the horrific 'remedies' applied by ignorant doctors. Kitty and Arthur were middle-aged and for both of them marriage, if it were to be achieved at all, was a matter of urgency.

A week after sending his reply to Olivia, Arthur was in Cheltenham, staying at the Plough, under the sign of Joseph Bickham – 'Foreign Wine and Spirit Merchant: Post Horses, Chaises, Saddle Horses: Livery Stables, extensive Coach Houses'. Arthur lunched on bread and cheese and beer, with a half-bottle of Madeira. Later in the day he had dressed salmon and sauce (3s 0d); a roast fowl (3s 6d), with mutton chops, pickles, potatoes and butter (1s 8d). He stayed there from 1 to 19 October, having visited the Marquis of Buckingham en route. His sister-in-law, William's wife, had asked friends in Cheltenham to help entertain him. 'He knows none there', she wrote. 'It would be a charity to look after him.'[1]

The diary of events as they actually happened in 1805 conflicts with an account Arthur gave Mrs Arbuthnot nearly twenty years later. He told her Olivia Sparrow had 'sent for him' on his return from India and told him a proposal was expected. This meeting he said, took place in Cheltenham – but there is little or no evidence that they met in Cheltenham or that any meeting took place during this crucial period. Arthur's and Kitty's letters to Olivia at this time are all addressed to her in Suffolk, either to Lowestoft or to Worlingham Hall, Beccles. During Arthur's stay in Cheltenham, Kitty received a letter from Olivia, dated 8 October, and immediately replied to her in Suffolk. On Arthur's return to London, he received two letters from Olivia, dated 24 and 26 October, one of which had been sent to Cheltenham in error – a mistake that was unlikely if they had both visited the spa at the same time. Olivia makes no reference to a meeting with Arthur in her letters to Kitty, which she would have done if one had taken place.

The evidence is all in favour of Olivia's contention that she did not bring undue influence on Arthur to propose. She was a partisan go-between, but Arthur needed no pressure from her to renew his proposition to Kitty. His only fear was of another defeat in a project he had come 'expressly from India to achieve'. The fact that years later he blamed other people for his decision to marry Kitty may have been a reflex response to one of his rare errors of judgement, one that reflected on his humanity and sophistication and which brought pain to them both.

It is not known exactly when he instructed Olivia to 'renew his proposition', but Kitty's distraught reply was written from Cookstown, where she was visiting her sister, Bess Stewart. She had received Olivia's letter, which is not recorded, just as she was leaving Langford Lodge, County Antrim, and must have considered her answer during her coach journey to County Tyrone.

Arthur's missing letter to Olivia could have been written from Stowe on or about 28 September; his decision to clinch the matter perhaps inspired by talk of old times in Ireland with Lord Buckingham. Olivia would have transmitted it at once to Kitty and it reached her at Langford Lodge on 8 October.

Kitty's letter from Cookstown is written on very poor quality paper, with much crossing out and few punctuation marks. She had been travelling all day in the coach and snatched a few minutes on arrival to write the reply she had been composing in her mind during the journey. As soon as she set pen to paper, her emotions gained the upper hand and the letter becomes almost incoherent in places. She was thirty-three and faced at last with a decision that would transform the fantasy of a long-remembered love affair into the hard fact of marriage.

She begins:

> Your letter arrived exactly as I was leaving Langford Lodge. Olivia, it has indeed agitated me and for a week I cannot hear from you again as I shall be either here on a visit to Mrs. Stewart or on the road all that time. What can I say – I can know nothing of his mind but what you have told me. You assure me he still regards me, he has authorised you to renew the proposition he made some years ago; but my Olivia, I have in vain sought in his letter for one word expressive of a wish that the proposition should be accepted of; there is indeed one circumstance that would make, as he says, my chance with him less than small – if he now speaks from any cause whatsoever than a thorough conviction that being accepted of would contribute to his happiness, I should be most truly wretched.
>
> It is quite impossible for me to express the apprehension that preys upon my heart at this moment. I think he wishes to be ordered abroad and perhaps he is right, for I am very much changed and you know it, within these last three years – so much that I doubt whether it would be in my power to contribute to the comfort or happiness of anybody who has not been in the habit of loving me for years – like my brother or you or my mother.
>
> Read his letter again, my dear Olivia. Is there one expression implying 'Yes' would gratify or that 'No' would disappoint or occasion regret? Either would remove the uneasiness of uncertainty and I cannot perceive that he

expresses any other. Perhaps when I hear from you again, which cannot be for a week, that this most painful doubt will be removed. Till then, what can I say? I have been witness to all the happiness arising from affection where it was mutual and can feel what would have been the misery had that affection existed but on one side. My dear Olivia, I cannot at this moment be certain that I write intelligibly – my mind is sadly oppressed. Indeed, I would not write today but that I know silence would give you more uneasiness than anything I could say. In the transaction of a former period, he must himself have disapproved of my conduct had I acted differently. I could not have done so without openly opposing or privately deceiving my mother, a mother entitled to the most open confidence and every act of Duty from me.

Adieu, my dearest Olivia.

This hurried letter, written under emotional stress, shows Kitty's genuine concern for Arthur's happiness above her own. She loved him – and had done so for all the years between their early courtship and this new proposal. Her fear was that this affection could only be one-sided.

It has been said of her that before she married she led a sheltered life – if so, she probably would not have been 'very much changed' over the years. Women in Ireland at this time had been living under the constant threat of rebellion and violence and in fearful anxiety for those they loved, both at home and abroad. The fact that she had changed is thus unquestioned but evidence about her appearance when Arthur returned from India is conflicting. That intelligent observer, Maria Edgeworth, visited Pakenham Hall in September 1805, and wrote to her aunt that she had met 'sweet Kitty Pakenham. . . . I never saw her look more animated and pretty'.[2] On the other hand, an Irish friend, Mrs Calvert, noted the following year that Kitty looked 'sadly altered'.[3] But much had transpired for Kitty between these two occasions.

The momentum of the correspondence between the three points of the triangle – Olivia at the apex, receiving and sending letters to her two friends – increased throughout October. Arthur and Kitty were still divided by the Irish Channel but, as the glorious autumn colours faded into the mists and fog of November, they saw their future more clearly than at any time since that first meeting eleven years ago.

The time was rapidly approaching when Arthur and Kitty would be able to correspond without a go-between. They had scrupulously observed the veto by Kitty's family against direct communication and without Olivia's enthusiastic intervention the embargo might have continued indefinitely. Whatever her motives, she had established that the bond between Kitty and Arthur had not been broken by a separation of more than ten years.

Had Olivia not intervened it seems likely, from Arthur's letters, that he might still have renewed his 'proposition' when he returned home. On the other hand, he might not have done so had he known how close Kitty had been to marriage with Lowry Cole.

Olivia lost no time in putting Kitty's agitated letter from Cookstown into Arthur's hands. His reaction was decisive. Her letter confirmed that she cared for him and would accept if he made a formal proposal. 'Your letters of 24th and 26th October, the former of which had by mistake been sent to Cheltenham, have removed most of the anxiety I felt when I wrote to you last,' he wrote to Olivia on 28 October.

> If your friend has felt confidence in the sincerity of my regard for her, she will only regret that I should so soon be sent away again without seeing her and she will be desirous of my early return. But if she should doubt me, she may imagine that I sought this service unnecessarily and that was what I apprehended when I wrote to you last.
>
> I received a letter from Lord Longford this day which I don't propose to answer 'til I shall hear from her. I may expect in a few days. I have heard no more of my departure. It is reported this day that the Austrians have been entirely defeated. If it should be true, it is possible the troops will not go immediately. They have certainly received a severe check but I doubt whether it amounts to a total defeat.
> God bless you, believe me yours sincerely,
> Arthur Wellesley.

Arthur had taken the irrevocable step by writing to Kitty's brother for permission to make a formal proposal and had 'this day' received a favourable reply. His proposal had been well received at Pakenham Hall. In a journal kept by Kitty's mother which recorded prayers concerning family events, she wrote on 28 October: 'How shall I express my gratitude to Thee, Oh Lord, for the prospect of my dear Kitty's happiness by her union with a man truly deserving and appreciating her worth....'

At last the way was clear. Both Kitty's mother and her brother were now favourably inclined towards him and at last Arthur could write directly to the woman he intended to marry and renew the proposal made in 1793. Her answer was only a few days away and although there was little doubt as to what it would be, he would not acknowledge Longford's letter until he had had her reply.

On 4 November, Kitty's letter arrived 'and two others', probably from members of the family. The next day he wrote to Olivia from William's house at Blackheath. Kitty had accepted, in a letter 'which I cannot part with', but he sent Olivia a copy.

'I should be the most undeserving of beings were I capable of feeling less than gratitude in return for the steadiness of your attachment,' Kitty had written.

> How much I feel, time alone will show. You are entitled to the utmost sincerity from me and shall ever receive it. To express what I feel at this moment would be quite impossible. I will therefore only say that in making the acknowledgment of regard I now make for you, I am conscious of a degree of happiness of which 'til now I had no idea.
>
> It is indeed my earnest wish to see you, besides the pleasure it must give me to meet again an early and truly valued friend, I do not think it fair to engage you before you are quite positively certain that I am indeed the woman you would have for a companion, a friend for life. In so many years I may be much more changed than I am myself conscious of. If when we have met you can tell me with the same sincerity which has ever distinguished you through life, that you do not repent having written the letter I am now answering, I shall be most happy. That I should ever have been the cause of your suffering anything like mortification, distresses me. That it may be the last time that I shall ever give you pain is the most earnest wish of C.D.P.

Arthur continues:

> There is the letter. Now, my dearest friend, you may wish me joy, for I am the happiest man in the world. Nothing could now prevent my happiness but this expedition. However, it is possible that I may not be sent immediately and if that should be the case, I shall have reason to believe that I can ask permission to go to Ireland without incurring the risk of being supposed to be unwilling to undertake this service. I will go there in a very short period of time. I have received no further communication about my departure; some of the troops are certainly gone or will go when the wind will change. You will hear from me as soon as I receive any further orders.
> God bless you, believe me ever yours most sincerely,
> Arthur Wellesley.

Kitty's letter emphasized her view of marriage as resting on companionship and friendship. He is entitled, she says to the 'utmost sincerity ... and shall ever receive it' from her. His letter must have contained a reference to his 'mortification' when she refused his first proposal. That rejection had rankled over the years and he was now snatching victory from defeat. Her letter was entirely satisfactory from his point of view and confirmed his belief that she had all the qualities he most admired. Her assurance that he was 'entitled to the utmost sincerity' was one he was not likely to forget. He dismissed her anxieties that he would find her 'much changed' as irrelevant. It was her mind he was in love with, he told a friend, and that would not alter.[4] He was a man of strong principles and believed that in Kitty he had found a woman whose hatred of deception and lies equalled his own.

Olivia's task as intermediary was now at an end but she still felt obliged to question Arthur on his attitude towards Ireland, knowing that nearly all the rest of the Wellesleys had deserted the country for England. Arthur patiently replied to her inquiries from his rooms in Conduit Street, on 8 November:

> You will have had an opportunity of forming your own judgement before this time of the manner in which my proposition to your friend has been received. I am perfectly satisfied and only wish it was at this moment in my power to fly to her.
>
> You ask me whether I propose to be an Englishman or an Irishman. All countries are alike to me, who have been so much abroad and who have had as unsettled life as I have. But I acknowledge that I rather prefer England because my friends and relations reside there; because hers must reside there during a great part of the year; because you reside here – and to tell you the truth, I must think that Ireland will not be a fit residence for any woman of this generation; and I acknowledge that if my profession should at any time call me away from her, which must be expected, I should feel the same kind of uneasiness about her, if she lived in Ireland, that I should at leaving her in a camp in the enemy's country.
>
> However, my preference for England is not of the strong kind to induce me to think of asking her to live here if she should prefer to live in Ireland and I will do in that respect exactly as she likes.
>
> I have heard no more of the expedition, excepting that the troops with which I am to go, have embarked at last and will have sailed by the first fair wind.

Even with the formality of the engagement behind him, he still could not 'fly to her'. Events were moving quickly and disastrously in Europe. The day following his declaration as 'the happiest man in the world', news of Nelson's victory at Trafalgar and his tragic death was announced in London. Pitt, the Prime Minister, was the hero of the hour as the nation's leader. Arthur was present when Pitt received the tribute of a dinner in his honour at Guild Hall, to celebrate the defeat of the French fleet. At this event Pitt made a brief but famous speech which appealed very strongly to Arthur Wellesley. 'I return you my thanks', Pitt said, 'for the honour you have done me; but Europe is not to be saved by any single man. England saved herself by her exertions and will, as I trust, save Europe by her example.'[5] 'Nothing could be more perfect', said Wellington, recalling this speech many years later.

But in spite of the sea victory, the land forces opposing Napoleon were crumbling. Arthur was closely in touch with Pitt during this anxious time and hourly awaited orders to embark for north Germany. By the end of December, he was still awaiting orders, this time in Deal where he expected to sail with an infantry brigade to reinforce British troops supporting a Prussian offensive against Napoleon. It was hoped that action in north Germany would relieve pressure on Russian and Austrian troops to the south. But the whole operation was too late. Napoleon had already defeated the Third Coalition at Austerlitz on 2 December, and when this news reached England, the blow to Prime Minister Pitt was mortal. He died three weeks later, in January 1806.

Arthur embarked at last, but his service in Germany was short-lived. In many respects this expedition mirrored the sorry episode in Flanders in the winter of 1794/5. Embarkation was delayed by contrary winds, and when the transports at last set sail for the mouth of the Weser, they were driven back three times by terrible weather. Again, hundreds of men were drowned when their troopship foundered on the Goodwin Sands; more than two thousand died when eight more ships sank among the Heligoland sandbanks.[6]

News of the storms and loss of transports reached poor Kitty in Ireland and, as her aunt reported later, 'She suffered a great deal of anxiety.' Just as she had feared him dead in the disaster of 1794, resulting in a nervous breakdown and serious illness now, as then, he had declared before sailing that he intended to marry her. Once more happiness might be snatched away by the terrors of the sea. 'She bears the traces of all this', her aunt Louisa informed a friend.

Kitty was not to know that this period of service abroad would be short. All she realized was that even if he survived the voyage, the rigours of winter among the icy marshes of Bremen could be fatal to a man weakened by Indian fevers and rheumatism. The ordinary hazards of battle were more bearable than fears of natural disasters and illness, to a woman of Kitty's volatile imagination.

Her fears were groundless. Not a blow was struck against the enemy and in February Arthur arrived back in England, with a posting to Hastings as part of a force assembled to resist a possible French invasion. He was now colonel of the 33rd, his old regiment, having succeeded Lord Cornwallis after his death in India. This promotion brought a considerable increase in pay and, although he was given only a minor command at Hastings, he accepted this with a good grace.

Arthur told his old friend Colonel Malcolm he had returned from the Continent 'a few days ago'. The letter announces that he is 'tolerably well in health and would be quite well if I can continue to spend a few weeks at

Cheltenham this summer.... The Regiment they have given me and the Staff [appointment] have made me rich'. There is no mention of his intention to marry, nor of the invitation to stand for Parliament made by the new premier, Lord Grenville, brother of his old friend Buckingham, who had also known Richard since boyhood. Grenville was now leader of the Whig/Tory coalition and needed support in the House to resist the attack against Richard, instigated by enemies of his Indian administration. He believed that Arthur, with his comprehensive knowledge of Indian affairs, would be an invaluable ally when speaking from the back benches. Richard was unpopular and, now that Pitt was dead, extremely vulnerable. Castlereagh, Secretary for War, advised Arthur to accept and he was offered the constituency of Rye. Time was short, proceedings against Richard already under way, and the election at Rye would be fought in April.

This was not the only subject occupying Arthur's attention. Plans for his marriage had taken a more definite form during the last weeks of March. Financially, he was now in a position to negotiate a satisfactory marriage settlement with Kitty's brother and the Dowager Lady Longford. He had returned from India with 'a little fortune of some thirty or forty thousand pounds'. The great bulk of it was prize money from the campaign of Seringapatam and Assaye and 'every penny of it legitimately earned', a friend reported at this time. 'Many men in his place would have accumulated, by means which were not frowned upon, three or four times that sum – for it must be remembered that in Mysore he was an absolute autocrat' and could have done as he liked with the power at his disposal.[7] To this was now added his command of the 33rd, which had made him 'rich'.

Proposals for a settlement on his 'intended marriage with the Honourable Miss Pakenham' were drawn up by his solicitors and involved the creation of a trust. The object was to provide for Kitty in the event of her husband's death. Kitty would contribute £4,000 of her own money (guaranteed by the family) with a further £2,000 from her mother. Arthur would contribute £20,000. It took 'eight skins' of parchment to define the proposals, with permutations as to how the trust would operate in the event of male children, female children, no children; his death before hers, hers before his, etc.

Such a document was in no way exceptional. Marriage between persons of property was strictly a business arrangement, with women in a very insecure position unless the wife's interest was defined in a marriage settlement. Without this legal safeguard, a woman had no right to own money or property – or anything else – once she was married. All her property passed automatically to the control of her husband. A woman's protection was for her family to ensure that an adequate sum from the future husband, combined with a contribution from the woman and her relations, was held in trust for her and any children of the marriage. Marriage with a man unable to make an adequate financial settlement would be opposed by the woman's family on her behalf. The Court of Chancery administered this section of the law, with much profit to the lawyers and little to the beneficiaries of disputed trusts. An unusual feature of Kitty's settlement was that the marriage took place before it was signed in August 1806. The trustees were the family solicitors, with Kitty's brother Edward and Arthur's brother Gerald to hold the ring in case of dispute.

The election for the Rye constituency had been fixed for 1 April and the first of the vital debates on Richard, Marquis Wellesley's impeachment would be on 22 April. Arthur was to be granted leave for the election and during this period he would just have time to rush to Ireland, marry Kitty and return to his parliamentary and military duties in time for the debates. In the meantime, he made several visits to his constituency although the issue was not in doubt. The people eligible to vote would do so at the direction of the owner of the seat, whether they knew the candidate or not.

What were Kitty's reactions to this strange progamme for their wedding? She probably felt that such a hurried celebration was not particularly flattering. Could she absorb the lesson that, for Arthur, domestic and personal considerations would always be subservient to public duty? Arthur would see nothing strange in expecting a woman he had not seen since 1795 to marry him in Dublin and part again in five days, if circumstances and obligations made it necessary. He expected Kitty to be as practical and committed to duty as himself – that was why he was marrying her – he had little time for sentimentality. The country was in a state of crisis, invasion was imminent; his brother needed his defence in a crucial debate in Parliament – and he had decided to marry at the first opportunity, a course of action to which Kitty had agreed. If these considerations left only five days for a reunion with his future wife and for their wedding, it would have to suffice.

Kitty's aunt Louisa, writing to Lowry Cole's sister Lady Florence Balfour in March/April 1806, gave her the latest news.

> ... and now, my dearest, about Kitty Pakenham, who tells me she has just received a most kind letter from you. I did not hear anything about Sir A. Wellesley 'til your letter, nor did I know that all was settled until two days ago – she wrote to you the same day. It seems it has been fixed these six months

but kept a profound secret. She has suffered a great deal of anxiety since, as he was ordered abroad, was out in the hurricanes, then in Germany and since his return very ill. She bears the traces of all this, for she coughs sadly and looks but ill, which we all lament as Sir A. is expected in a very few days. They have not met for about twelve years and some little agitation she suffers at being altered since [then], but not much, as she seems to have the most perfect reliance on him, both in affection and all other things and to think him the very first of human creatures.

I do think she is and will be, I trust, very happy and certainly an affection that has subsisted twelve or fifteen years promises very well. His stay in Ireland is expected to be very short. So I dare say a month will take her away from us. All her family are happy and delighted about it....

She continues the letter with news of Kitty's mother and sisters and then

put it by for a day or two because of spending most of my time with Kitty Pak, of whom I shall now see little more....

Sir Arthur and his brothers arrived this morning and I hear he must be in England again by the 16th, so that the agitation and hurry will be great. They all like him vastly and think him but little altered by his Indian absence.[8]

Louisa's letter reveals that the engagement had been kept secret, even from close members of the family, for six months and it is difficult to understand the reason. It may have been that Kitty could not bear the publicity of an announcement until she and Arthur had actually met again and he had confirmed in person (as she had asked in her letter) that he still wanted to marry her. This was a prudent decision and it is almost unbelievable that a meeting was not arranged either in Ireland or England. To announce an engagement before the reunion would have given rise to endless gossip, speculation and ribald humour at their expense. Nobody anticipated that a meeting would be so long delayed and, as the months passed, Kitty's position became difficult and worrying – engaged to a man who could not find time to come and see her. Her response, at least in public, was as Louisa described – an exhibition of perfect trust in Arthur's affection and assurance that in this, as in everything else, he was 'the very first of human creatures'.

But the strain was considerable. From the 'animated and pretty' woman Maria saw at Pakenham Hall in the previous September, Kitty had now become a prey to anxiety, 'coughs sadly and looks but ill, which we all lament', as Arthur was expected in a few days. Those few days had now elapsed and Arthur had arrived, supported by his brothers, on 8 April, with the by-election at Rye behind him and the necessity to take up his seat in the House by 16 April.

There is no record of their first meeting. The unkind remark he is said to have whispered to Gerald when he first saw her (and of which no written evidence remains) – 'She's grown ugly, by Jove' – seems unlikely. Arthur had been warned that she had changed and had discounted it. He was essentially a kindly man and intensely loyal. The fact that the woman he was about to marry was looking tired and thin was more likely to have touched his sympathy than evoke a harshly critical remark at their first encounter.

It is not hard to imagine the tumult and 'agitation' in the minds of all concerned in this strange affair. The long-absent hero descending on Dublin with his brothers to confront the anxious Pakenham family and his future bride; everyone furtively watching his reaction to 'sweet Kitty Pakenham' and hers to the stranger she was about to marry. Not only was Kitty feeling the effects of the strain of the reunion, but she was deeply concerned for her widowed sister Helen, whose health had sharply deteriorated since her husband's death and the posthumous birth of his last child. Louisa reported that Helen 'coughs and is very delicate ... she has been a good deal overcome by this business' of the wedding and her little boy Edward 'is not very well'. Kitty had probably been helping to nurse the invalid as well as trying to prepare for the hurried ceremony, hampered by her own ill-health and personal anxieties; an inauspicious start to married life at the age of thirty-four. But now, in a few days, the problems and frustrations of the past years were to be resolved – for better or worse.

CHAPTER 9

# Five Dublin Days

The day of the marriage had now arrived, 10 April 1806. The 'agitation and hurry' was over and in the calm of the Longford drawing-room in Rutland Square, Kitty and Arthur stood side by side, April sunshine through high windows falling on a diminutive figure, on soft brown hair under a wreath of flowers, on a pale, oval face and expressive grey-blue eyes, lowered now in acceptance of the marriage vows. The light caught her thin, white hand resting so lightly on another – hard and strong, sinewy from many battles and burnt with endless riding across sun-scorched plains. She would have prayed for strength to stand without a tremor or faintness beside this man whose absence had dominated her life and who was already a famous military commander and national hero.

As his brother intoned the familiar words of the marriage service, did she also hear a confusion of noise, a clash of sabres, the scream of a piked horse? She was marrying a soldier she hardly knew. The life he had led was beyond her imagination. He was not the Dublin Castle ADC who had walked with her beside Lough Derravaragh, played the violin in the drawing-room at Pakenham Hall, who went hunting with her brothers or stood patiently beside the Viceroy, ready to perform some trifling errand. He was not the man she had laughingly commanded to obey her slightest wish, who had said he was unworthy to ask for her hand and yet was determined to make her his wife if circumstances changed. In those days, she was the centre of admiration, the unattainable object; he, one of a band of devoted admirers. Now he had returned, to crown successes achieved in India by marrying the woman for whom the effort had been made. Their roles had completely changed. She was now nervous, unsure – he, dominant and admired. She had realistically acknowledged that she was no longer the woman he had loved so long ago; begged him not to commit himself to something that existed in his imagination rather than in fact. He had not listened, had not understood, and she had been swept on by his determination, trying to believe that the marriage could be what they both wished. The small hand trembled as the service continued, her feelings a confusion of fear and happiness.

For Arthur, this was the moment when the humiliation of his rejection by the Pakenham family was purged at last. He had gained his objective in this as in the rest of his early ambitions, by the single-mindedness of his purpose. The way was now open for a further advance. Time was not given to a soldier to waste – the essence of success was rapid movement from one target achieved to the next. The woman beside him was now his wife who would share his duties and obligations in the national interest. The marriage had been successfully concluded in the shortest possible time to everyone's satisfaction. He would now concentrate on the immediate problem of his brother's defence, while waiting the inevitable call to active service and possible early death in the field, which he did not fear. In the meantime, he would do his best to provide a comfortable home for Kitty, where he and his friends would find relaxation from the increasing pressure of work as the international crisis deepened. He would give her the honour and consideration due to a loving wife whose high principles matched his own.

It was over. The marriage registered at St George's Church, Dublin: 'The Honourable Sir Arthur Wellesley, KB, to the Honourable Catherine Dorothea Sarah Pakenham of this parish, by the Reverend G. Wellesley.' From the hushed stillness of the service, the drawing-room filled with noise and conversation as guests congratulated the bride and groom; toasts drunk, old friendships renewed.

It is not known how many brothers supported Arthur at his wedding. Gerald was there, conducting the service, and probably William Wellesley-Pole with his interests in Ireland. Henry might have attended, but it seems unlikely that Richard could leave London in view of the crisis facing him in Parliament.

On Kitty's side, Longford gave his sister away. Edward was there, newly returned from abroad; Bess and her husband had probably come from Tyrone, while Helen may have been well enough to attend the bride with the youngest sister Caroline. Her aunt, Elizabeth Rowley, had helped to organize the proceedings and had acted as Kitty's chaperon before the wedding. Louisa and Tom and their family from Coolure would have been among the guests, trusted friends of both Kitty and Arthur, whose open-handed hospitality and good nature endeared them to all. Kitty's mother seems to have played a minor role in the hurried festivities, perhaps through ill-health. Congratulations on the event were sent by the Edgeworths to aunt Elizabeth and not to the dowager.

The recently widowed Olivia was not present. Two days later Arthur wrote to her from Dublin:

> The enclosed letter will apprise you of the events which have occurred here within the last few days and I cannot mail it to you without adding a few lines to express to you the sincerest sense I entertain of the obligation I owe to you for all the happiness I enjoy.
>
> Kitty has informed me of your kindness in offering us the use of your house in London 'til we should get one; but I believe I have one already, or at all events shall have one before I shall arrive there; I should be sorry by these means to deprive myself of all hope of meeting you in London on arrival or shortly afterwards.
>
> We leave this place tomorrow if the wind should be fair, or the next day whether it is fair or otherwise. I wish to be in London on Wednesday and I shall accomplish that object if I should be able to sail tomorrow.

In the event, Arthur sailed without Kitty, whose health may have been too poor to risk a bad crossing. She followed later, escorted across the Irish Channel by Gerald.

This strange and romantic marriage caused surprise and pleasure to their friends and food for gossip to all and sundry. Although the engagement had been arranged in October 1805, the secret had been so well kept that even members of the family were not informed. Edward, on his return to Dublin from the West Indies just before the wedding, expected to find Kitty engaged to Lowry Cole.[1]

Maria Edgeworth's stepmother wrote: 'I hope the imagination of this hero and heroine have not been too much exalted and that they may not find the enjoyment of a happiness so long wished for, inferior to what they expected. Pray tell dear, good Lady Elizabeth, we are so delighted with the news and so engrossed by it that, waking or sleeping, the image of Miss Pakenham swims before our eyes. To make the romance perfect we want two material documents – a description of the person of Sir Arthur and a knowledge of the time when the interview after his return took place.'[2] There was not much chance, once news of the marriage began to circulate, that gossip could be avoided about the extraordinarily brief interval between the reunion and the wedding.

When Kitty crossed to England with Gerald the Harley Street house, for which Arthur was negotiating, was not ready. Arthur, on 24 May, was still in his rooms at 14 Clifford Street, having given up his Conduit Street address, and wrote from there to an unnamed correspondent, presumably

Olivia, expressing concern that he was not able 'To be so much with you as I could wish, but you must be aware how painfully and constantly I am engaged and you must excuse me. Let her go and I will follow her if possible at an hour as early as I shall be at liberty'. The 'her' must refer to Kitty, who was probably forced to stay with Olivia at her London house until 11 Harley Street was ready. 'Let her go....' Was Kitty becoming impatient? Was she insisting on moving into the new house whether it was ready or not? Her irritation and embarrassment would be understandable. After waiting nearly twelve years, a sudden marriage within a few days of being reunited, followed by another separation, and then to find she must live in a friend's house while Arthur maintained his rooms in Clifford Street, emphasized the relatively low priority her happiness and convenience had in Arthur's plans. She would be painfully aware that she was the subject of endless speculation and gossip in London society. Curiosity prompted friends to call – and what could she say to them, except that Arthur's 'constant and painful engagements' prevented them living together? A further worry was that she was to be presented at Court almost at once. Yet another reason for her irritability she may not have fully comprehended. She was in the first stages of pregnancy.

Arthur's preoccupations were mainly concerned with Richard's case. He made three major speeches in Parliament between 22 April and 8 May. The situation was serious. Not only was the Marquis under attack but also his brothers. Arthur himself was called an 'accessory' to the alleged financial mismanagement and a pack of fellow Members were in full cry after the Wellesleys.

The workload was enormous. Charges were being brought by an Anglo-Indian merchant named James Paull, a Member who had developed a vindictive antipathy to the Wellesleys in India, supplied with ammunition by Richard's enemies in the East India Company. William and Arthur employed a clerk to copy the vast numbers of papers produced by Paull, Arthur composing his replies with care and great attention to detail. His recorded speeches are excellent – well reasoned and contemptuous of politicians who knew nothing of India, with their trumped-up charges against his 'noble relative'. In his usual direct and logical way he hammered at the opposition to produce proof – which they could not do. He spoke again at the end of May and beginning of June and the affair was not concluded until 10 July 1806, when he made a long, brilliant and detailed speech on Indian finance, the treaties with various Indian princes and the complex military situation in relation to the operations of the East India Company.[3]

In all these exertions it is obvious that there was little time to devote to

Elizabeth, Countess of Longford, Kitty's grandmother. A pastel attributed to H. D. Hamilton, *c.* 1785.

Edward, 2nd Baron Longford, Kitty's father, wearing the uniform of a Post Captain, R.N. Probably by Hamilton, *c.* 1785.

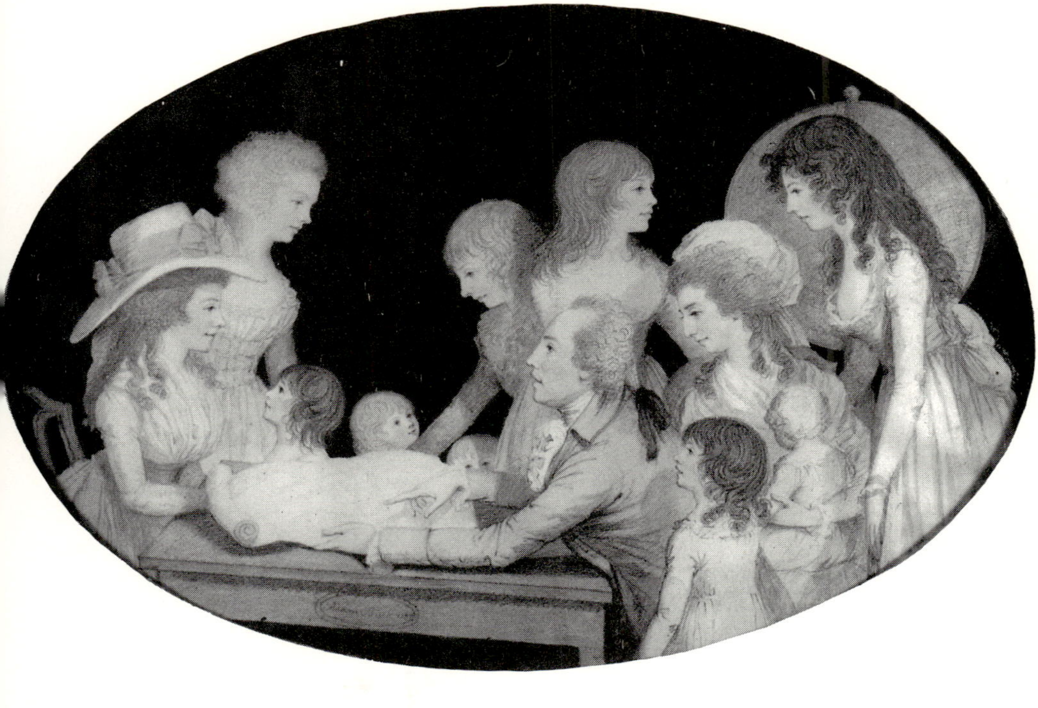

The Edgeworth family. A water-colour by Adam Buck, 1787. Maria is seated opposite her father, Richard Lovell Edgeworth, scientist and philanthropist. Around them are some of his children and his third wife, Elizabeth Sneyd.

The Hon. Arthur Wellesley, Lieutenant-Colonel of the 33rd Foot, aged twenty-seven, before setting sail for India in 1796. By John Hoppner.

Catherine (Kitty) Pakenham, Viscountess Wellington, aged thirty-nine. A portrait in pencil and coloured chalk by Josiah Slater, done at Tunbridge Wells and dated 1811. Kitty disliked sitting for a picture and very few likenesses of her exist.

Pakenham Hall (now Tullynally Castle), County Westmeath. Drawing by James Sheil, architect, in 1820. The process of gothicizing the original Georgian house was carried out by Kitty's brother, Thomas, 2nd Earl Longford.

Edward Pakenham, Kitty's favourite brother, a distinguished soldier and Arthur's devoted friend. Killed at New Orleans, USA in January 1815, aged thirty-seven. Lithograph by de Jobard.

Hercules Pakenham, who served with distinction under his brother-in-law until seriously wounded at Badajoz in 1812. Miniature by Andrew Plimer.

The Upper Court, Dublin Castle, from a print by James Malton, 1792. The State Apartments and Throne Room were entered by a broad staircase from the colonnade.

Lady Olivia Sparrow (*née* Acheson), daughter of the 1st Earl of Gosford and Kitty's lifelong friend. She was widowed in 1805. From a portrait by Bückner.

General Sir Galbraith Lowry Cole, Kitty's suitor before joining Wellington's forces in the Peninsula. Engraving after Lawrence, *c.* 1815.

The Irish Packet off Liverpool by Robert Salmon, c. 1800. Ships of this type supplied a fast and regular service (weather permitting) carrying mail and passengers between Irish and British ports.

A bill from Robert Birchall's 'Musical Circulating Library', New Bond Street, dated 19 September 1805 – Arthur's first purchase after landing from India the previous week, following nine years abroad. His choice included a number of love songs and duets.

Arthur (Douro) and Charles Wellesley. A water-colour by Henry Edridge, *c.* 1810, which their father pasted on the lid of his dressing-case and carried with him throughout the Peninsula campaign.

The Pantiles, Tunbridge Wells. A water-colour by J. Green, 1793. The raised band-stand was an added attraction to the fashionable parade where Kitty and the boys went shopping and visitors promenaded on their way to take the waters.

Spoof letter making fun of her new title, written by Kitty to amuse the children, inviting Margaret Packer, a young friend from Dublin, to spend the day at 11 Harley Street, London in 1813.

Catherine Marchioness

Whereas our right trusty cousin & counsellor the Hon'ble Lord Mayor, having this day laid before us a certain written document touching the coming of Margaret Packer to N° 11 Harley Street on Wednesday next the 31st inst. we did, as the case appeared urgent, forthwith our well beloved cousins & counsellors Dowse of the Lord and the King Charles, champion general, Jenny, cossy of the House and Caske guardian of the family and did command them to take said matter into their most serious consideration and to report unto us the result of such mature consideration———

We are happy to declare to Margaret Packer that she is graciously commanded to be ready at ½ past 11 on Wednesday A.M. at which hour we the undersigned will send our carriage to convey Margaret to N° 11 Harley Street and will also convey said Margaret back again at night, on certain following conditions.

1st that Margaret Packer shall not overturn or otherwise damage or deface the splendor of the carriage.

2nd that said Margaret shall not kick up a row in the streets, by hooking out of the window, making faces at or otherwise annoying his majesty's subjects who shall pass on their own concerns thro' the streets.

3rd If that said Margaret shall not stop in returning home at night, to Mug herself at the Public House at the corner

Arthur, Marquis Wellington, after crossing the Pyrenees. Engraved on the back of this miniature: 'Painted by T. Heaphi [sic] at Head Quarters at St. Jean-de-Luz, France, in December, 1813 and sent by Lord Wellesley to his niece, Priscilla, Lady Burghersch [sic], who received it at the Allied Head Quarters in France in 1814.'

Catherine, Duchess of Wellington, as Ambassadress. A miniature by Louis Marie Autissier (1772–1830), probably painted in France c. 1814/15 (identified by Evelyn, 3rd Duchess of Wellington).

Water-colour of spring flowers by Kitty, found with her paint-box and easel at Stratfield Saye.

Kitty. Arthur and his brothers' efforts were crowned with success and the charges refuted but the affair contributed to the ruin of Richard's career. It was also the undoing of Paull, who shot himself in a gambling club some years later.[4] The conclusion of this episode did little to relieve Arthur of his burden of work, nor did it halt the smear campaign of the Whig faction against the Wellesleys. Their attack included malicious innuendoes against Arthur and his implied 'neglect' of his wife and her company, which may have been helped by Kitty's indiscretions in complaining to her friends of her lonely state.

At the same time London society swept Kitty and her relations into a whirlpool of parties, receptions and Court functions. Prominent party-givers were the old Ascendancy families from Ireland, who had moved to London after the Union. In all this activity there was little time for Kitty to adjust to her new life and Arthur was seldom available to help her.

The most important event was Kitty's presentation at Court in May. The strange tale of Kitty and Arthur's marriage had caught the attention of good Queen Charlotte, who was curious to know the details. When Kitty appeared at her Drawing-room and the formalities of presentation had been concluded, the Queen told her she was 'happy to see you at my Court, so bright an example of constancy. If anybody in this world deserves to be happy, you do'. She then inquired: 'But did you really never write one letter to Sir Arthur Wellesley during his absence?' Kitty replied: 'No, never, Madam.' The Queen pressed for more details. 'And did you never think of him?' 'Yes, Madam, very often . . .,' Kitty modestly replied. Her aunt Elizabeth, present at this function, sent an account of what took place to the Edgeworths. Maria commented drily: 'I am glad constancy is approved of at Courts and hope the "bright example" may be followed.'[5]

On the eve of the King's birthday celebrations, 3 June 1806, Kitty and Arthur attended the most important function of the London season: a party given by an old friend of the Pakenhams – the newly married Mrs Thomas Hope, daughter of William de la Poer Beresford (later Lord Decies) from County Galway. It was the young matron's first 'assembly' in her wonderful new house in Duchess Street, Portland Place. She and Kitty had both been married in April that year and the great house had been created by her husband, who was already a famous antiquarian, designer and architect, as a setting for his bride. She would be the most treasured possession round which to assemble his great collection of antique vases, marbles, sculpture and furniture, many of the items purchased from Sir William Hamilton, husband of the notorious Emma.

This comparatively modest intention was soon to expand, under

Hope's enormous creative energy and huge fortune, into an extraordinary example of his eclectic virtuosity. He decided that the State rooms should represent different styles of interior decoration encountered during his extensive travels and some of his own artistic invention. From his notebooks he produced detailed drawings of furniture, ornaments, drapery, lamp-holders and wall decorations for each style, to be created by an army of craftsmen under his personal supervision. If the result was intended to shock and amaze London society, it succeeded. Reports of the inaugural assembly could not only be read in London but in the Dublin papers.

*Saunders's News-Letter* describes how 'thirteen State Apartments' were thrown open to the 'one thousand, five hundred fashionables' who attended, headed by the Prince of Wales, the Dukes of Cumberland, Cambridge and Gloucester and as many London notables as could get invitations. The originality and extravagance of these interiors would have appealed particularly to the Prince of Wales, whose longing for entertainment included enjoyment of experiments in design. Thomas Hope's fertile imagination was to excite admiration and imitation throughout Europe.

Were Kitty and Arthur impressed? On this first viewing, among so many people, the effect was overwhelming and confused. Kitty was to become more familiar with this strange house as she and her old friend exchanged visits.

The *News-Letter* informs us that guests entered through an ante-room 'fitted up a la Grecque' and moved on to the 'Black Velvet or King Henry VIII room' and then to the 'Blue or Etruscan room' with walls and ceiling of blue and crimson satin; from there to the 'Star room, which is fitted up to resemble the Celestial regions'. Already dazzled, the reporter found himself in the 'Ottoman room or Boudoir ... the ceiling in strict costume, as representing the awning over a Turkish tent'. The dining-room was furnished 'a la Egyptienne; the chairs, tables, sideboards and pedestals all being composed of the most beautiful mahogany, inlaid with ebony. In this room are the first mahogany antique candelabra in the known world'. By this time the correspondent was becoming slightly confused but persevered into the 'seventh public room, the Drawing-room' with its 'brass and gold furniture, magnificent mirrors of vast magnitude ... candelabra, tripods ... and two real gold chandeliers or Grecian lamps, richly chased'. From there, undaunted, to the 'Statue Gallery ... illuminated by an immense number of silver lamps with patent burners' and the Picture Gallery adjoining was lit in the same manner. His amazement satiated, the report concludes with the bare statement that the tenth, eleventh, twelfth and thirteenth rooms, in the corner wings of the house, were all in the 'Grecian style'.

An assembly of this magnificence began late in the evening. 'The company began to arrive at 11 o'clock. About one, what was called a "Sandwich Supper" was set out in different rooms. This supper consisted of every delicacy.... On this occasion were displayed several large gold cups, resembling vases. There were many other articles of gold plate displayed.' The correspondent describes how guests entered the house between rows of servants in 'rich State liveries ... more servants out of livery lined the great staircase.... About two o'clock the celebrated Milanese Minstrels arrived from Mr Augustein's house in Pall Mall'. Apparently, this gentleman had begun the evening with a grand entertainment for the Prince of Wales and the guests had moved on from there to the Hope's assembly 'at a late hour.... It was not until five o'clock in the morning that the party broke up'.[6]

The guests would hardly have got themselves home to bed before it was time to begin preparations for an appearance at the Queen's Drawing-room at St James's Palace that evening.

This time, the *Freeman's Journal*, Dublin, reported 'to our fair readers, an account of the Irish ladies of distinction who attended ... and of the dresses in which they were presented.... Among the great variety of the Irish nobility and gentry, the following appeared to be the most distinguished'. Those in attendance are then listed in order of precedence, beginning with the 'Duchess of Leinster; Marchionesses Thomond, Ely, Downshire, Headfort [Kitty's cousin], Donegal, Waterford; Countesses Kenmare, Barrymore, Athlone ...; Viscountesses Castlereagh, Charleville and Templetown ...; Ladies Newport, H. Fitzgerald ... Longford ... and Wellesley'. Kitty had made the required appearance at the Drawing-room with her mother and the 'Honourable Misses Pakenham'. Among the 'Sirs' present: 'Arthur Wellesley'.

The list of Irish nobility in London for the King's birthday celebrations included archbishops, bishops, generals, colonels and a long train of 'others'. It fills a column of close print in the paper and provides the correspondent with a surprising and vituperative conclusion to his report on the Irish element in London society.

But first, for his 'fair readers', the correspondent describes in great detail the dresses worn by the 'distinguished representatives of the Irish nobility' on that June night at St James's in 1806. It is fairly obvious that the ladies or their dressmakers supplied the reporter in advance with details of the creations worn. One or two examples are sufficient to illustrate the richness and extravagance of the scene. For instance, the

Marchioness of Headfort, Kitty's relative, wore 'a primrose sarsnet petticoat festooned with white patent net and primroses, train of the same. Head-dress: Primrose-coloured feathers ornamented with diamonds'. The Marchioness of Waterford was in 'white crepe, embellished with silver à la Maltese; a superb border round the petticoat and drapery, the latter festooned with uncommon rich tassels'. The Marchioness of Thomond: 'A white crepe petticoat over yellow sarsnet, ornamented with wreaths of lilac in coloured voile, intermixed with shaded voile green leaves – from the centre of the festoon, a large sprig of the same flowers. A yellow train of sarsnet, sleeves drawn up and fastened with diamond. Head-dress: Diamond bandeau, white and green feathers.' The report continues through the various degrees of nobility with their 'reverse skirts wholly composed of Brussels lace', their superb tassels, their pea-green crepe petticoats and trains richly embroidered in silver, their head-dresses of feathers and diamonds ...'. Near the end of the list Miss Pakenham is mentioned, wearing a 'white petticoat, richly embroidered with silver and festooned with apple blossoms, train of white crepe and silver body'. This was Kitty's youngest sister Caroline, wearing an appropriately youthful dress of white and silver. Kitty's gown is not described. Her taste was simple and unlikely to attract attention even had she given the details in advance.

Having done his duty in supplying his 'fair readers' with enough material to keep them gossiping for weeks to come, the reporter suddenly erupts in an explosion of anger. 'What claim', he storms, 'have the husbands of these ladies to IRISH GRATITUDE? What benefit does this brilliant show at St James's confer on Ireland? Will all this finery and profusion of diamond exhibited on this occasion by IRISH ladies add a feather to our national pride? No; we sicken at the recital of such profusion.'

In the bitterest language he contrasts the emptiness of the Irish Court, which 'only attracts ten men of title from upwards of three hundred' at any of the Viceroy's Levees, with the attendance at the Drawing-room he has just described in England. After the Union, he continues, Irish men 'of property and rank' deserted their native shores to 'shoulder themselves into the ranks of a nobility which treats them with indifference or ridicule'. He laments that money 'drawn from the groans and labour of this country' is expended amongst the wealthy English. He grants that Great Britain complains 'loudly and justly of the abundance and load of her taxes – great they are and unquestionably beyond precedent.... Yet with all her burthens ... compare her circumstances with ours. All her noblemen and gentlemen when not attending to their

## Five Dublin Days

Parliamentary duty, reside on their Estates. They cheer the tenantry by their presence; they spread comfort over the face of the country; they find work for the poor and they PAY THEM WELL.'[7]

During the Summer Recess of 1806, Arthur and William made a tour of Ireland to inspect the coastal defences, while Kitty remained with her family at Pakenham Hall. By the end of July they were back in England; Arthur resumed his regimental duties in command of 'a few troops' at Hastings. He and Kitty lived in rented accommodation there while purchases were made to complete the furnishing of the house in Harley Street. They were still in Hastings towards the end of October, when Arthur told Richard, 'We shall be very glad to see you' if he should be visiting the town.[8]

Kitty, half-way through her pregnancy, already realized how anxious Arthur was to return to active service. Four out of five regiments under his command had been sent to Deal in October, preparing to embark for Europe. In a desperate letter to Richard, dated 26 October, Arthur hopes he will be joining them: 'I don't care in what situation; I am only afraid that Lord Grenville does not understand that I don't want a chief command if it cannot be given to me; and that I should be very sorry to stay at home when others go abroad, only because I cannot command in chief.'[9]

At last the Harley Street house was ready and Kitty installed in London. But Arthur was not with her. He had moved to Deal with his brigade and from there he sent the first recorded letter to Kitty since their marriage. It is dated 6 December. 'My dearest Kitty,' he writes,

> I send underneath an Order for £50, but I wish you would not send it 'til you want the money, as the bankers will not have it in their hands 'til they have disposed of some stock of mine. George is to have 14/- a week board wages; and if he should want more and not be satisfied, give him warning, for it is high time to draw a line. Ever yours affectionately, A.W.

Probably the cost of setting up the Harley Street house had been more than Arthur expected and he was forced to use his capital to cover expenses. He had little experience of servants in civilian establishments and found the lack of discipline irritating when compared with the simplicity of life in a military camp. He liked plain living, although he enjoyed good company and entertaining. Many ordinary household expenses he considered unnecessary and extravagant. 'It is high time to draw a line' was an almost automatic response to requests for housekeeping money; he suspected domestic bills were fraudulent and many of them were. It was the lack of honesty and control that infuriated him rather than the actual sums involved.

A few days later he wrote again to tell Kitty he would be in London the following week. She was in the last stages of pregnancy; their first child would be born in about six weeks' time.

CHAPTER 10

*An Enemy's Country*

The cost of running a London house in winter, with bills for coal, food, servants, carriage horses and the entertainment of a stream of visitors and relations, gave Kitty little concern. She had never felt the want of money at Pakenham Hall and now the shops and entertainments in London were there for the enjoyment of those she loved. Money must be spent to make provisions for the new baby, for improvements to Harley Street and for the support of her old 'pensioners'. In January a 'Mahogany Crib-bedstead' was delivered to the house, with 'pillars to screw out ... and enclosed with mahogany sides and best brass socket casters', complete with a set of dimity curtains, two fine blankets, a marella quilt and two mattresses of the best curled hair.

She saw Arthur at infrequent intervals but the house was seldom free from members of her family and friends from Ireland. He was unused to the trivialities of family life and conversation limited to tittle-tattle on domestic dramas. She could not easily join in talk with brother officers from India or on political matters with the rest of the Wellesleys. In her drawing-room, mixing her pious mother and aunts and her loquacious Irish friends with Arthur's military and political colleagues would have been uncomfortable for all concerned. Could Kitty, and perhaps her mother, resist showing disapproval when the company began to get boisterous and Arthur's huge laugh echoed round the room? Or when the conversation became deeply serious on matters they considered unsuitable for a social occasion?

Fortunately for him, temporary relief from domesticity could be achieved in the hunting field, and Lady Salisbury was glad to receive him for several days at a time at Hatfield House. In January he was again hunting in Hertfordshire and instructed Kitty to forward 'this night' any letters for him. He told her that if the thaw continued, he would not be in town till Sunday. 'If there shall be a frost, I shall be in town tomorrow.' His return depended on the possibility of riding or not riding to hounds – no word of anxiety for her in the last days of her pregnancy. What woman has not experienced that sudden pain to the heart when a tiny incident reveals indifference, insensitivity to her state of mind by the person she loves? Her thoughts were concentrated on him, on her need for support and affection; his were on hunting. Spending so little time together, they had not assimilated the tolerance, consideration, understanding and good humour – not to mention love – required for a happy partnership.

On 3 February 1807, their first child, a son, was born at 11 Harley Street; her mother and numerous others round the bed. She was thirty-five and married just under ten months. Her health was not good and the attention of doctors and midwives was more likely to end in disaster than success. As was to happen so often throughout her life, in a crisis she seemed to find strength and courage of a high order. She and her son survived.

Arthur was not in the house when she was in labour, having accepted another hunting invitation. This was not unusual; men were not encouraged to participate at the time of childbirth, leaving the field clear for female ministrations. He wrote a polite and graceful note from Hatfield House to Kitty's mother three days later:

> I am much obliged for the good account you sent me yesterday of Kitty's health, of the continuance of which I am sanguine in my hopes that there is not now the slightest doubt. I hope also that considering the superior interest that I have in her safety and welfare, I may be allowed to take the opportunity of expressing my appreciation and acknowledgement for the great attention and kindness which you have shown her in the late disturbing and critical moments.... Ever your most grateful and affectionate, Arthur Wellesley.

Arthur refers to 'the late disturbing and critical moments'. Presumably the birth had not been without complications.

Towards the end of the month Arthur was seen about in London society and Frances Calvert in her diary recalls meeting 'My old friend, Sir Arthur Wellesley, at Lady Mansfield's assembly. I don't believe I have seen him for twenty years'. Shortly afterwards, Frances called on Kitty and found her at home with her 'nice little boy of three weeks old. Sir Arthur was there too and Lady Salisbury and the Ladies Cecil came in while I was there'.[1]

Kitty and the baby, little Arthur, were now the centre of attention at

Harley Street while his father's thoughts turned to India and the political situation there. He had intended to write to his old friend John Malcolm earlier in the month but 'I was hunting at Hatfield'. On 3 February, having heard that 'the Indiamen are to sail immediately', he sent a long letter on Indian affairs and on his efforts to get Malcolm appointed to the British Embassy in Persia. Although wishing his friend was in England, Arthur warns him not to be in a hurry to come home. 'Expenses here are very heavy and fortunes very large. Notwithstanding all the taxes and a rise in the prices of every article in life, there is more luxury than ever.... You could not exist in the way you would like under a much larger fortune than you possess.... You will lose nothing by staying away from England a little longer. Pray remember me to all my friends.... God bless you.'[2]

Why did he not mention the imminent birth of his first child? Could he have been so bored with female chatter on the subject that as soon as his interest in India was revived, domestic matters sank out of sight? His ability to concentrate on the matter in hand to the exclusion of domestic and personal interests was a characteristic that a wife might understand only after years of chilling experience.

The weariness of a woman after the birth of her first child is usually compensated for by tranquil moments with husband and baby at home. Kitty was not so lucky. When their son was seven weeks old, a political crisis developed in which four of the Wellesley brothers were deeply involved.

On 27 March 1807, the Government resigned over a disagreement with George III on the Catholic question. The old Duke of Portland was sent for to form a new administration. With its dying breath the untalented 'Ministry of All the Talents' passed a piece of reforming legislation – it abolished the slave trade in countries and shipping under British control.

Much to the annoyance of all the place-seekers, no less than four lucrative appointments were offered to the Wellesley family in the new government. Richard was to have the Foreign Office, but declined on the grounds that the parliamentary inquiry into his Indian administration had not yet published his vindication. William Wellesley-Pole was appointed Secretary of the Admiralty, and Henry was given a junior minister's appointment as a Secretary of the Treasury. Arthur's old friend, Lord Castlereagh, had the Department of War and Colonies; Lord Westmorland, to whom Arthur was ADC in Ireland while courting Kitty in 1791, was in the Cabinet as Lord Privy Seal.

Arthur's new appointment was owed to another old friend and contemporary, the Duke of Richmond, who had reluctantly accepted nomination as Lord Lieutenant of Ireland. He chose Arthur to be Chief Secretary, with ministerial but not Cabinet rank, and a salary of £6,500 per annum.[3] Richmond, a good-hearted man of considerable ability, selected him not only for his knowledge of Ireland and known hatred of corruption, but perhaps also out of consideration for his domestic situation. The Chief Secretaryship would give him useful employment at home and time to devote to his family after years of foreign service.

Arthur could hardly refuse, although he was longing to return to active service. He would be the most powerful man in Ireland under the Viceroy and the experience of holding ministerial rank would be invaluable. On the other hand, he disliked working as a civil servant and wanted to pursue his Army career. He accepted, with the proviso that as soon as an opportunity for a military appointment occurred he would be released from his civil duties for service abroad.

Kitty was probably not informed until after the decision had been taken. She was overjoyed at the news, even if it entailed moving from the newly found security of Harley Street to a new home in Dublin and the responsibilities of wife to an important public figure. Soon she would be back in the country she loved and where she belonged.

Her contact with Ireland had been maintained by correspondence with family and friends. Recently, she had heard from Maria Edgeworth, describing a visit to Pakenham Hall and Coolure, where Admiral Pakenham 'was very entertaining and appears very amiable in the midst of his children, who dote on him'. During this visit Kitty's brother Edward fell asleep by the fire and scorched his instep when a burning turf fell on his foot, 'At first to everyone's alarm' and later to their amusement. Soon she would be home, sharing family laughter and peaceful evenings by a turf fire or walking in the cool, green countryside. In Harley Street, carts and carriages rumbled by, hucksters called their wares, coal fires smoked and there was no sign of spring.

By the end of March, the house was becoming Arthur's temporary office for his duties as Chief Secretary, and letters were already pouring in – on patronage, on political jobbing or on any subject that would advance the writer in the esteem of the man who held the key to public appointments and private gain in Ireland.[4] At the same time, Arthur's increase in pay allowed for improvements to the house. He intended to retain Harley Street during his appointment. He would need to make frequent visits to England and it would be prudent to keep the property and to make it more comfortable. A new black and yellow Kidderminster carpet was ordered – forty-five yards at 4s 6d a yard, a four-poster bed, chests of drawers and plainer furniture for the servants' rooms.

On 14 April he was summoned to Dublin Castle to join the new

Viceroy, taking with him all the bustle and business that had filled the last few weeks. Kitty remained in the silent house with her servants and baby, but this time the separation did not cause her anxiety. Her doubts about their relationship were behind her; now everything would go right. Arthur had shown great affection and was in excellent spirits on their first wedding anniversary, just before he sailed. She looked forward with happy expectation to life in the Chief Secretary's house in Phoenix Park.

The longed-for letter from Dublin Castle, dated 17 April, arrived at last; very brief and to the point. 'My dearest Kitty....' He reported that he had arrived on Wednesday, 15 April, after a bad crossing from Holyhead. He had seen her aunt Elizabeth at Bess's house, when he had called. Her younger sister's children were staying there and had been ill with influenza. As Bess was apprehensive 'that her's will catch it, I believe the young Hamiltons are going to my house in the Park.... Ever yours, most affectionately, Arthur Wellesley'.

A few days later he sent her further news: 'The little Hamiltons are better; Harry Stewart [Bess's husband] very ill; all the rest pretty well. Lady Longford is arrived this morning, as I see from the return from the Post Office, but I have not seen her yet. I have had no sore throat....'

So short and curt a note – no word for her or the baby, nothing about the new house, simply a minimum report on the only subject he seemed to think would interest her – her family. Harley Street had suddenly become a prison and Kitty prayed for help to overcome a momentary weakness and despair – rationalizing the perfunctory note as due to pressure of urgent business. In this she was probably correct. Arthur's day was an endless round of interviews and visits; the evenings spent in writing scores of replies to endless requests for jobs, for pensions, for privileges of one sort or another. On top of the routine correspondence he submitted a number of official reports on defence, internal affairs, the political situation and other topics, to his seniors in England – mainly Lord Hawkesbury, Secretary of State for the Home Department, better known in later years as Lord Liverpool, a much criticized Prime Minister.

In May he wrote: 'I lay it down as decided that Ireland, in a view to military operations, must be considered as an enemy's country'. The threat of invasion by the French and the likelihood of a rising to support the invaders, should they establish a landing, was immediate. 'I am positively convinced that no political measure which you could adopt would alter the temper of the people of this country. They are disaffected to the British Government: they don't feel the benefits of their situation; attempts to render it better either do not reach their minds, or they are represented to them as injuries.'[5]

No letters from Kitty to Arthur for this period survive. Throughout his life he destroyed personal correspondence as soon as read but carefully preserved anything that concerned his official duties. It is not difficult to reconstruct her letters to him. He told her nothing of his work, so she probably did not inquire on this subject. Her interest concerned his movements and his health; after that she wanted news of her family and friends – questions about them he answered meticulously.

Concern for his health was a recurring topic. Had he caught cold during the voyage? Had he got over the sore throat he had in London? Although Arthur had always been careful to maintain his physical fitness – survival in India depended on it – he did not like to be reminded of minor weaknesses. Kitty could not restrain her longing to do something for him to demonstrate her concern and love, mistakenly believing he would appreciate her inquiries and offered remedies. Her attempts to fuss over him were coldly rejected. 'I have no sore throat. . . .' The curt statement should have been a warning.

She joined him in Ireland in May, but already he was making plans to return to England for the parliamentary session at the end of June, mustering the Irish Members to support the government. He was not neglecting his long-term objective to return to active service and an expedition to Denmark might provide the opportunity. He wrote to Castlereagh from Dublin Castle on 1 June 1807: 'By all accounts you are advancing the preparations for your expedition to the Continent. . . . I hope you will recollect what I said to you upon this subject. . . . I am determined not to give up the military profession. . . . If you send the expedition, I wish you would urge Lord Hawkesbury to fix upon a successor for me, as I positively cannot stay here, whether I am to be employed with it or not . . .'[6]

On the same day he wrote to Lady Elizabeth Langford refusing her request to 'do something for Mr Sherlock', Kitty's uncle by marriage. Arthur told her: 'You must be aware that I am in a very delicate situation in this country: and being connected with it myself, it is my duty . . . to avoid pressing upon the Government objects . . . in favour of my friends and connections.'

However, he suggests she ask Lord Longford, her nephew, to put forward Mr Sherlock's claim to a government appointment – to avoid 'embarrassment' which would 'retard the accomplishment of your wishes. Ever your most affectionate . . .' – his standard ending to members of the family.

It was not only Kitty's relations who were asking for favours. His sister Lady Anne Smith asked him to appoint a Mr Marshall 'to command a

Dublin packet boat'. He replied on 10 June: 'There is no vacancy... and I cannot pretend to make an engagement to dispose in any particular manner of a vacancy which may occur.... It may be expected that the Duke of Richmond or I, who have been all over the world, have naval friends of merit, but not rich, to whom we may be desirous of giving such provision.'

On 22 June, Arthur was writing to Kitty again – a single page from Harley Street, in the coldest terms – no name, no endearment. It begins: 'I arrived here on Saturday morning. I shall be very much obliged to you if you will let me know what day you propose to leave off your mourning....' She was in mourning for her sister Helen Hamilton, whose children were with her at Phoenix Park.

Kitty was now sure she was pregnant again, the result of the sudden burst of affection and euphoria in April at Harley Street, when Arthur was on the point of departure for Dublin Castle.

Helen's death, after a long illness, added a fresh complication to Kitty's life. Her sister had made a will shortly after her husband's death two years before, in which her chief concern was for her infant daughter, Catherine. She begs her friends not to send Catherine away to school. 'If my sister Kitty is unmarried she will, I know, be a mother and a tender mother to her and will, I hope, take her entirely under her care. It is my particular wish that she should. My sister knows perfectly all my wishes respecting her education. She is also acquainted with the sentiments of my child's most excellent father. I have nothing more to say, for my child in such hands can hardly be said to have lost a mother.'

She added a codicil in 1806, leaving small legacies to her servants but not altering her desire that Kitty, now married, should look after her little daughter. The two elder children, both boys, and their sister were placed under the official guardianship of Kitty's unmarried brother Edward. For the time being, they were all to live at Secretary's Lodge, Phoenix Park, or at Pakenham Hall with their grandmother. Arthur was fond of children and made no objection to this arrangement.

It was probably a matter of indifference to him what domestic arrangements Kitty made. His plan to join the expedition to Denmark was now approved. He would not leave his post until the last moment, joining the troops at their point of embarkation. Kitty was not to be informed. As late as 24 July, Arthur was writing to the Duke of Richmond on his doubts as to whether or not the expedition would be sent. 'In this state of uncertainty I have not written to Lady Wellesley upon this subject; and it is as well not to say anything to her about it 'til it will be positively settled that we are to go.'

By 27 July 1807, the decision was taken. Napoleon's plans to seize the neutral Danish navy for a possible invasion of England had been confirmed. The Danes had refused an invitation voluntarily to surrender their fleet to the British and it had been decided to remove this threat by a combined land and sea attack on Copenhagen, where the ships lay at anchor. Arthur would have command of a brigade during this operation, which was expected to be short as the Danish militia could offer little more than token resistance. The Lord-Lieutenant wished to keep him in office as Chief Secretary during the expedition, returning to his administrative duties after the campaign. Writing from Harley Street to a political friend, Arthur explained that when he accepted office in Ireland it was conditional on his being free to rejoin his profession when opportunity offered. 'No political office could compensate to me the loss of the situation which I held in the Army and nothing should induce me to give it up.'[7] The Army was his life. He had a genius for command and he knew it. It was not ambition that drove him on; he was on the threshold of a brilliant career in civilian life. It was the necessity to exercise his capabilities to their maximum extent. He hated bloodshed, but loved the excitement and responsibility of leadership, of patriotic endeavour to protect his country from her enemies and preserve the rule of law. For this duty he felt he was uniquely chosen by God and endowed with the gifts the task required. To fail to answer the call would be dishonourable and cowardly. The most courageous men were those who were the least obsessed with themselves. Arthur always considered he was expendable in achieving God's purpose and this humility gave him his characteristic coolness in the face of danger.

The expedition to Denmark was now certain, and in the interval Arthur was enjoying the London social and political scene, relieved from the begging letters of Irish opportunists and the necessity to placate and manipulate the Irish Members. His letters to Kitty became more considerate. He knew he was to have a second child early in 1808 and listened more tolerantly to Kitty's accounts of domestic dramas. When little Arthur had measles, his father wrote: 'I have no apprehension for the measles, being convinced that it is a mild disorder and one that has no bad consequences if the patient is well taken care of as it is going off. You have not said whether you have had the measles yourself?'

Kitty's next letter told Arthur of the suicide of one of her maids at Secretary's Lodge, on account of being seduced and made pregnant by, it was alleged, one of the gardeners – a man she had now dismissed. Arthur replied sardonically from London on 13 July. He hoped that 'the remainder of the maids of the Park will put up with the misfortunes of this world and not destroy themselves. Let that gardener be taken back. It is evident that he has nothing to say to the death of this woman.... I enclose a letter from a bricklayer. I thought that you had paid him. Let me know whether you have or not. I shall be able to get away from here in about a fortnight or three weeks.'

She wrote again on 14 July telling Arthur that the Hamilton children had recovered from an illness and of a family upset at Summerhill, the home of her mother's relations. Arthur, in his reply, suggested that Catherine Taylour, the troublesome daughter of the Marquis of Headfort, ought to be married: 'They should find a husband for Lady Catherine; and fix upon a common fellow, if they cannot prevail upon a gentleman to submit to the misfortune of being united to her Ladyship. If some measure of this kind is not adopted, she will soon be confined in a Mad House.... Let the law take its course in respect of the gardener; but if there is no evidence or suspicion that he was concerned in the poor girl's death, it would not be very charitable to dismiss him from my service ... and I shall certainly not dismiss him.' He adds that he cannot call on Lady Longford at Langford Lodge in Ulster, because he cannot yet 'fix a day for my return to Ireland; but I suppose it may be in about a fortnight from this time'.

Kitty had been anxiously awaiting his return but could not pin him down to a date. She and Arthur had only had a few weeks together at Secretary's Lodge since coming to Ireland and now she was three months pregnant and feeling far from well, her condition not helped by having to manage her baby son, the Hamilton children, her household of servants and the payment of bills. She resented Arthur's easy commands regarding the reinstatement of the gardener; it was obvious he did not trust her judgement, although quite prepared to leave her alone to contend with the problems of managing a large and unfamiliar house.

She admitted to Arthur that the bricklayer's and other bills had not been paid, her excuse being that she did not want to ask him for money. He replied on 25 July, beginning 'My dearest Kitty' and attempting to restrain his annoyance. 'I am much concerned that you should have thought of concealing from me any lack of money which you might have experienced. I don't understand how this want occurred or why it was concealed; and the less that is said or written upon the subject the better.' Then his irritation bursts through: 'I acknowledge to you that the conclusion I draw from your conduct upon this occasion is that you must be Mad and that you must consider me a Brute and most particularly fond and avaricious of money. Once for all, you require no permission to talk to me about any subject you please; all I request is that a piece of work may not be made about trifles and things of ordinary occurrence and that you may not go into tears because I don't think them deserving of an uncommon degree of attention.'

At this point in the letter Kitty must have thought how little time there had been to talk to him 'on any subject you please'. It was his chilling impatience with trivial matters that made her fearful to speak of money and bills, which he always assumed were excessive or fraudulent. She read on: 'My principal reason for writing now is to let you know that I am going abroad with the Expedition. I expect, notwithstanding this, to be in Ireland by 1st of September. I request you therefore, to remain where you are.'

Was she not to be allowed to see him before he went abroad? Would he not see his little son before leaving? He expected to return by 1 September, but in between there would be a sea journey, a military action – were they not to say 'Goodbye'? Tears were falling already – this was certainly a 'piece of work' and Kitty felt the suffocation of anguish as the letter continued with its crisp information and attention to detail. 'I don't know yet whether I am to retain my office or not . . . but remain where you are 'til you hear further from me. I rather believe I shall retain my office; but upon that point, as well as upon the probable period of my return, I request you to say nothing to anybody. I shall write again before I sail.'

Letters had crossed in the post and his next communication, dated 26 July, began without an endearment: 'It would be imagined that I had acted harshly by you in desiring that the gardener might not lose his place, from the answer I received this day on that subject; and certainly nothing was ever further from my thoughts. But it is to be hoped that at some time or other I shall be better understood. It is useless to enter into details upon this subject but it appears that your letter is written purposely to give me to understand that I have not allowed you authority to act and that I had expressed my desire upon it. This will never do.'

Again Kitty's tears were falling – the letter was unfair – Arthur had told her he would not dismiss the gardener and had countermanded her decision – but nothing mattered now. He was going away. The old terror of storms at sea which had so nearly claimed his life on two occasions years ago were added to her fears of death on active service. How would she manage alone, with two little children, if anything happened to him? How could she live without him? Through her tears she read her orders as to what she should do 'if any permanent successor' to his post as Chief Secretary should be appointed during his absence. 'You had best come over to England . . .' – with the baby and another expected? More tears. She must hand over 'everything I took from Mr. Elliot [the previous Chief Secretary] at the same rate I paid for it . . . and my successor must pay for all. You have the valuation papers. There are twenty of Tom Pakenham's cows among my stock which must be returned to him if I should not return.'

Poor Kitty was convinced that all these instructions were for the event of his death, not merely his replacement as Chief Secretary; he was giving her his last wishes.... She could read no more. Servants hovered about her, offering smelling salts, a little brandy. The Hamilton boys began to cry.... 'Have my salary transferred to Mr. Smith and as soon as he has received the money, I request you pay all the bills ... amounting I believe to £500.... Look over the stock of wine and ascertain the quantity that has been used since I have been in office. I must pay Mr. Elliot for that quantity and my successor must pay for the remainder of the stock.'

The careful, precise instructions continued: nothing forgotten, every detail covered – foresight, order, discipline, scrupulous honesty. Here was General Wellesley in command. 'If you should come to England ... bring my plate, including silver articles which I have bought in Ireland; your carriage and horses and harness and my curricle harness; and leave everything else behind. Let my curricle be sold.' This was the longest letter (six pages) she had received from Arthur and, in Kitty's vivid imagination, his last.

CHAPTER 11

# The House in the Park

Arthur's arrangements for joining the expedition to Denmark were complete. He felt relaxed and happy on arrival at Sheerness, where he was to embark, and could write to Kitty in kindlier terms than in recent letters. 'My dearest Kitty, I arrived here this day [30 July] and shall embark in the Prometheus fire-vessel this evening or tomorrow morning. I received your letter of Saturday last night but had not time to answer it before I left town.'

Kitty had asked permission if her mother could come to live at Secretary's Lodge, or the Park, as Arthur called his house. Arthur, now in good spirits, had little concern what went on there, so long as he was not at home. 'Lady Longford is perfectly welcome to the Park and all that it contains; and I am only sorry', he added, tongue in cheek, 'that I am not there to receive her.... Pray tell Tom Pakenham that I have not written to him because ... I have nothing to say.... Remember me to him most kindly.' He informs Kitty that Longford has gone to Deal to see another brother, Hercules, embark and he would be 'under my command. God Bless you, my dearest Kitty and believe me ever yours most affectionately, A.W.' In a postscript he tells her to write to him via his London house where 'Mr Wyatt will forward your letters'.

Kitty and her mother were anxious not only on account of the Danish expedition, involving Arthur and Hercules, but another brother, Edward, was waiting to embark at 'Humbermouth' for an unknown destination, possibly the West Indies or North America. The indefatigable, kindly Longford, having seen off one brother from Deal, set out for the north to give 'God speed' to another. By 9 August, Edward informed his mother: 'My excellent friend, Longford, has just left me and as the wind seems inclined a little more in our favour... we hope to be quite off tonight. It is vastly satisfactory your being together at this time, for a dear friend of ours [Kitty] may much benefit by the company of those she loves, which I hope will rather keep her silent than make her speak; the world is a strange one and we must not be surprised whatever occurs.'[1]

He might have been even more surprised if he could have seen what Arthur had written a few days before. He had drawn up a new will as soon as he boarded the *Prometheus* on 31 July 1807. 'As I am about to sail upon an expedition with the Army and Navy, I make this my last will and testament, by which I revoke all instruments of the same description.' The previous 'instrument' had been drawn up in 1805, at Fort St George, Madras, just before leaving India. In this earlier will he had made various bequests to brother officers, to Mrs Freese and to his godson Arthur Freese. The remainder of his fortune he had left to his brother Gerald, with £10,000 for Henry, and specific instructions that his papers should be destroyed 'and not looked at'.

Now, two years later, as the ship bucked across the North Sea, he wrote: 'When I married in 1806...' he had settled £20,000 and a further £6,000 'in the manner pointed out in my marriage settlement'. He now directed that the £20,000 should be left to his son, Arthur Richard, after the death of his mother. The remaining £6,000 'I leave to whatever child may be brought forth by Lady Wellesley, my wife, within nine months of this date'. If there was no issue surviving at the time of Lady Wellesley's death, the whole £26,000 would then go to 'my nephew and godson, Arthur Wellesley, the son of my brother the Honourable and Reverend Gerald Wellesley'. After other contingencies had been provided for, he appointed his brothers Gerald and Henry as executors and guardians of his children.

So far the will was a careful and predictable document; but at this point Arthur made an extraordinary declaration: 'I particularly desire that my son, Arthur Richard and any child I may have as a consequence of the existing pregnancy of my wife, may not be allowed to live in Ireland or even to go there or to have any connection with that country'.

The will continues with directions that his children are to have 'the best education that can be given to them and then to choose their profession; but let it not be believed that a finished classical education is not necessary for a gentleman in a military profession'.

Two points were uppermost in his mind for the future of his children as he returned to active service, apart from normal financial considerations. The first was to direct that they be barred from all contact with the land where he and his wife were born; the second, that they should have a 'finished classical education' whatever profession they chose to follow. His own unfinished schooling had been a source of deeply felt regret, a deficiency he tried to rectify all his life by systematic reading in a wide variety of subjects, so that his knowledge would be equal to the responsibilities placed on his shoulders. Education, particularly in the classics, was the key to honest and unbiased judgement in public affairs, to the ultimate benefit of the nation as a whole.

What did he fear from the influence of the 'enemy's country' on his children? It could have been the reaction of a man sickened by the ceaseless demands for patronage, privilege and rewards for political services with which he had been inundated as Chief Secretary, combined with unbridled and cynical corruption more general and scandalous than he had encountered elsewhere. Or was his disgust centred on the treachery and betrayal he had experienced from persons he had worked for and trusted – the feeling that however much he applied his mind and influence for the benefit of the people and the country as a whole, his efforts would be discounted or misrepresented as being the opposite of what he intended? Was it the realization that a part of the population was only waiting for a signal from the French and a successful invasion, to place themselves under the military dictatorship of Napoleon, hated throughout the rest of Europe, whether still free or already subjugated? Was he revolted by the mindless cruelty of Irishmen against Irishmen; by the horrors of Wexford Bridge and other atrocities, which had sickened hardened soldiers; or by the terrible reprisals inflicted by the military and civil authorities – violence mounting upon violence, cruelty on cruelty? Had Ireland come to stand for a country of fear, where innocent people were caught between rival gangs and murdered; a land without pity?

It might be that his dislike of Ireland was linked with his wife and her family – or with his wife alone. There is no reason to think that Arthur was not on good terms with the Pakenhams, with the possible exception of Kitty's mother, who had disapproved of him in the past. It is obvious that he greatly valued the bravery and loyalty of Hercules and Edward, serving under his command; while his affection for the Coolure Pakenhams was sincere and enduring. As for Kitty herself, he may have realized already that she was not capable of the standards he had attributed to his imaginary wife while in India. Accusations of 'neglect' from her mother, which stemmed from Kitty's complaints to her family, cast doubts on her loyalty, but all these imperfections did not amount to a cause for regretting the marriage, at this stage. It must be assumed that Ireland itself was responsible for Arthur's antipathy – made more bitter by his lost love for that Siren land, whose beauty covered degradation and death.

## The House in the Park

The will concluded with bequests of £1,000 each to his sister's children Caroline and Georgiana Fitzroy by her first husband and to Arthur Freese, his godson. The balance of his fortune was left 'to my son, Arthur Richard Wellesley ... on the day he is twenty-one'. Attached to the document was a list of his assets, amounting to approximately £53,400, plus 'Prize-money still due me in India'.

He was still on board the *Prometheus* on 7 August when he wrote: 'My dearest Kitty, One line to inform you that I am quite well. I have not seen or heard anything of your brothers; but I have not sailed with any of the convoys.' On the fourteenth he wrote to tell her that he had 'removed from the fire-ship to a "74" [the *Goliath*] where we have more room, although we are not more comfortable'. He had not yet seen Hercules, but communication between ships 'is very difficult. Your brother Edward is not arrived yet'. He had sailed from the Humber, not to the West Indies as anticipated, but to join the Danish expedition.

Three weeks went by before Kitty had more news. On 5 September he wrote from Braesenborg in Denmark: 'I received three letters from you yesterday, all written before the last, the receipt of which I acknowledge, for which I am much obliged. We fought a battle and gained a victory on 29th August, which was gained by my Corps. I saw your brother Hercules after the battle in very good health. I think that this battle is likely to accelerate our return; and I still hope to see you in the course of this month. Ever yours...'.

A single page, bare facts, but much to be thankful for – he was well. Hercules was 'in very good health' and the battle might 'accelerate our return'. Best of all, he was hoping to see her before the end of the month. Kitty could build great hopes on his 'hope to see you' and suddenly life at the Park and her pregnancy assumed an aura of happiness.

A few days later another letter arrived, headed

> Headquarters before Copenhagen, September 8th, 1807. My dearest Kitty, I was sent for here on the day before yesterday in order to settle the capitulation of Copenhagen, which I did in that night; and I returned to my troops this day in order to draw them in. I will ask leave to return to England in a day or two, so that I hope to arrive in England shortly after this letter. I saw your brother Edward last night quite well. Hercules is with my Corps in the country and very well also.

Kitty was overjoyed. Arthur, crowned with success, would be home at any moment, might already have landed as she read his letter. Preparations for a welcome were put in hand; all was bustle and rush to finish preparing the house in the Park for his return.

By almost the same mail came the inevitable anticlimax. Her implacable rival, his public duty, had intervened. 'I landed yesterday and had proceeded thus far on my journey to London when I received a letter from Lord Castlereagh to request that I would go to him at Lord Hertford's. I am therefore obliged to turn back and shall not be in London 'til tomorrow. I will go to Ireland as soon as possible. I left your brothers very well.'

The letter was dated 29 September. Kitty must wait still longer for her reunion with Arthur, a reunion that for her was to be a new start to married life. Arthur too, during his absence abroad, probably decided to be more tolerant and understanding in domestic affairs. Absence may have made the married state appear more attractive, or at least worth a new effort to achieve success. He hated to fail in any situation.

Unfortunately for his good intentions, he was still under tremendous pressure of work. The capitulation of Copenhagen and the successful capture of the Danish fleet had not silenced critics of the Government at home. The brevity of his letters to Kitty was balanced by the long and detailed reports and analysis of the Danish situation, with its implications for the defence of Europe, he was sending to Hawkesbury, Castlereagh and his brother William Wellesley-Pole at the Admiralty.[2]

Such matters were not to be discussed with Kitty or even hinted at. He had decided, on the evidence of her behaviour during the little time they had spent together, to exclude her from discussion of his problems, other than domestic affairs. She desperately wanted to please him but lacked the qualities of calm and tranquillity which a man involved in great events needed at home. If he could have given more time to their relationship, she might have overcome her tense anxiety, her effort to be his intellectual equal, her fatal propensity to talk when she should have listened. Their lack of mutual understanding was largely due to her pregnancies during nearly the whole of their first two years together. Her preoccupation was with childbirth, his with international affairs. When she attempted to enter his world she cloaked her lack of understanding with dogmatic statements that infuriated him. His answer was to avoid her; she responded with reproaches. The gulf between them became unbridgeable. Kitty floundered in a morass of sentiment, resentment, muddle in running their domestic affairs, and a cloud of gossip. There were peaceful interludes but these were too infrequent to form a basis for mutual respect and affection.

Kitty had to wait until the second week of October before Arthur landed in Ireland. If he intended to give his marriage another lease of life, the intention was short-lived. It was soon evident he would be thankful to escape again into the world of the professional soldier.

## The House in the Park

On 17 October he wrote to Canning at the Foreign Office from Dublin Castle, reporting on 'the disturbances in the Southern Counties', and concluded by remarking that he would 'be happy to aid the Government in any manner they please and am ready to start for any part of the world at a moments notice'.[3] Arthur did not think he would be sent back to India. Writing to his friend Colin Campbell at about this time, who was still serving there, he said: 'I have got pretty high upon the tree since I came home and those in power think I cannot well be spared [to return to India].'[4]

Their son was now eight months old and Kitty's second child expected soon after Christmas. She was happy knowing Arthur was settled at home and that he liked the house, pleasantly set in the middle of Phoenix Park looking down over the city of Dublin. It had been built in 1776; a low, commodious building on two floors with large bays at either end. Neighbours were few; there were only three other houses of note within the Park, one of which was the official residence of the Viceroy. It was a pleasant carriage ride through the high, undulating landscape into the city, to call on friends and relations or for business at Dublin Castle. There was plenty of room in the house for guests, and the Hamilton children, who normally lived with their grandmother at Pakenham Hall, were frequent visitors. John, the eldest, was now seven, Edward five and the baby, Catherine, three. John recalled one of these holidays at Secretary's Lodge in his memoirs when, after an illness in 1807, the three children convalesced 'with our kind Aunt, Lady Wellesley'. He describes an incident that had vividly impressed itself on his memory.

It was November and the autumn days were getting short. Sir Arthur was at home and another uncle, Kitty's brother Henry, aged twenty, was staying with them. The two uncles took John and his brother for a walk in the pale sunshine of a winter afternoon and, talking and striding out across the Park, the men forgot the tired little boys trying to keep up with them – not very strong after their illness. A red sun was low in the sky and the hour for dinner approaching – about five o'clock – when suddenly the uncles realized how late it was and how far they were from home. To save time and help the children, Arthur took one boy on his shoulders and Henry the other – and so they began to jog on. Soon the pace quickened and the uncles were racing, their passengers bumping up and down with squeals of excitement. Arthur, thirty-eight, was no match for Henry at first, but as the race lengthened stamina began to tell. Henry could not keep up his cracking pace and Arthur drew level. Shouting with laughter between gasps for breath they ran at top speed towards the gates of the Lodge, Arthur with a great bellow of triumph rushing through first,

Henry close behind. The astonished watchman ordered them to halt, not recognizing in the dusk the Chief Secretary of Ireland as one of the hooligans disturbing the peace of the evening.[5]

Kitty had rarely seen this boisterous side of her husband's character. There has been too little laughter and horseplay for Arthur's liking in the last two years. He loved a house full of people or a headquarters full of good fellows and their pretty wives, with plenty of music, dancing and amusing company at dinner. Dublin Castle and his house in the Park had stifled him – the one with unremitting paper work and intrigue, the other with domestic responsibilities that irritated him and a wife seven months pregnant.

Arthur announced to the family in December that Kitty was 'in a situation which will not permit her to go from the neighbourhood of town at present'[6] and she would not be able to join the usual jolly party assembled at Pakenham Hall for Christmas. Maria Edgeworth was there and reported to her brother in London: 'This is really the most agreeable family and the pleasantest and most comfortable Castle I ever was in. We came here yesterday ... and a few minutes after we came, arrived Hercules Pakenham – the first time he had met his family since his return from Copenhagen.... Lady Wellesley was prevented by engagements from joining this party at Pakenham Hall; both the Duke and Duchess of Richmond are as fond of her as no tongue can tell; the Duke must have a real friendship for Sir Arthur; for while he was in Copenhagen His Grace did all the business of his office for him.'[7]

Edward was not at Pakenham Hall but in London, waiting to join his regiment in Sussex. On Christmas Day he wrote to his mother for news of Kitty's health, now she was so near her confinement: 'I do suppose you now in town on account of our Kitty – whatever she is most anxious to add to our strength, either King or Queen, God send that safety and good fortune may attend – with my remembrance, say I shall only object to anything of lower rank than the above.' The letter continues in praise of Hercules: 'Whatever opinion you may have formed [of him], it cannot be too high.' The Pakenhams were a close-knit family; their letters to each other show strong affection and solidarity. Kitty must have been sadly torn between staying dutifully at the Park with Arthur or joining the happy family reunion at Pakenham Hall over Christmas, however close she might be to her confinement.

Christmas made little difference to Arthur's routine. He spent part of the day at Dublin Castle, writing official letters and memoranda. The following day, 26 December, he was not at his desk – he had gone shooting: 'The Chancellor [Lord Manners] and I went out yesterday,' he wrote to Richmond, 'but we saw only two brace and the day turned out so bad that we were obliged to return at one o'clock.' Kitty had stayed at home without the pleasure of a whole day in Arthur's company. There were still three weeks to wait for the birth of their second child.

Did this Christmas season bring Henry Pakenham to the house in the Park, begging his sister's help to save him from his creditors? Did she, in a moment of resentment at Arthur's neglect and pity for her younger brother, lend him money from the housekeeping account? It is difficult to say; all correspondence relating to this period was later destroyed. Conjecture and an entry in Kitty's diary indicate that at about this time she did something she was to regret for the rest of her life and for which Arthur never forgave her.

In January, Arthur was beginning his usual round-up of Irish Members for the next session of Parliament. It was at this season that the demands of constituency owners for patronage became most insistent; requests for favours combined with veiled threats that, if not satisfied, their MPs would be 'unable' to attend at Westminster and vote in support of the Government. On the day Kitty was in labour, 16 January 1808, Arthur was at his desk in Dublin Castle as usual, giving short shrift to an MP who said his health would prevent him attending the next Session in England.

After a full day at the office, Arthur returned home to find Kitty delivered of another fine boy. He left Ireland for London four days later and on 22 January was back in Harley Street, annoyed that he had been unable to settle the Ordnance accounts before he sailed. Writing to the officer responsible for the delay, he told him a start must be made to put the matter right. Vouchers or a reasonable explanation for expenditures must be furnished 'as fast as you can' or he would incur Arthur's serious annoyance.[8] Where money and accounting was concerned, he would have no nonsense – as Kitty already knew only too well. If she had lent from the housekeeping account, a recurring anxiety would be whether Henry would repay before Arthur noticed the discrepancy.

Winter weather in London had undermined Arthur's health. Writing to the Duke of Richmond on 1 February, he begins by reassuring the viceroy's concern at the threat offered by a French squadron of ships at Rochefort. 'We have nothing to fear of a possible invasion from that quarter ... but those damned parties in Donegal will destroy us.... I have not been very well for these last two days.... Don't tell Lady W. that I have been unwell, as it is only making a piece of work about nothing.'

Kitty on this occasion may not have had time to 'make a piece of work about nothing'. The new baby, Charles, was privately baptized on 12 February and entered in the parish records of Castlenock. Plans for a public baptism were put in hand for a later date.

Family concern for Kitty was increasing on the subject of Arthur's 'neglect'; his inability or unwillingness to spend adequate time with his wife and children was a subject discussed by her relations and gossips in Dublin. Edward, writing from Halifax, Nova Scotia, had heard from Hercules of Kitty's complaints and unhappiness. In a letter to his mother, he writes: 'I have an excellent letter from my friend, Hercules. . . . How is Kitty? I should like to write – the case is so singular that silence is best, though perhaps at the expense of being negligent; you will not allow that. Give my best regards to her and all my friends – in the event of our sailing [for Europe] I should have a letter to go . . . 'til then, my excellent mother, adieu.'[9]

Throughout March, Kitty continued the routine of life at the Park. Her second wedding anniversary would be on 10 April, and already she had two healthy babies to care for. Fortunately, she had many friends in Dublin, including the Richmonds; the Duke was only four years older than Arthur and understood him pretty well. The Chief Secretary was a popular visitor at Viceregal Lodge and a particular favourite of the Duke's young family. Georgiana Lennox, then thirteen, and her sisters would ride with him every day from a rendezvous in Phoenix Park to the Dublin Gate, giving him company on the way to his Castle office.[10] Cantering across the Park with the girls on their ponies in the early morning was a brief respite from the burden of administration, which he found increasingly irksome.

Knowing and admiring Arthur's character and ability, the Richmonds were also sympathetic to Kitty and the situation in which she found herself through no fault of her own. Arthur was utterly honest and would have made no secret of his attitude to his marriage, which he regarded as normal in the circumstances. He was immersed in a huge volume of work on political and international affairs of the first importance. He would lose little sleep in worrying about his domestic responsibilities or the chatter the so-called 'neglect' of his wife caused in family circles. Kitty bore the burden of local gossip and would have to parry the 'kind' inquiries as to when Arthur had last been with her at Secretary's Lodge. She could and did complain to her family but her essential loyalty to Arthur inhibited this outlet for her feelings. The seclusion of Secretary's Lodge became a refuge from the curiosity of friends and her two babies an excuse to withdraw from Dublin society.

Spring brought promotion for Arthur to lieutenant-general, the youngest in the Army and a further step up the tree on which he had 'climbed so high'. He was in London on their second wedding anniversary but paid a flying visit to Dublin on 19 April and was back in London on 26 April, by the fast Irish Packet, Dublin to Holyhead.

Arthur's friendship and respect for the Duke of Richmond had deepened with their close association over Irish affairs. In a letter at this time, Arthur congratulated him on his popularity but expressed his own contempt for popular acclaim. He pointed out that Richmond had acquired popularity without effort and had always acted regardless of the impression made on individuals or the public. 'You have governed the country as you thought best yourself. Popularity may not last.' If popularity were lost, the Viceroy would be consoled by knowing that he had acted as he thought right for the country and that would 'always be a satisfaction to you, let what will become of the "bloody popularity" as Falkiner calls it'.[11] Arthur and Richmond shared the view that they would never compromise their principles to please anybody.

It was now nearly certain that Arthur would have command of an expedition to Portugal and on 4 June he explained the situation to Richmond in a letter from London, which concludes: 'Don't mention this subject to Lady W. 'til it will be positively determined.' But the chance of keeping such a secret from the Dublin gossips was slim. It seems likely that as soon as she heard of Arthur's possible departure for Portugal, she set off for London, leaving the children (Charley was now five months old) to the care of a nurse and her mother at the Park. Allowing three days for her journey from Dublin to London, she could have been at Harley Steet on 10 June. John Wilson Croker, politician and journalist, who was also an old friend of the Wellesleys, claims in his memoirs to have been invited to dinner at Harley Street with Sir Arthur and Lady Wellesley at this time, when arrangements were discussed for his duties as 'stand-in' Chief Secretary in Ireland, during Sir Arthur's absence.[12]

Another subject for urgent discussion, as far as Kitty was concerned, was the public baptism, not only of little Charley, but of Arthur Richard, privately baptized in London the previous year. She would have insisted that their father be present at the ceremony and they probably left London for Holyhead together, crossing to Ireland on 19 June. Arthur did not waste a moment of time. While waiting to sail he wrote two long official letters from Holyhead, one to the Duke of Portland, the other to Lord Hawkesbury. On 22 June he was back at Dublin Castle, attending to his usual duties.

He took a day's holiday to be present at the double baptism on 27 June 1808, arranged by Kitty and her family. The ceremony was held at Secretary's Lodge under the direction of the Lord Bishop of Limerick. The impressive list of sponsors for Arthur Richard included 'The most noble Marquis Wellesley; the Earl of Longford; the Countess of Mornington...'. For Charles, the 'Duke of Richmond; The Earl of Harrington [Commander of Forces in Ireland]; Lady Longford...'.

Two days after the christening, Kitty purchased 'a silver comb and hair ornament' in Dublin, as a present for her younger sister Caroline, who was about to marry Henry Hamilton, distantly related to her late brother-in-law.

A week later, Arthur left Dublin to take up his temporary command of the expeditionary force to Portugal. The Braganza dynasty had been dethroned by Napoleon the previous November and forced to flee to Brazil. This was a golden opportunity for Britain to activate the ancient alliance with Portugal and secure a foothold among a friendly people from which to strike at Napoleon's dominance in the Peninsula; a dominance which rested on a seething mass of resentment, unrest and shame at the lip-service paid to Napoleon by their rulers.

Fuel was added to the flames in May when Napoleon's dynastic obsession led him into a fatal error. He forced King Ferdinand VII of Spain, whose father had been his uneasy ally since 1804, to abdicate in favour of his brother Joseph Bonaparte; an insult to the Spanish people whose smouldering insurrection burst into spontaneous combustion wherever the unfortunate French troops found themselves in a vulnerable situation. No soldier was safe from murder outside his camp site; stragglers and the sick were picked off silently by shadowy figures or by village traders who a moment before had been selling oranges and joking with their French customers. Retaliation from the troops was swift – peasants tortured and executed in blind fury, villages burned as soon as they had been sacked. Unspeakable crimes were committed by both sides. It was always the policy of French forces to live off the countryside and feed themselves as best they could by commandeering supplies, usually without payment. It was to take advantage of this hatred of the French that the British Government decided to support the Spanish rebellion.

The first step was to secure a base in Portugal. The limiting factors, as always, were money and supplies; the operation would be further impeded by the reverence for seniority among the High Command in the British Army. Command could not be given to the most able and experienced officers if they were junior in rank to older and inexperienced generals. Thus Arthur's command was temporary and provisional. Diplomacy was another factor inhibiting the strategy of an expeditionary force. The Spaniards claimed to have large numbers of troops under their own generals – the British expeditionary force, once it entered Spain, would be required to support the Spanish initiative. History would show how fatal this policy was at the first attempt to invade Spain. Sir John Moore and his forces were sacrificed to false information on the efficacy of Spanish support in the winter of 1808/9. All this was still in the future. It was now July 1808, and it had been decided that while Arthur was away Kitty should remain at Secretary's Lodge in much the same situation as when Arthur left for Denmark; but this time no letters survive from her husband.

Clouds of gloom and disappointment seemed to have settled over the house in the Park. With two little boys to her credit, Kitty might have expected a better relationship with Arthur. But her only serious rival, the Army, had triumphed again. Once more he was embarked on a long sea voyage, this time to the surf-washed coast of Portugal. This time, Kitty was determined to put a brave face on the absence of her husband. She wrote to her brother-in-law Richard on 19 August from Phoenix Park, after a successful landing had been made but before news of the first battle had reached her.

> My dear Lord Wellesley, I am more obliged to you than I can possibly express for your kindness in giving me authentic information from abroad. Even the hopes with which the newspapers are filled are too agitating not to give great uneasiness; but I am a Soldier's wife and the husband of whom it is the pride of my life to think, shall find he has no reason to be ashamed of me. All promises well, the Cause is a glorious one and please God, we shall see our friends return safe and successful. My boys are well and lovely. Adieu, my dear Lord, believe me, your ever obliged and sincerely affectionate C.D.S.Wellesley.[13]

Arthur's reiterated lesson had sunk home. A soldier's wife must bear frequent partings and tears had no place when duty called.

Following quickly after Richard's letter came a number of conflicting reports. First, news of Arthur's victory at Vimeiro; then the sudden arrival on the battlefield of elderly generals from England with massive seniority over Arthur, their arrival coinciding with a controversial armistice. Then came the news – Oh joy! – a recall to England. He would be coming home. Kitty had all this information from the viceroy, who told her of Arthur's victory almost in the same breath as the order for his recall. Arthur had kept closely in touch with Richmond and told him that Kitty's brother, Captain Hercules Pakenham of the 95th, had been slightly wounded on 25 August, in a skirmish before Obidos. He had sent the news first to Longford, so that he could tell the family and avoid excessive lamentations and exaggerated fears. Always careful of detail, even in the middle of a complicated military situation, Arthur told Richmond: 'I have written to Longford to desire him to apprise his mother and his family of his brother's wound; but if he should be out of the way, and you should have reason to believe that Lady Wellesley will hear about it before she will see Longford, give her the enclosed letter.'[14]

Richmond replied on 6 September:

> Many thanks for your various accounts of your progress, which all reached me on the 4th. It is not possible for anything to have been better managed than the whole of your glorious campaign.... I trust nothing will stop you coming here [to Dublin]; the business must be over and they can't want you under so many senior officers.... Lady Wellesley is quite well, and highly delighted, as you may suppose. Louisa and Charlotte [his daughters] say: As you have killed all the French, you must now come back. Yours, dear Arthur, most sincerely, Richmond.[15]

At the beginning of October, Arthur was in London, and by the end of the month, back at his desk in Dublin Castle and in the bosom of his family. His financial position was now quite good and Kitty had probably put from her mind the troublesome loan to her brother, which had not yet been repaid. Bills with Dublin traders often went unpaid for years without remark, and they could wait a little longer. Yet there was a nagging fear that Arthur would discover what she had done; an action she now very much regretted.

After the brief and unsatisfactory campaign in Portugal, Arthur continued with his careful plans for improving the administration of Irish affairs. His correspondence is full of schemes, carefully worked out and revised, e.g. for improvements to the 'Inland Navigation'; he wanted more priests to attend the Catholic College of Maynooth, believing that a better informed and educated priesthood would guide the population away from bloodshed and towards a more constructive and prosperous future. He put forward plans to improve the defences of Ireland and to modernize the port facilities. He had inaugurated a police force for Dublin to control street crime, footpads and drunkenness. He would not tolerate corruption in any part of the administration for which he was responsible. At the same time he was dealing with the routine reports of the usual outrages: 'Magistrates unwilling and afraid to act.... Acts of personal malice and revenge ... are no longer a matter for astonishment in Ireland....' These quarrels and murders usually arose from disputes over the tenancy of land and the splitting of farms between rival claimants as one generation succeeded another.

In November, he was in London attending a Court of Enquiry into his part in the unpopular Convention of Cintra and the armistice in Portugal which preceded it – drawn up by his seniors and to which they had requested he should put his signature. There was still not much time for family life, but Kitty was encouraged when he returned to Dublin just before Christmas, having managed a few days' hunting at Hatfield with the Salisburys before leaving England.

Letters rolled out of Dublin Castle, signed by Arthur Wellesley, on 23, 24 and 25 December; and so on until the end of the year, without a break. Not even half a day's shooting this year to mark the festive season. On 9 January 1809 he wrote to John Villiers: 'There is no news here. I shall go to England for the meeting of Parliament and mean to join the Army as soon afterwards as I shall be allowed to go.'

The next day he went to a Dublin jeweller and purchased 'Three plain hairbrushes, set in gold' to be delivered to Lady Wellesley. Had he forgotten to buy her a Christmas gift? Did his conscience prick him a little with the thought that soon he would leave her again, not only to go to London for a week, but to return to military service as soon as he could?

Towards the end of January, Kitty was completing arrangements for leaving the house in the Park. She had now accepted that Arthur would resume his army career and the Irish interlude was over. Maria Edgeworth mentions that a large number of people had gone to the Park: 'To Lady Wellesley, who gives a parting Ball, then follows Sir Arthur to England.' This festivity followed a large gathering at Pakenham Hall. 'We sat down 32 to dinner ... at supper, so crowded that Caroline Pakenham and I agreed to use one arm in turns ... to reach our mouths! Caroline grows upon me every time I see her; she is as quick as lightning, understands with half a word literary allusions as well as humour.... We stayed till between three and four in the morning.' On the way home, the carriage in which Maria was travelling with Henry Pakenham and her mother overturned in a ditch, but no one was hurt.[16]

There was little time left. The gallant Sir John Moore had died at Corunna and the initiative in the Peninsula had been lost. On 28 March 1809, Arthur wrote to Richmond: 'Lord Castlereagh has offered me the command of the troops in Portugal which I have, of course, accepted. This will separate me from you, at which I feel much concerned.'

How had he broken the news to Kitty? The same words would have served: 'This will separate me from you' – but how much concern? She seems to have shown considerable fortitude, giving a farewell party for Arthur's friends and fellow officials 'before following him to England'. For once, his absence from her side was easily explained. She would have made an admirable impression on the guests, expressing in charming simplicity the appropriate sentiments on behalf of her absent husband and herself; gratitude and sorrow at leaving so many honoured and trusted friends.... The call of duty ... service to King and Country.

Everything was now moving at a tremendous pace. The house in the Park had to be vacated, this time for good. Loose ends of business had to be tied up and – catastrophe – Arthur insisted all outstanding bills must be paid. Where was the money? Why had this bill and the next been neglected for so long when he had given her ample funds to cover them? Would she please explain and furnish detailed accounts....

Letters relating to this domestic crisis were destroyed years later because of their 'harshness'; but it is not difficult to imagine the icy politeness which covered Arthur's fury at the deception or, when the fury burst through, his blunt accusation that she had dishonoured his name by getting into debt and thus implying that he kept her short of money for household expenses. Above all, it was her lame excuses, her lack of frankness in telling him of her difficulties, that he could not forgive. It was the lack of moral courage he could not understand or tolerate in a woman who, all her life, had expressed the highest moral principles; strength of character and sense of duty were the characteristics for which he had married her. The day of reckoning had arrived, and Arthur's cold fury cut to the heart.

The Wellesley family were now in London. As usual in their married life, there was no time for reconciliation before public duty called him away and great events eclipsed, for him, the immediate domestic tragedy. Only Richmond seems to have spared a thought for Kitty and her children. Arthur had made one unalterable decision – they should not go back to Ireland. The Richmonds were deeply concerned. Knowing Arthur had been making inquiries for a suitable house in the country for Lady Wellesley without success, the Lord Lieutenant wrote to him on 3 April: 'I have understood you wanted a place in England for Lady Wellesley.' He mentions that he has a very comfortable small house a mile from Goodwood. 'If you think it would suit, the distance from London is under sixty miles. The situation is very pretty and retired. Chichester is four miles off, with good medical people.'

The offer was not taken up. On the day before Arthur left London for Portsmouth to join the expedition for embarkation, he wrote to Richmond. 'I am obliged for your letter of the 3rd. I rather think Lady Wellesley will go to Malvern Wells as soon as the weather is sufficiently warm.' Detached, impersonal, Arthur would attend to Kitty and his family in due course. Meanwhile, they could remain in Harley Street.

## The House in the Park

Her deception added fuel to his growing conviction of her general inadequacy as a wife. It confirmed his views on the disastrous influence of Ireland on standards of conduct and reinforced his determination, expressed in the will made the previous year, that Kitty and his boys must never live in or even visit that alien land. In their last stormy confrontation, she had tearfully promised to respect his decision in this and in anything else that might mitigate his anger and begged him to believe she would never deceive him again.

Arthur's temper could pass as quickly as it was aroused. It is likely that a truce was established before he sailed, although he may have told her frankly he could not find it in his heart to make an easy reconciliation. Once trust had been breached, things could never go on quite the same as before.

On 9 April, Arthur was still writing official letters from Portsmouth while waiting for a great storm to abate. The terrible weather delayed the expedition for nearly a week. Once more Kitty's fear of the sea was justified. Before the *Surveillante*, in which Arthur had embarked, reached the Isle of Wight, the weather worsened again and the ship's Master warned his passengers that they must get ready to abandon the vessel. When an officer woke Arthur with this message, asking him to get up and put his boots on, Arthur replied that he could swim better without them and would stay where he was, so as not to add to the confusion on deck.[17] He was probably feeling seasick and, with his usual fatalism, decided that death below was preferable to facing the cold deck and heaving seas above; the vessel survived and the voyage continued.

Kitty, waiting in London with her little boys, listened to the wind whistling round the chimneys of Harley Street and prayed for Arthur's safety. Prayed for his forgiveness, prayed for God's mercy. Kneeling by the great bed in the draughty room, she confided her sins and fears and repentance to the Almighty, her only hope now that earthly happiness with Arthur seemed dead for ever.

# CHAPTER 12

# *'Till my Husband Returns'*

For the next five years Kitty did not see Arthur. He never returned to England on leave or on duty during the whole of the campaign in the Peninsula. His letters to her were infrequent, short and formal. Occasionally he asked her to send some article he required or acknowledged her little gifts of things she had made for him, often with criticism or a request for practical improvements. Yet he carried in the lid of his dressing-case throughout the campaign a watercolour of his two little boys which she had sent him.

He had forbidden her to go to Ireland with the children. Their last quarrel over her 'misappropriation' of housekeeping money, and possibly a more serious breach of confidence, had not been healed before he left England. He wrote several letters to her on this subject which were destroyed by his grandson, because of their extreme 'unkindness'.

Kitty's family did what they could to alleviate her anxiety and unhappiness. In the first few weeks after his departure she stayed in Harley Street with the children, putting on a brave face in public when unable to avoid social gatherings. Not all was gloom. On 26 May 1809, about six weeks after Arthur's departure for Portugal, she woke to hear guns firing from the Tower of London and in Hyde Park, announcing a victory. Soon the news reached her – Arthur had taken Oporto, but details of this brilliant action and the famous crossing of the Douro were not yet available. Two days later she called on Mrs Calvert, an old friend from Ireland, who noted in her diary: 'I had a great many visitors after Church. Lady Wellesley among the rest. She told me they were in momentary expectation of very interesting news from Portugal. Poor little woman! She is very much attached to Sir Arthur and must be very anxious, but carries it off very well. She brought two nice little boys with her.'[1]

Kitty was trying to 'carry it off well'. The empty days passed in small routine duties, forgotten as soon as performed. Her kind brother Longford was a frequent visitor and tried to cheer her, though secretly worried at the unfortunate turn in her relationship with Arthur.

In Portugal, Arthur had maintained his pressure on the French occupation force and in four weeks from the initial landing had driven them out of the country. Without specific orders to pursue the enemy into Spain, and without adequate supplies, Arthur was forced to rest on the frontier while the French regrouped. At the end of June, fresh orders and additional financial resources freed his hand. He crossed into Spain and joined supporting Spanish forces under the old General Cuesta. Lack of discipline and capricious leadership made these allies of more than doubtful value in contrast to the unrelenting and effective guerrilla warfare of the peasantry against the hated French. It is perhaps interesting to note that the Spanish word *guerrilla* was first used in this context before its meaning became international.

War in the Iberian Peninsula was endless marching across mountains and arid plains, interspersed with battles and sieges of immense ferocity. The lifeline of the British forces, as they probed deeper and deeper into Spain, was supplies from home, shipped with Royal Navy protection through the friendly ports of Portugal. Three times in three winters Arthur and his generals fell back on the western seaboard where, near Lisbon and the mouth of the Tagus, he had ordered the construction of permanent defences on the Lines of Torres Vedras. From this secure base his forces recouped their losses, renewed their supplies, retrained their men, restored their wounded. With the spring, the marching resumed, the same ground recaptured, the same citadels stormed – and still Napoleon poured fresh forces into this ulcer in his empire to preserve his dynastic obsession, represented by his brother on the throne of Spain, and the self-created myth of invincibility. He himself never came to take personal command, knowing, perhaps, that this war of attrition was one he could not win, preferring to conduct more grandiose battles and expeditions where victory was certain – until his shattering retreat from Moscow in 1812.

At last, in 1813, the British attack surged to the foot of the Pyrenees. At the battle of Vitoria, Joseph Bonaparte abandoned his Spanish crown and fled with the remnants of his brother's army across the mountains into France, followed by Wellington and his veteran soldiers and the vengeful contingents of Spanish and Portuguese. The last victorious battles of the

Peninsula campaign were fought on French soil, at Orthez in February and Toulouse on 10 April 1814. The last day of March saw the Allies in Paris. On 6 April, Napoleon abdicated and three weeks later began his first exile, on the island of Elba in the Mediterranean.

On 15 July 1809, Kitty began to keep a journal: 'If I delay any longer, what I have proposed to do every day from the 8th of April, will probably never be even begun. Three months have passed of which I can give no account. I now begin to mark the time as it passes and will continue to do so till my husband returns.'

She begins with a typical entry, which recurs with minor variations on many days throughout her record: '15 July 1809. Rose at nine; breakfasted, played with the children, gave each a lesson; finished their shoes.' Making shoes was a fashionable hobby for ladies at that time. Probably Kitty had learned this new 'science' from her friend Mrs Calvert, who refers to shoe making in her diary. The entry continues:

> Sir Walter Farquar [her doctor] called on me; he approves of my taking the children to the sea. By his advice I have procured Dr. Neal's 'Letters from Spain and Portugal', which I propose sending to Sir Arthur. From twelve to three spent with Mrs. Brodrick. Longford called on me. Wrote letters till half past five. Attempted to give the children a second lesson, but Arthur [aged two and a half] was not inclined – begged the book might be put up. His request complied with. He must not fear being forced to learn. Dined alone: went to Lady Harrington's in the evenings: company – Duchess Dowager of Newcastle, Colonel Craufurd, Lady Mulgrave and some strangers. The evening very dull. Home at eleven.
>
> July 16th, Sunday. Very late this morning: Major Quin [an Irish friend] breakfasted with me. Heard Arthur a lesson. Arthur Freese his catechism.'

This was Arthur's godchild, son of his friends in Madras. Little Arthur had been returned to England for his education and health, to live with his aunt while his parents remained abroad with the younger children – but when he reached England, his aunt was dead. Hurried arrangements were made for him to be brought up in his godfather's household and Kitty gladly accepted this additional responsibility. The boy became devoted to her. The entry continues:

> Lady Templetown spent an hour with me. General Cole called this morning with Longford. [This was Galbraith Lowry Cole, who had courted her before Arthur's return from India.] Longford and I dined at Coombe Wood [the home of Lord Hawkesbury, later Lord Liverpool]. A pleasant day.
>
> July 17th, Monday. Rose very late from fatigue. Wrote to Sir Arthur. Walked with Longford to see Sir Arthur's bust at Nolleken's – it is indeed as

like as possible.... Longford and I dined early and went tête à tête to the play 'The Foundling in the Forest' and 'Killing no Murder'.

July 18th, Tuesday. Preparing to leave London. Dined alone: spent the evening at Lady Mornington's [her mother-in-law].

July 19th, Sittingbourne. Left London, slept at Sittingbourne. The children pretty well.

July 20th, Broadstairs. Arrived at Broadstairs. Got a house immediately. Dear Longford! Slept at the inn one night to allow for airing the house.

July 21st. Longford and I went to Deal. A more magnificent sight cannot be conceived than that of the Fleet now in the Downs. Above five hundred sail of transports, including fifty men-of-war. God Almighty protect our brave men, success attend them! [This assembly of ships was for an expedition to attack Walcheren, under Lord Chatham.] I wrote this day to Sir Arthur.

July 22nd. Walked to Ramsgate this morning; no troops were then embarking. Went again in the evening and saw several transports put to sea to join the Fleet in the Downs; the cheering of our men as they passed really went to my heart, God bless them! Left Longford at Ramsgate and spent the evening in reading 'Roman Comique de Scarron', which I got today from the Library. The children began to bathe today.

July 23rd, Sunday. Heard each of the children a lesson before Church. Longford and Arthur Freese with Martha [Kitty's companion], Cook and I went in the carriage to Church – wrote to my uncle [Tom Pakenham] and to Colonel Torrens [military secretary at the Horse Guards]. Walked with Longford till two o'clock. Longford dined at Ramsgate. I dined alone and went for an hour to the Library in the evening. At six, took the children in the carriage for an hour. Drank tea with A. Freese. The remainder of the evening reading.... I propose beginning a regular plan of occupation tomorrow. Longford came home before eleven: walked for half an hour on the Terrace with him.

July 24th, Monday. Began the day wretchedly. God forgive me!

Then the usual daily routine: walking, lessons for the children, a letter to Arthur. 'Drove part of the way to Canterbury' to see Longford on his journey. He had settled his sister at Broadstairs and was now returning to London. 'Worked at shoemaking; finished first volume of Scarron – cannot like it.'

Interspersed in her daily record, she copied news of Arthur's movements in the Peninsula from the *Gazette* and newspaper reports; sometimes turning back pages of her diary to enter events when they happened, not when the news reached her at a later date.

'July 25th, Tuesday. Sir Arthur at Talavera. A despatch from Sir Arthur, dated 29th July, brought over by Lord Fitzroy Somerset [on 14 August] states that the enemy ...' – and then follows details of troop movements, etc., carefully recorded. Secondhand news was better than none and to record it at the time it happened made the story more immediate and easier to follow.

> July 27th. ... Took my children to Ramsgate. They were delighted walking on the pier. They proposed to make a necklace for me of the cannon balls! Completed a pair of shoes in the evening. Read; and wrote to my mother.
>
> July 28th. Bathed today for the first time ... walked two hours: went to Barfield's Library and was detained there by rain. A gentleman, who was also detained, played some airs with variations so pleasingly that, if I find him to be a music master, I am much tempted to take lessons from him.... My little Arthur's disposition distresses me: his shyness ... gives him quite the appearance of ill-temper and tonight (when walking on the Terrace) I saw plainly that those who spoke to him thought him envious of his brother and it is not so. This disadvantage must, if possible, be overcome. I have completed a galoche this evening.

Kitty relied heavily on the various libraries in the town to pass the time. Not only could she borrow books there, but she found them centres for social activity and entertainment. Reading was the main purpose for her visits. At the end of July, she noted in her diary: 'Of all the improper books that were ever written, the one which I chose yesterday and whose name I have blotted out, is the most improper.' She carried it back to the library and tried to slip it in unnoticed, but 'Mr Muckle, [the librarian] picked it out and examining the number, had it marked down in the catalogue. I never felt such shame!'

On the same day, Longford returned to see her and she called on Irish friends staying in Broadstairs. She notes with pride: 'Sir Arthur wrote the despatch from Talavera: he also wrote to me.'

A few days later her spirits were drooping once more. 'I fear indolence is again creeping about me. I am fatigued by a regular course of insignificant occupations and dissatisfied with myself when idle. I took poor little Arthur Freese to Ramsgate, whence he was to go in the stage [coach] to school. I am glad to see that my little boys miss him. Arthur wished much to go with him to school.'

The following day she was still in low spirits. 'I was so far from well today as not to be able to get up till late: fatigue and cold oppress me. Received a letter from Sir Arthur today [1 August] of 30th June from Castello Branco.'

She mentions Arthur's letters without joy and apparently did not keep them. They were almost certainly short reports on the state of his health, on family matters and about her brothers' situation, etc. Cold comfort for Kitty, except for that touch of pride – the victor of Talavera had written a despatch all England was reading; at the same time, he had written to her!

The chilling effect of his letter was still with her twenty-four hours later. 'Ill and idle. I have nothing to say of this languid day.' She notes how much her children benefit from Longford's 'steady care', but he is leaving tomorrow and she walks with him to Ramsgate.

> August 4th, Friday. Heard today that the house which Sir Arthur wishes me to enquire about is disposed of. Longford is gone. Almighty God bless him! To me he has been a saving angel.... Tomorrow I will again begin my regular occupations. In another week Arthur will begin to learn the small letters: he knows the great ones perfectly.

It is clear from her diary that she was already involved in making inquiries about her husband's personal welfare, movements, etc., from members of the headquarters staff. She had begun a correspondence with Colonel Torrens, military secretary, which may have been on routine matters but which she also hoped would provide information to augment Arthur's dry, perfunctory letters. She was so much alone, and her mind so constantly occupied with thoughts on their relationship, that she convinced herself she was only asking for details her husband would have supplied if he had not been so burdened with military matters.

Kitty was short-sighted and this physical disability at times reflected her mental inability to foresee the effect on Arthur of what she considered to be normal and loving concern. She probably asked Torrens not to worry Arthur with knowledge of her anxieties. Arthur's reaction, on discovering this correspondence, can be imagined. He would have been furious on at least two counts: first, the implied criticism that he was neglecting to write adequate letters to his wife; second, that she had behaved again in a deceitful manner to his discredit. Her motives had nothing to do with the issue, as far as he was concerned.

'August 5th. Broadstairs. Saturday. Much as yesterday, languid and dawdling ... heard today from Caroline, Lady Liverpool and from Colonel Torrens that Arthur was at Plauntia on the 15th.'

On Sunday, Kitty was too late to attend church. 'God forgive my neglect of my own duty! Wrote to Caroline, to the Duchess of Richmond, to Mr Pole [Arthur's brother], to Colonel Torrens, to Sir Arthur.... Took my children walking on the pier at Ramsgate.... Sir Arthur passed Castello Branco on his march to Plauntia.... My dear children continue good. Please God they will be all their father could wish them to be.'

To pass the time, Kitty was considering taking up the harp or pianoforte again and tried to buy an instrument in Margate. 'Not being able to procure either ... agreed to take a barrel-organ for the boys. The evening was so fine that I went walking alone on the Terrace, but it was too late, the company was bad: I therefore returned and spent the evening in writing. Firing heard the whole of this day from the French coast.... Henry Wellesley, who is arrived at Ramsgate, called on me. He looks ill and low. His children are not yet come.... I am tired. This unvaried life fatigues but must be endured. I bought the organ: my boys will be pleased by it.'

Henry's arrival was to introduce a new responsibility into Kitty's life. After his wife Charlotte's elopement in March 1809 with Henry, Lord Paget (later first marquis of Anglesey, the distinguished cavalry commander), he had led a miserable existence with his three sons and a daughter, all under five years old. The youngest child, Gerald Valerian, was born in 1809 and Henry Wellesley believed the child was not his. Since serving in India he had suffered periodic attacks of fever and at times was seriously ill. The children arrived on Friday 11 August and Kitty went to see them.

She had bathed in the morning with her children and had noticed how beautiful they looked when coming out of the water. Henry's boys seemed tired after their journey from London but her little Arthur was delighted with his cousins. On Saturday she took them all for a walk on the pier at Ramsgate. 'Poor children, they are a strong instance of the evil of not having a mother's care. The girl [Charlotte] is for the present ruined; but children, with judicious management, in a very short time recover from the effects of that kind of spoiling: her maid appears to me much too severe. The older boys are lovely children, the youngest a miserable little being. God Almighty will protect the forsaken.... Merciful God will, I trust, assist and strengthen me. The past cannot be recalled: it was bitter, so bitter as, I fear, to injure me for the remainder of my life: but while there is life there is hope and God is very merciful.'

The next day, Sunday, she heard that her brother Edward had arrived safely in England and she hoped to see him in a day or two. 'How ungrateful I am conscious of being. It has pleased God to deny me one blessing: on that one I had fixed all my hopes of happiness and every other blessing, which Heaven has so liberally bestowed, fails to make me even easy. Perhaps in time God will pity the agony I suffer: perhaps it is inflicted as a punishment for my ingratitude. Oh Merciful Father, forgive and pity a very weak and suffering being. My fault is great, but my punishment is most severe. God Almighty, look on me with mercy! I will not again give way to these unavailing regrets.'

She had bathed as usual in the morning and wrote a number of letters after church. The evening was wet, too wet to go out. She notes in her diary: 'From the time my children go to bed, I find my mind torn with the most hateful recollections, but I will not so soon break the resolution I have thought it prudent to form: I will therefore write no more tonight.' She passed the next day 'in the most depressing reflections' but, to her joy, in the evening a messenger arrived with news of Arthur's victory at Talavera and that he was well. Overhearing the servants planning to celebrate this event at a public house, she thought it better for them to keep their rejoicing at home. 'I therefore gave them some spirits and liberty to make themselves as happy as they could without being quite drunk. I had the satisfaction of hearing them pass the evening in the most good humoured merriment, without riot and retire at a reasonable hour. I was myself incapable of anything. Walked up and down the room till, quite exhausted, I went to bed.'

On 15 August 1809, she received further particulars of the battle which had taken place more than five weeks before. 'Surely the hand of God almost visibly protects the life of my husband. Blessed God, continue to protect him. His fatigue, his anxiety must be extreme: but he is well. He has fulfilled his duty and he is happy.... I had the comfort of receiving a few lines from Sir Arthur himself, written on the 29th – this was indeed a satisfaction; it was everything to me. My brother [Hercules], who joined him after the action, writes me word that he is and looks well and happy, thank God, thank God.'

Edward had now joined her at Broadstairs. 'This has been a friendly day. Thank God for it.' Sunday, 20 August brought her an 'express' from Mrs Wellesley-Pole, William's wife, containing an account of the King's 'intentions' towards Arthur. 'Nothing can be more gratifying than the honours and the manner of conferring them, accompanied with expressions of approbation which Sir Arthur so well deserved.' The King was to create Sir Arthur Wellesley a viscount and this was confirmed in September 1809.

After a brief rest at Broadstairs, Edward was obliged to return to London almost at once. Kitty had a flood of correspondence to deal with but managed to find time to help poor Henry Wellesley. 'Henry is much to be pitied; he called here today and his dejection went to my heart. Every attention that I can show him he shall meet with from me.'

A few days later she had the little Wellesleys to dine with her children. 'They are strong instances of the evils which the loss of a mother inflicts upon children; they are well-disposed and clever but ill-managed. I pity them, I pity their poor father. Let no degree of suffering, Oh my God, tempt me to forsake my children.... I heard today from Edward that he has met Longford and was appointed to take out the despatches to Sir Arthur.'

By the end of August, the news from Spain was not so good and Kitty was full of anxiety. 'He has, I believe, retreated some miles. The remainder of the report it pains me to think of; although no degree of blame can attach to him, I know he will be abused, even at the moment he is most deserving of praise. I saw Henry Wellesley today: his dejection I think increased. God help him.' A visit from a friend 'saved me from an evening of uninterrupted misery'. Lady Nelson (Horatio's sister-in-law) and her daughter had visited Kitty in the morning. 'From them I heard that there were gloomy reports. God Almight protect our dear friends! I received today a very kind letter from Lord Castlereagh concerning Edward.'

A few days later a friend called to 'congratulate me on Sir Arthur's peerage. I regret his former style and title – that of Wellington I do not like, for it recalls nothing. However, it is done and I suppose it could not be avoided.'

Kitty's comment on her new name had some justification. Arthur's victory at Talavera in July 1809, some seventy miles west of Madrid, gave a tremendous boost to morale not only in Britain but in Europe, whose subjugated countries had begun to despair of release from French domination. Arthur realized this success was transitory – 'Don't halloo until you are out of the wood', he warned his admirers. Nevertheless, a grateful Sovereign, prompted by Castlereagh, decided to create him a viscount. His brother William, precipitated into a decision to provide a name for the new peer, selected the hamlet of Welleslie in Somerset, from which the family was said to originate, and the nearby village of Wellington. From these names, which the College of Heralds said were available, he composed the title 'Viscount Wellington of Talavera and of Wellington and Baron Douro of Welleslie in the County of Somerset' and in a long letter to his brother, concluded: 'I long much to hear that I ought not to be hanged for my arrangement respecting your title. God bless you.'

Subsequently, the Douro titles were transferred to Arthur's heir, an arrangement which gave Kitty great satisfaction. Writing to Lady Hood in 1813, she told her: 'My little boy's title is Baron Douro. They wanted to change his title and raise his rank, but I roared and screamed. The passage of the Douro, the most brilliant and least bloody of all his father's achievements, shall not be forgotten, and he shall keep the name.'

Wellington's connection with Somerset was given increased validity in 1812 when, at Lord Liverpool's suggestion, he purchased 'the Borough or Manor of Wellington, from which you take your title', together with some 400 acres of farmland (but no house); the land was let and it is doubtful if Wellington visited his manor more than once or twice in his lifetime.

The diary continues:

> My dear Longford came today [29 August]; he tells me that Edward sailed on Friday. Heaven protect and prosper him. Longford and I called on Henry Wellesley in the evening ... but he had unexpectedly gone to town. We walked back and went for a few minutes to Barfield's Library; we found the company raffling and apparently very gay. Longford, who has been travelling night and day for ten days, was very tired and we retired early.
>
> August 31st, Tuesday. A happy morning; I received a letter from Sir Arthur of the 8th; although they had been obliged to retire, they were safe and well, thank God. I have now received several letters directed to me 'Lady Wellington', so I must assume the name. This day has been too hot and too uncertain to venture to walk far. Longford has left me.... I bathe now regularly every second day and teach my children every day: they will learn without difficulty. I have made several acquaintances – Lord and Lady Nelson and their daughter, Lady Charlotte Nelson; Miss Blakeney, Mr. and Mrs. Forsyth, who I must call on tomorrow. I must also go to Ramsgate and call on Miss Dashwood, Miss Burton and Mrs. Rawdon.

In spite of her efforts to fill her days with useful activities – shoe making and music, as well as lessons for the children, etc. – she found the lonely evenings particularly trying. 'Strung the harp, which I am determined no longer to neglect.... Spent the evening alone and wretchedly! I must try to regain the favour of the Almighty!...' Her thoughts were nearly always of Arthur.

> Surely Heaven will protect the good, brave man! I need not trouble, but with all my soul I wish he was at home. His despatch in the Gazette today is most agitating: it is evident that, far from having everything to hope, he had everything to fear from the Spaniards, more I think than from the enemy. He wrote to me on the day on which he wrote that despatch: that he should have leisure of mind or body for any other object than that on which he is engaged, is really wonderful. How quiet, how uniform is my life at the moment when fatigue and anxiety is preying upon him. Heaven in mercy restore him to his home, his country and his children.

The daily routine continued. 'Bathed this morning and received permission to put up a netting at the bathing place – my children may then run and play without danger.' She finds her life most uninteresting but 'I trust in God it is innocent. Oh that I had strength to curb my unavailing recollections. I will pray to God, for God alone can assist me'.

Arthur would have been a little alarmed if he had known of Kitty's ambition to make Broadstairs safe for her children. 'I have given directions for railing-in the dangerous bridge and tomorrow I shall receive an estimate of the expense of railing the whole Terrace.' On 6 September she notes: 'Part of the railing is completed.... Dined with Henry Wellesley. He is miserable.... My darling children, may no degree of suffering tempt me to forget my duty to you. I little imagined the extent of my crime when I so earnestly wished to die.'

Her diary, although in the main recording humdrum events, frequently reveals the strength of her love for Arthur, epitomized in her literal acceptance of the marriage vows – love, honour and obey, for better, for worse. To maintain these vows in spite of rejection by her husband demanded great strength of character. Kitty, beneath the too easy display of emotion and perhaps too conscious piety, possessed massive reserves of fortitude and a sense of duty to Arthur and the children greatly to her credit.

There is no doubt she had been tempted to leave him; the example of Henry's predicament brought to the surface painful recollections of that moral struggle. She might have decided to return to her family in Ireland during his long absence and this would have caused little comment. The scandals of the day were full-blooded, rumbustious affairs involving royalty, nobility and lesser dignitaries. Adultery, incest, bigamy, blackmail, chicanery of all kinds, duels and murders were the diet of the public with no censorship and few inhibitions about libel. The return of a virtuous wife to her family would have been small beer for the gossips, at least until his return, when custody of the children would have raised serious problems. Her reward for maintaining the marriage was her two boys. She had little hope of a change of heart in her husband, although she could not stifle her yearning for him or disguise her pride in his achievements.

In spite of her depression and anxiety, she tried to keep her accounts in order. 'I find I have been much imposed on but must reform, for I am ruining: it will be a hard task, for Martha [her companion] has no inclination to assist me, not from ill-will but from an idea that it is mean to pay any degree of attention to household business.'

Housekeeping accounts were to become an albatross about her neck for the rest of her life. She was kindhearted and therefore easily deceived by servants and others. Those employed by the gentry found nothing wrong in purloining their master's property, within reason. Gentlemen were not supposed to count the small change and Martha's attitude – 'it is mean to pay any degree of attention to household business' – was typical of the snobbery among servants.

For Arthur, whose life had been spent in maintaining military discipline and enforcing law and order for the survival of those under his command, theft was a serious offence. Since childhood, money or the lack of it had been a problem. Debts and scandals in the family, followed by his own experience of debt as a young officer in Dublin, had never been forgotten. Lack of money caused his initial rejection by the Pakenham family and this humiliation had rankled throughout his service in India.

As a commanding officer, every move he made was dependent on funds from England – and funds were always short of what was necessary for complete success. For this reason, he required to know that every penny was spent to good purpose. Cheating and pilfering from public funds was equivalent to murdering his soldiers – every penny lost meant less ammunition and supplies. Arthur became obsessed with the need to conserve resources, both in public and in private life. Those who defrauded funds under his control attacked his integrity and efficiency.

Kitty was now confronted with an example of the waste of men and resources Arthur most detested. Her pleasant walks on the pier at Ramsgate were discontinued 'on account of the numbers of sick, dying and dead which are disembarking there every day. The sight of the Fleet is as dreadful as it was magnificent some weeks ago'. The expedition to Walcheren she had watched assembling in the Downs in July had ended in disaster. Lord Chatham had returned with thousands of sick and dying soldiers, victims of Walcheren fever, a form of dysentery, the result of inadequate preparation and supplies.

Most of her evenings were spent at the library. 'It is not pleasant, but I am conscious I am not to be trusted quite alone.' She was still enjoying some social life. Mrs Calvert brought her daughter to visit friends at Ramsgate. She notes in her diary: 'Lady Wellington dined here. In the evening came the Duchess of Manchester, Lady Saltoun, her son and two daughters and several other people. There was a fiddle and twelve couples danced till past twelve o'clock. Isobella was very happy.' Kitty's record of this event simply states: 'I dined at Ramsgate today with Mrs Calvert and in the evening went to the Library.' She did not make one of the number who danced until midnight.

On 25 October celebrations were arranged to commemorate the fiftieth year of the King's reign. Kitty gave money and helped to arrange a dinner of meat and beer for the poor. After a thanksgiving service at church, 'we assembled on the Green and saw the people at dinner; they really seemed to enjoy it. My children were not the least startled by the report of the guns, though quite close to them. In the evening, had supper at the Library, where we ended the day most loyally by singing and drinking punch.' The next day she heard the subscription had been sufficient not only to give five hundred people a good dinner but also to buy a provision of blankets for the winter.

It was now time to make arrangements to return to London. On 28 October, Kitty wrote: 'After my children's lessons, worked the whole morning to finish the frock which I have begun, before I leave this place.' The frock was for little Arthur, not yet breeched. 'I have paid my bills and shall be ready to go on Tuesday. The evening as usual, at work at the Library.'

> October 29th, Sunday. Went to Church. Wrote the remainder of the morning. In the afternoon went to Ramsgate to pay farewell visits. Passed the evening in writing. The success of the Jubilee is really delightful and must be most highly gratifying to the good old King. 'Tis the voluntary act of the people from affection.
>
> October 30th, Monday. Finished this morning all the jobs and made all the preparations necessary for the journey tomorrow.

They went back to London via Sittingbourne, where they slept the night, and on 1 November 'arrived in London, found my house as comfortable as poor Martha could made it, clean in every part. The children delighted to find all their old playthings'.

The winter in London started badly. The children were ill and Kitty far from well.

> It is decided that my poor children have got the whooping-cough. May God spare them to me and may they escape the dreadful consequences which I have known from this dreadful complaint. So uninteresting, so unvaried, is my life that to keep a daily journal is almost impossible and yet by not doing so I lose the pleasure of knowing how *he* and I were employed at the same time, which to me is a great pleasure.
>
> For this last fortnight I have been occupied by attending to my poor little children, who are in the whooping-cough, and in knitting a blanket which, when finished, I propose sending to Lord Wellington – may it contribute to his comfort and save him from cold.... My time, I am conscious, is terribly dawdled away.

By the end of the month the children were better. Kitty learned that Marquis Wellesley had been appointed Foreign Secretary and had returned to England from Spain, where he had been ambassador. She noted in her diary: 'Lord Wellesley has been in town some days. It is rather mortifying to me that not one of his suite, all friends of Lord Wellington's, should have sent me even a line to tell me how he was. Spent this evening with Lady Mornington [30 November] and met there that insufferable puppy, young Pole.' This was William, son of Arthur's brother

William Wellesley-Pole. The 'insufferable puppy' was to give the family a good deal of trouble in later years.

In desperation for news of Arthur, Kitty wrote to Richard on 1 December. With some annoyance she comments, 'Perhaps he may be civil enough to send me an answer.... Edward Pakenham has escaped the West Indies and is returning to Ireland: he dined and spent the evening with me today. My children are mending every day.... the covering of the blanket is nearly finished.... not a word from Lord Wellesley.' but on 9 December she received a 'penitential letter from Lord Wellesley' and he promised to visit her 'tomorrow'. After his visit, Kitty noted in her diary: 'Nobody has the power of pleasing more than he has.'

A few days later she records dining with 'Mr. and Mrs. Drummond and met Lord and Lady Liverpool and Mr. Arbuthnot: pleasant, but fatiguing for me. I have been too long secluded from company not to feel fatigued by meeting even a few'. The next day Lady Liverpool dined with her. 'She approves my blanket.' In the morning she went out in her carriage to purchase the *Life of Cobbett* for Arthur and on Friday sent the parcel with her blanket to 'Lord Wellington' by a messenger of Lord Liverpool's.

Arthur Freese had now returned to spend the holidays at Harley Street with Kitty and the family. 'That boy gives me much thought: there are faults in his character which, if not arrested early, will involve him in contempt and ruin. I will pray to God Almighty to instruct me in what manner I can fulfill the duty I have undertaken with respect to that boy.'

Arthur Freese had been well taught at school and 'is much advanced in learning ... began today as I mean to do every day during Arthur Freese's holidays. By reading with him the Psalms for that day.' Her fears regarding his character were reinforced the following day when she received a note from his school 'which gives me great uneasiness. It proves that Arthur Freese is by no means cured of that odious vice of lying. My earnest wish is to lead that boy right – may heaven assist me'. After some consideration, Kitty decided to send him back to school for due retribution.

Christmas Day was spent alone and the following day she sent 'the remainder of Lord Wellington's commission to Spain'. On the twenty-seventh she dined with Lady Liverpool and 'began a shoe'. On the thirtieth she notes: 'alone and sad'. New Year's eve, Sunday: 'Took the maids to Church. Heard two lectures of Porteus. Sir Walter [Farquar, her doctor] cheered me with a visit. Dined with Lady Gosford and so ends a melancholy year! Heaven spare me from such another!'

CHAPTER 13

# *The Public Gaze*

Kitty's New Year resolution was to avoid pessimism; her first diary entry for 1810 was determinedly cheerful: 'Wishing every happiness to my husband, comfort to those who need it and a continuation of happiness to the happy.' She went to see Arthur's mother and received a visit from her brother William. 'I look on it as a good omen that a Pakenham should have come to me on the first day of the New Year.'

Lord Liverpool, in a letter on official business to Arthur, included news of his family. Writing in April, he told him: 'I had the pleasure this day of seeing Lady Wellington and your little boys.... They are all well. Arthur is grown quite stout. They have no remains whatsoever of the whooping-cough and appear to have received great benefit from Lady Wellington's excursion to the country.'[1]

Kitty did not record this country visit and her diary is blank until 25 June, when she writes:

> Near six months have passed in which it would hardly have been possible for me to have marked the events of a single day without some degree of pain. Yet the time has not been totally lost. I have, in some degree, mixed with the world, made some acquaintances and tried to perform some duties – but so many of my resolutions, and those my best, have been broken. Though so little has been done as it should be, that I think with shame of the lost time. Arthur Freese is now come home and I feel that, to perform my duty to that child, I must live a very different life. Indolence must be conquered, hours must not be wasted, attention must be paid or the child is lost and I break a most solemn engagement. Today has been tolerable. From this day I shall keep an exact account of my time and deceive myself no more.

On 1 July her new plan seemed to be working.

> Last week has passed more to my satisfaction than any in the last six months. I have not omitted what I hope was right; I have attended to my duties and will continue earnestly to entreat the assistance of the Almighty in judging well with respect to the children under my care. I have given a Master to my little boys and have begun to teach Arthur Freese French. My present object is not to leave town for a month, that the boys may have all the advantage they can derive from their Master. Arthur Freese will then return to school and I will endeavour to continue with my children what they will have begun. God is merciful and good and will strengthen my weak and rectify my erring judgement. I have been engaged in making enquiry for a house: none that has yet offered will answer. This is Sunday; I have heard A. F his catechism, have been at Church, have seen Robert Taylour [Lord Bective's son]. Have written so far and will now read till tis time to take out my children.

On 11 August, Arthur Freese returned to school. 'I have, I hope, done all in my power to make him good and happy. Heaven will assist me, as it is my decided and sincere wish to do my duty by that little boy as by my own. Everything has been arranged for leaving town; my children, maids and myself got into the carriage at two o'clock and reached Tunbridge at half past eight; a slow and wet journey.'

Her next two months at Tunbridge Wells seem to have been more sociable than life at Broadstairs. Her diary is full of names and appointments; of pleasant excursions to Penshurst Place, etc., carriage drives, walks on the Pantiles, frequently in the company of Miss Mary Chester, a niece of Lord Bagot, who was to become in 1822 the second wife of Lord Liverpool. Kitty kept up her correspondence with her family. In a letter from the Peninsula to his mother, written in July 1810, Edward told her: 'I hear constantly from Kitty, who seems in reasonable spirits and indeed so far as relating to her husband's public duties, she ought to be most proud – for not many under such circumstances ever did such justice to the charge reposed in him.' Lord Wellington 'looks as well as possible and I never saw him in such high spirits'.[2] At this time Arthur was planning his masterly retreat to the Lines of Torres Vedras in Portugal and enjoying the prospect of Massena's fury at the move.

Although Kitty received a number of invitations, and frequent visits from friends to her home (she had rented Sydenham House, conveniently situated near the Pantiles), she did not wish 'to go into company' nor did she intend to 'dine at other places'. She preferred to call on her friends informally.

'August 16th. Dined at home. Walked a little in the evening and drank tea at Mr. Greville's. A most pleasant evening.' The next day the weather was very hot – too hot 'to go out till late in the day. Rose at nine – taught my children ... began with Cook the explanation of the Sacrament: wrote my letters. Strung the harp. After this I dressed. Carried my letters to the post. Called on Lady Robert Seymour. Spent the remainder of the morning at the Library reading the newspapers. Dined at five. Walked till nine with Miss Chester. Read the Grecian History for an hour and a half. Wrote ...'.

On Saturday, she 'gave an hour to the harp and another to reading French'. On Sunday, she met met young Pole (her nephew by marriage) in the churchyard. 'If his object is what I take it to be, I will give no assistance. It is much too serious.' Did he want to borrow money? 'Colonel Shawe joined us on the Pantiles. Pole dined with me: he must continue to be satisfied with the very plainest fare.... Walked in the evening to Mr. Legge's with William Pole: drank tea there which was much more agreeable to me than a tête à tête at home would have been. We were joined by Colonel Shawe on our return home: both stayed with me till ten o'clock.'

She was a great believer in fresh air and exercise, although walking with her children she found 'very fatiguing. They stop and turn and look at everything.... Mr. Legge is very kind to me.' She called on a sick woman and gave her 'wine and money ... my dear little boy gave her bread'.

'Young Pole', as she called him, was paying her a lot of attention, but she understood him better than he thought. 'Dined alone. Young Pole came in the evening. We walked an hour, then he left me on the pretence of settling his bills – Oh why pretend at all? – In fact, to go to the play. Drank tea with Mrs Legge: read half an hour when I returned home.'

> August 30th. I finished that which I wish to read with Cook and I trust that God will bless us both in this endeavour to obey the command of our Saviour. At twelve, Mr. Legge and Miss Chester called on me and we went to Stonelands, a most beautiful though not a large place. The Duchess of Dorset was not at home.... The weather almost intolerably hot. Went to the Pantiles in quest of a rake for the boys. Young Pole was to have dined with me – sent an excuse at five o'clock – I was much rejoiced, as his conversation is extremely foolish, boasting and fatiguing. Walked in the evening with Miss Chester and drank tea with Mrs. Legge.

On 4 September, Kitty packed her belongings and moved from Sydenham House to Bowling Green House – the servants complained of the move, but she took no notice. The next day she took the children to Harrison's Rocks, 'which are uncommonly beautiful and the day was delightful.... Dined at home and played with my boys till their bedtime'.

She visited Buckhurst Park with a group of friends – Lord Whitworth, the Duchess of Dorset, her son and two daughters, Count Munster (Hanoverian Minister to England), Miss Whitworth, etc. 'A cheerful, quiet day. On my return home, I found my children asleep.' She went to 'Bayham Abbey, a most beautiful ruin', with Mr Legge and Miss Chester. She took part in raising funds for charity. 'Spent most of the morning in walking and distributing tickets for the play. Dined at Mrs. Legge's. Went to the play in the evening and had the satisfaction of seeing a very full house.'

Her children gave her endless pleasure. 'Walked with my children, who improve as much in mind as in looks. They are not greedy, which at their age is a great merit.' Arthur was now three years and seven months, Charles two years and six months.

She renewed her interest in playing the harp. 'Finding myself dropping asleep [in the evening] went to the harp, which had hardly power to rouse me.' On another day she was 'prevented from reading with Martha by the noise the harp-tuner made'.

Her outspokenness still got her into social difficulties. 'Dined with Mrs. Legge. The evening as usual but that I expressed, I fear too strongly, my disapprobation of Espriella's "Letters from a Spaniard" – to a friend of the author's: they are bad.'

Her mother arrived from Ireland on 15 September with Kitty's brother Henry. 'Thank God, in perfect health and spirits. My mother, Henry and I walked to the Pantiles before dinner. Dined at five. The evening walking and talking of absent friends.'

The next day she 'drank the waters' for the first time. She was still reading the *Spanish Letters* and found 'much amusement in the book but it is not one to be approved of. We have just received intelligence of the intended visit of HRH [the Prince Regent]. I think it better to be out of the way than to fly after arrival.'

She did not enjoy public functions and came more and more to avoid them. It does not need much imagination to see how difficult was her position in society, married to a man of national fame, who never came home on leave and who seldom wrote to her. On public occasions she would be singled out for special attention as the wife of the hero, questioned on the latest news from the Peninsula – and what answer could she give? Her news was nearly all secondhand or derived from reading the *Gazette* and the newspapers. Her embarrassment would have been acute. She was not naturally shy and enjoyed the company of friends, but her marital problems forced her to shun society and unnecessary exposure to the malicious gossip of the day. A wise decision, although she was often censured for her 'retiring nature' as being unsuited to the wife of a famous man.

To avoid the celebrations and entertainments provided for the Prince Regent's visit to Tunbridge Wells, she and her mother decided to spend a few days at Brighton. 'I do not half like leaving my children but it is only for a few days. Left Tunbridge about twelve o'clock, reached Brighton about six. Walked a little before dinner to see the Steyne, etc.... I never saw a less inviting place of residence than Brighton. Lady William Bentinck and young Greville called on us in the evening.'

The next day they walked and drove about the town and went to hear the Prince of Wales's Band play at the Pavilion. 'Saw the Pavilion with some difficulty and a more tawdry habitation never was built or furnished. His Royal Highness's taste in houses at least, is not manly.... The evening was pleasant.'

On 21 September they returned to Tunbridge Wells, having bought two monkeys as presents for the boys. 'Received by my children with a degree of noisy delight that quite enchanted me.' The day following began with a quarrel. 'Charles spit on Arthur's monkey and Arthur beat him for it: two minutes and two kisses set all right.'

She began reading Scott's newly published *Lady of the Lake* to her mother in the evening. At the end of the month she started riding exercise and rode every day, weather permitting. She also set in hand 'the most disagreeable of all operations – sitting for my picture. Sat nearly two hours: it is quite impossible the picture can be the least like'. The artist she had chosen was Josiah Slater, reputed to have been a pupil of Sir Thomas Lawrence; a watercolourist, whose pencil and wash drawings were popular with Kitty's friends in Tunbridge Wells.

Dr Mayo called to see her on 5 October and gave her advice 'which I believe will be absolutely necessary for me to follow.' The nature of her health problem is not mentioned. The doctor, who was physician to the Prince of Wales, 'cupped' her mother on the same visit. She had fallen heavily on the Pantiles a few days previously and bruised her face. 'I never saw so horrid-looking an operation, but I do not believe it is attended with pain. My children sat for their pictures: theirs, at least, will be extremely like.' Over the next few weeks she continued to give Slater a number of sittings for the portraits.

Once more it was time to return to London for the winter months. On 12 October she payed all her bills 'previous to my departure'. She called on her friends to say goodbye and observed that her children were 'well and lovely. I regret taking them to town'.

The next day they left Tunbridge. 'After a sick journey we arrived in town, where I found a letter which has most deeply wounded me. No matter – I was originally to blame, but I think I could have felt more forgiveness, more indulgence: it is now, however, at an end for ever. Dined with my mother; began to read *Gil Blas* in the evening.'

It is obvious that although Arthur's letter was deeply wounding, it was not unexpected. Philosophically, she bravely accepted this retribution for her faults in the past. 'No matter – I was originally to blame.'

She mildly criticizes his total lack of forgiveness and 'indulgence' – but realizes there is nothing more to be said. She had written to Arthur seeking reconciliation or at least a relaxation of his total rejection of her affection. This was his answer, uncompromising and decisive. There was no question of the marriage being repudiated, only that their personal relationship was 'at an end for ever'. Perhaps Kitty read more into Arthur's reply than he intended, but her intuition told her that, for the present, she was in limbo – her pleadings could not reach him.

Her resilience was demonstrated the next day. 'October 14th, Sunday. A very wretched night certainly gave no presentiment of the happiness this day was to bring. My husband and brothers are safe and victorious, thank Almighty God.' She had just heard of the battle of Bussaco, fought on 27 September, where Wellington had repulsed Massena with severe losses on the French side and far fewer casualties among the Allied troops.

As soon as she heard the news, she sent an express letter to Arthur's mother, living in retirement in a 'grace and favour' apartment at Hampton Court. Lady Mornington commented to Richard that Lady Wellesley had told her of 'the late splendid victory and conduct of our dear hero. We have indeed reason to be proud of him'.

Kitty continues the entry in her diary: 'I cannot describe the agitation of this day.... From the absence of all the Ministers, no more intelligence could be gathered than that contained in my letter. At last, at night came Captain Burgh [Arthur's ADC], who gave us all the particulars. All was glorious and, thank God, our loss but trifling. We cannot be sufficiently grateful.'

She was besieged with callers during the next few days and wrote letters to all those in her circle who might not have heard of Arthur's victory. Lord Liverpool called on her and, after the usual congratulations, offered her the use of his house at Coombe Wood, away from the unhealthy atmosphere of London – an offer he had made to Arthur the previous year. Kitty declined – 'but am most sincerely obliged'.

When the excitement had died down, she continued with her usual routine: teaching the children, ordering shirts for 'Lord W.', looking for a house to rent, as Harley Street was now too small and the area too congested for the health of her children. She made more clothes for the boys and cut out leather shapes for more shoes. Among her visitors were

Dr Mayo and Surgeon Hume, to look at a spot on little Arthur's lip. Colonel Torrens, the Military Secretary, called. Her mother was staying with her in Harley Street and her brother Henry was a frequent dinner guest. These days she was seldom alone and time passed quickly and pleasantly enough. She inspected a house in Putney: 'In my life I never saw such an old rattery.' In the evenings, she read *Gil Blas* aloud to her mother and continued to work through the *Memoirs de Sully* to improve her French. Among her acquaintances on whom she called was Lady Cremorne, an American known as 'Philadelphia Hannah', daughter of Thomas Freame of Philadelphia and a granddaughter of the famous William Penn of Pennsylvania.

On 26 October, Lord Liverpool called and spent half an hour with her. She then wrote 'a most painful letter'. Was this a result of something Lord Liverpool had told her or simply an overdue reply to Arthur's 'wounding' letter of two weeks before?

Her callers were not all friends and relations – a few days after Liverpool's visit, she was told that

> a poor woman, a soldier's wife just returned from Portugal, was below with her infant. Her story, the gratitude and regard she expressed for my husband, went to my heart. I gave her money, linen and flannel and I hope she may get safely home.... My dear children, too, divided their toys with the baby. Before this woman was gone, Surgeon Hume came to see little Arthur and Alice [a kitchen maid who had hurt her hand]. Both going on well. He saw this poor woman too, and advised her to remain in town to rest, but she was determined to pursue her journey....
>
> The next person who came was Hughes, the house broker, who ... gave information of a house in St. James's Square, which I think would answer....
> I should certainly think it would suit us if the price is not beyond our means.

Kitty acquired a large tin box for her papers: 'the bills and other papers having so much accumulated in four years....' On 2 November she notes: 'The unfortunate Princess Amelia died. The good old King is far, very far from well.... What will become of this Kingdom? No news yet from Portugal. This prolonged anxiety is very, very wearing.... Taught my children, written to Longford and Henry [who had returned to Pakenham Hall], marked a dozen shirts for Lord Wellington and worked at my boys' trousers.... Finished *Revolutions in Portugal* – it astonished me to find how alike the events of a hundred and fifty years ago are to those of the present day in Portugal.'

The King was now so ill that a number of people, including Kitty, 'went to the Palace to enquire for the King each day'. Among her other activities, she had taken considerable trouble to have a locket made for Mrs Freese, mother of her ward Arthur, to contain some of the boy's red hair. An aunt of his was sailing for India and would take the locket with her, together with a letter from young Arthur to his mother.

Kitty was meeting more and more people in London society, although still avoiding public functions. Lord and Lady Liverpool gave her frequent invitations to dinner at Fife House, their London home, which she usually accepted. She kept in touch with the 'two little Lennoxs' – the little girls who were Arthur's favourites among the Duke of Richmond's large family. In spite of everything, she was still subject to fits of depression. 'The desperate dejection which has oppressed me thus for some days past, will destroy me. I must pray for a calmer mind, for power to calm myself. I was not well enough to go to the Palace today. My mother went and brought back a better account of the King, thank God.' Kitty, although suffering from a bad cold, had hoped while her mother was out that 'some person should call on me and see them alone, which certainly would have been pleasant. There is a degree of restraint in the protectoral presence of a third person which, from the habit of being constantly alone, I feel oppressive. I was, however, disappointed. Nobody came.... Dined with my mother. During dinner, a message arrived from the Admiralty, saying no battle had taken place during the last month.' Kitty, in her emotional state, misread the message and was sure there had been a battle and was 'much agitated' by the news. 'Never, never, shall I forget the feeling expressed for me by my children. My little Arthur held me in his arms... Charles, who was further away, in the most melancholy voice cried out "I am too far from you, Mamma". Heaven bless my children and God Almighty give me a grateful heart that I may feel and acknowledge the blessings which I possess. The dreadful oppression of this evening prevented me from attempting to read.'

She suffered from sleeplessness, which made her late in getting up. 'The best part of the day is over before I have begun the business of it.' In Arthur's phrase, which she often uses in her diary, 'This will never do.' In spite of this disability, she made valiant efforts to keep up with her housekeeping accounts, to write to her friends in Portugal in time to catch the mail and to entertain her mother-in-law. She had considerable affection for the tough and disingenuous old Lady Mornington and made her welcome at Harley Street. 'Company seems in a great measure to remove the dreadful oppression under which I labour in the evening. This has surely been a happy day. I have heard from abroad, have spent an hour with Lady Liverpool and know that the King is better.'

She continued to sit for her 'odious picture', which she insisted on having altered. She settled with Slater 'that he should again draw my children'. Among her correspondents was her old friend the widowed Lady Olivia Sparrow, now living in Huntingdonshire but a frequent visitor to London. Unfortunately, her efforts to keep herself occupied could not always overcome fits of depression: 'I will not think of the feelings of this wretched evening. Heaven forgive me.'

Her domestic problems included a dishonest coachman – his exorbitant bills for fodder at last aroused her suspicion and she checked them with Dr Hume and her relative, General Taylour. 'There could not be a more shameless imposition than the bills that were brought to me for the provisions for the horses.' The man was dismissed. The same day, she heard that her sister-in-law Charlotte Wellesley, Henry's divorced wife, had married Lord Paget. 'What a complication of infamy and vice', she commented.

Later in the day she went with friends to see 'Nollekens, the Statuary; the sight of the figures suggested to me the idea of borrowing from him some of them and drawing from them. If I succeed, I shall have a delightful resource and occupation'. A few days later, Nollekens sent her a small bust of Arthur, as a present.

By mid-December she notes: 'My sweet little Arthur has changed his dress today and is delighted.' He was now nearly four and ready to wear boys' clothes for the first time, instead of petticoats. Just after Christmas she was 'extremely provoked to find the cook had cut my boys' fine eyelashes'.

She saw the Liverpools nearly every day. Lady Liverpool was in poor health and enjoyed Kitty's company. There were a number of pleasant evenings at Fife House with small groups of friends or tête-à-tête with the Liverpools, who valued her friendship and admired her character. He was Secretary of State for the Colonies and War Department, a powerful political figure, soon to be Prime Minister. The bond between them included memories of Ireland and Arthur's service as Chief Secretary.

Between her social engagements, Kitty was hemming handkerchiefs for Arthur and on New Year's eve, started a new knitted blanket for him. 'received letters from Portugal today. Lord W. wishes a larger blanket, which he shall have as soon as it can be made: bought worsted and bespoke needles for it.... So ends 1810.'

The new year did not begin very well.

> January 1st, Tuesday. The first heavy snow of this winter. Taught my children after breakfast, wound several balls of worsted. I was extremely shocked to hear of the loss of poor Miss Stewart [Arthur Freese's aunt], on her passage to India. I will not tell it to poor little Arthur Freese today: New Year's Day

should not be a melancholy one.... Lady Liverpool kindly asked me to spend the day with her. I did so: the company, a set of stupid Lords, who were anything but pleasant. I behaved very ill and expressed what I thought of them. After they were gone, I wound more worsted: needles not yet ready ...

The locket Kitty had prepared for Mrs Freese would now reach her by another hand.

The next day Olivia Sparrow came to town unexpectedly and Kitty spent the evening with her at the house of another friend, Lady Hood. 'It is very strange,' Kitty noted in her diary, 'Olivia and Lady Hood, taken separately, are extremely agreeable; together, are perfect romps.'

Her mother had returned to Ireland and was replaced at Harley Street on 4 January by her brother. 'Longford is arrived, which I am delighted at.' After teaching her children, as she did every day, she worked on Arthur's blanket. 'Till my quilt [sic] is done I shall not think of a book. Olivia called on me and liked the children.... Worked all evening.'

On the whole, her life was full and pleasant in that winter of 1811, with plenty of friends to see and to call on. A typical entry is for 12 January. 'Morning as usual, teaching the children and reading psalms with Arthur Freese. Worked all day. Dined at the Speakers [Henry Addington, Viscount Sidmouth]. A remarkably pleasant day. Company, Lord and Lady Castlereagh, Lord St Helens, (who I like very much) Clancarty and other pleasant company.... The room in which we dined is under the House of Commons; it was a chapel and is still preserved in the old style of Gothic architecture. It would have been worth dining there had there been no other inducement than to see the room. Spent the rest of the evening with Mr and Mrs Pole, Mr Villiers [Mrs Pole's brother-in-law] and Lord Rivers.'

She was still reluctant to appear in public. 'Dined with Olivia today with the intention of going to Astley's [Assembly Rooms] in the evening, but finding there was a probability of Lord Wellington's name being introduced, I did not want to encounter the public gaze. Returned home when they went.'

'January 21st, Monday. Made up my quilt this morning and took it to the Admiralty. Called on Mrs. Brodrick [a relation]. Returned to the Horse Guards and gave my quilt in charge to Colonel Torrens.' The next day: 'wrote my letters to Portugal; carried them to the Horse Guards. Spent half an hour with Olivia Sparrow. Dined with Lady Liverpool; in the evening went to Mrs Brodrick's.'

A few days later Kitty 'went to the play, where I was extremely amused by the "Beehive"'. She now had Arthur Freese and his little sister Jesse staying with her. 'Arthur and his sister, added to my own two, made such a racket that I myself can do nothing but work; I have therefore begun a shoe.... Dined at Mrs Hope's; a large company, few of whom I knew. Mrs Hope's boy is a fine child. The dinner not unpleasant. In the evening I went to Mrs Pole's, where I was astonished to meet Lady Mornington; the evening would have been very pleasant if there had been less harpsichord. I met there Gerald Wellesley, whom I have not seen for months. I engaged him to dine here on Sunday next.'

A new interest was about to enter Kitty's life. Since meeting Gerald at Mrs Hope's she found her mind occupied with concern for little Gerald, Henry's son, deserted by his mother when she ran away with Lord Paget. The little boy had been in the care of his uncle, Gerald. 'This young Wellesley preyed on my mind', Kitty wrote. 'My dreams were all of Gerald Wellesley. The first thing I received this morning was a letter from his Uncle Gerald, requesting me to take the child. It has very much agitated me. I have decided to do it; the wretched infant is rejected by everybody. My own family would be very angry, but in some cases I must decide even against better judgement than my own. I have written to Gerald to desire to see him. I have called on Lady Mornington; they all think the child will be happy – I will try to make it so. Many people have called here today.'

In his letter, Gerald had reminded Kitty of an offer made some time ago, when his younger brother Henry had left England, that she would take 'the little infant'. The child had been living with Gerald and his wife. 'Since then we have had an addition to the family which makes his remaining with us a serious inconvenience.... If you are still of the same mind ... you will be doing me a very great kindness and ... obliging Henry in such a manner as he will never forget.' Kitty replied: 'You may be sure that my mind will never change when being of service to a Brother and a Wellesley is in question.... Gerald, if entrusted to me, shall be to me as a child of my own ... with the same tenderness as my own.' Gerald, a chaplain to the Royal Household, replied from Hampton Court Palace on 1 February: 'I have received your letter which is, like yourself, everything that is good-natured and amiable.' He would call on her in London tomorrow 'to talk over everything about little Gerald'.

The next day she wrote in her diary: 'On reflection, I thought it right to know Lord Wellington's opinion before I take charge of the little Wellesley. I have therefore sent him Gerald's letter. I am also resolved not to take the child unless it's father lets me know he wishes it.'

Arthur Freese was just about to return to school. 'A good boy and happy. I have sent by him a draught for the amount of the last half-year's expenses.... Dined at home alone. Olivia came to me in the evening. My cold is still very heavy.'

Her cold continued to make her feel ill and uneasy for the next few days. The following night she 'dined alone and spent a heavy evening hardly able to keep myself awake till ten o'clock, when Lady and Miss McKenzie came. Olivia soon joined us and we got into a chat which lasted till one in the morning'.

In the morning, Gerald called 'and has shocked me by explaining that the child is to see it's mother. I had no idea of this and it staggered me with regard to taking the charge. I will get advice and try to act for the best'. Lady Charlotte's elopement with Lord Henry Paget had excited a great deal of abuse against the couple, and particularly against Charlotte. The Wellesleys were extremely bitter at this betrayal of a member of the family and expressed their anger in a number of letters. Arthur referred to Charlotte as 'that blooming virgin', while other epithets included 'hell-cat' and expressed a general contempt for her lack of moral standards. Her action immediately made her an outcast from society and Kitty's consternation at the idea of little Gerald seeing his profligate mother is therefore understandable. To desert husband and children was considered a terrible and callous act, a crime that could not and should not be forgiven; to allow such a wicked woman to see her abandoned children was almost unthinkable. In spite of these disturbing events, the routine of life at Harley Street continued.

'February 6th. Immediately after breakfast I took my children to Mr. Slater's. It is a most sad job, that of sitting for their pictures. I do not think I will ever attempt it again. While they were there, I went to Lady Liverpool and spent a most delightful hour with her.' The next day, she received a present: 'Lady Liverpool brought me a shawl from Lord W. I hope it really was from him!' Kitty's doubts about the shawl were justified. Arthur, at the beginning of November the previous year, had asked Henry, now in Spain, to send some shawls to Lady Liverpool from Cadiz. Henry replied that where he was, Isla de Leon, no shawls were to be had, but he would do his best to get some.[3]

At last, the final visit to Slater's was made on 6 February and now the sittings were over Kitty decided to take drawing lessons from the artist herself.

This London season had passed pleasantly. Kitty had been a modest social success. Many of her diary entries conclude: 'Dined with a large party ...', 'Dressed and went to the play ...', 'Dined and spent the evening at Fife House, Lady Liverpool's, where there was a pleasant society ...'. The people she was meeting were mainly Tories, Government supporters. When she visited 'opposition people' she felt herself 'a restraint upon every mouth in the room'. On one occasion, when dining with General Stewart (Castlereagh's half-brother) and his wife, she notes: 'The company consisted of a number of military men; the Duke of Clarence [later William IV], Lady Darnley, Lady Selina Stewart. The dinner was pleasant. Immediately after dinner the ladies retired to their own rooms, leaving me alone in the drawing-room till a few minutes before the gentlemen came up. Tip-top quality breeding!' Her temper was still quickly aroused and her comments outspoken.

At the end of February, Gerald called on her, asking her to take Henry's little boy at once, on a temporary basis until 'Lord Wellington's wishes should be known.... I have consented. Please God, my own sweet children will not suffer for it'. She asked Longford's advice. 'He did not disapprove of my intention of undertaking the charge.'

On 6 March, Gerald brought the child to Harley Street. 'It appears a miserable little infant.' Her sister-in-law Mrs Wellesley-Pole called later and offered to take the boy, provided Kitty would look after him while the Poles were in Ireland. 'I will do no such thing', was Kitty's answer.

The 'poor little boy' did not at first settle down in his new home. 'Spent a miserable night.... On examination, I find he has been badly neglected. May it be in my power to make him well, good and happy.' Little Gerald was about two years old, his mother having run off with Paget soon after his birth in the spring of 1809.

For some time, Kitty had been expecting a letter from Arthur. She had sent him shirts, handkerchiefs and the large knitted blanket he had asked for. She had tried to fulfil all his instructions and requests and waited with muted optimism for signs of a thaw in his attitude.

'March 12th. At last my letters are arrived and, if I have not done all that was expected of me, at least what I have done was not wrong. I must try to make up my mind to repeated disappointments.' The score for her work had been a low one – not wrong, but not all that was expected of her. The winter of her hopes continued, although all around was spring.

She had a bad cold; Dr Mayo called: 'A very bad and melancholy day.' Her morale and enjoyment of life were reduced once more to zero. Arthur's infrequent letters were often harbingers of depression and loss of confidence. 'My cold so heavy and the effect of the medicine so sickening, as to force me to keep my bed most of this day. My heart, too, is very heavy; I feel a great disappointment. No matter, I have endured still worse.... At home, alone.'

As always at such moments, her children were her lifeline. Now she had another to care for. 'Little Gerald is coming on; my own boys are very well.' The same week, Alice (her maid-servant) died. 'The poor girl, whose life has been for some months in so precarious a state, is released. She died this evening. She was a good and gentle girl.'

On Sunday, 17 March she was still unwell, but walked to her mother-in-law's house for a visit. The next day: 'Much better. I will not give way to this preying dejection.... Dr Mayo has been of great service to me, so has my dear and excellent friend, Lady Liverpool. I haved dined with her and am still better.'

The following day she wrote to Portugal. 'When shall I feel at ease? Spent the day at home and alone. My children going on well. This has been a sad week.... Longford dined with me; this was a comfort.'

In spite of Longford's sympathy, she was having great difficulty in shaking off her depression, which coincided with poor health. She wrote: 'I can hardly account for the languor, the depression, that preys upon me. I really feel incapable of exertion or even occupation. I am glad I am to spend next day at Putney; it is a difference from other days and I shall be forced to exert myself. Poor Alice was buried this day. I remained at home and in a most distressed frame of mind, till five o'clock. Mayo spent part of this day with me. To effect a cure, I know that a wound must be probed; when that wound is in the heart, how torturing is the process.' Before going to Putney the following day, she spent the morning sorting letters. 'An occupation that has entirely lowered and oppressed me.'

As women often do, when feeling depressed, Kitty went shopping, and ordered a 'pianoforte, which is to be sent on Monday'. Her brother came to see her nearly every day – 'Dear Langford, dear brother'. Gradually her normal spirits returned, thanks to the efforts of her friends. 'Dined at Lady Liverpool's in company with Lady Mulgrave; a most friendly, pleasant day.'

On 4 April, Olivia Sparrow gave a ball, but Kitty did not go: 'I cannot bear the questions and observations to which I am subjected.' She was still prone to fits of intolerance: 'Lord Burghersh... appears to be an insignificant, chattering, blockhead.' He was to become a member of the family in later years, marrying one of Arthur's nieces.

William, her brother, was among her many visitors. He had at last been given command of a ship, much to the relief of the family, who feared his naval career was not prospering too well.

Little Gerald was still giving trouble. He cried at night and Kitty decided to 'keep Gerald in my room and watch him every night, till this wakeful habit should be broken. My servants are very angry – no matter. Dined at home alone today: in the evening went to my room and remained there all night. Gerald had a bad night but is in some degree in awe of me and, from stopping him the moment he begins to cry, I am certain I shall in time break the habit'.

CHAPTER 14

# *Homecoming*

Kitty's journal breaks off at this point, 21 April 1811, and is not resumed until September 1812. In the intervening sixteen months the news from Spain was inconclusive. Sieges, surrenders, advances, retreats – a conclusion to the campaign in the Peninsula seemed nowhere in sight. Few women in Britain could not number killed or wounded among their relatives and friends.

Edward and Hercules kept up a flow of reports on the military situation as they saw it, with news of casualties sustained, victories achieved. Lowry Cole was wounded twice but soon resumed command of his division. 'Every officer wounded more or less, many of them having lost limbs', Edward reported on 29 May 1811, during one of the sieges of Badajoz. In this action, where casualties were heavy, 4,000 British, 2,000 Spaniards 'and some Portuguese Cavalry' were lost.

Hercules had been appointed Arthur's adjutant-general with Edward as his deputy, although he was soon to have a brigade. 'Wellington, though quite the Commander of the forces, is positively my brother in all our dealings', Edward informed Longford, and vowed to repay his debt of gratitude to Arthur whenever possible.

In August, Edward, replying to letters from Longford dated 1 and 17 June containing news of Kitty, commented: 'I am pleased to hear that our Kitty, (under all the circumstances of various anxiety) keeps up so good a countenance – the more so as I am in hopes that it will give her a degree of firmness which may render her more happy, and at all events give domestic calm, which heretofore her stock of philosophy was not equal to command.'[1] Edward's letter is headed 'Sarnadas, near Castel Branco', Portugal; the main body of the army was on the move and had crossed the

Tagus, heading for their old lines in front of Ciudad Rodrigo. Edward was soon to be promoted to brigadier. He was thirty-three and had served 'near seventeen years'.

During this period Kitty continued to make a more satisfactory life for herself than seemed likely from her recurring fits of depression. Although previous extracts from her diary had underlined these attacks, in fact they were widely dispersed. She had enjoyed the London season and had taken her children back to Broadstairs for the summer and prolonged her stay into the autumn. About this time, one of the children had a sudden and serious illness. Her brother-in-law Marquis Wellesley was a frequent visitor to Ramsgate and was on hand during this crisis. Kitty wrote to him on 10 November 1811, from Broadstairs, just before returning to London, thanking him, in her usual effusive terms, for his help, 'when the situation of my child was most desperate ... on this subject I am not able to dwell. My boy is almost miraculously preserved and his dear and excellent father will, I trust, receive intelligence of his recovery, almost as soon as that of his danger'. She cannot express to him her 'affectionate gratitude ... and can only say and repeat – Good God bless you. Most affectionately yours, C.D.S. Wellington'.[2] Her nephew, the insufferable William, had also helped her in this crisis, a service for which he claimed consideration many years later.

While Kitty was struggling with this emergency, Edward had contracted fever in Spain and as soon as he could travel would return to England. Hercules told Longford how impressed he had been with 'Lord Wellington's kindness' during Edward's illness, a subject soon to be eclipsed by an even greater family disaster.

Young William Pakenham, who had waited so long for command of a ship, was now captain of the *Saldanha* and wrote cheerfully to his mother from Lough Swilly (Donegal) on 25 November 1811: 'Here we are again ... had a good and pleasant voyage – I shall be in port about three weeks.' When he set sail once more, patrolling the Irish coastal waters against the dangers of a French invasion, a winter gale swept across the lough with the treacherous force of a hurricane, overwhelming the *Saldanha*, pressing her into the waves so that she filled and sank with the loss of all hands.

Edward, staying with his sister at 11 Harley Street, wrote to his mother on 14 December, confirming that William was dead. 'England has been deprived of one of her most devoted servants. . . . God give me true resignation, for such an event must need it. Write to me a line, my mother; it may ease you and relieve a remaining son. Kitty's steadiness has quite astonished me. She is calm to a degree that only could proceed from goodness and religion.'

Arthur, on 5 January 1812, had the sad duty of breaking the news to Hercules: 'The mail has not yet arrived but I am concerned to have to inform you ... of the loss of your brother, William. I don't know the details ... but it appears that the *Saldanha* was wrecked in a gale of wind off Lough Swilly and all on board perished.... It is useless to pretend to offer any consolation ... indeed I can suggest none.... I think, however, that you will bear your misfortune like a man, and will seek to divert your mind from reflecting upon it, by attending to your duty in the new scene which is opening before us. Believe me, ever yours most affectionately, Wellington.'[3]

Before this cloud of sadness descended on the Pakenhams, Maria Edgeworth had visited them. Writing to Mary Sneyd in November 1811, she describes her arrival at Pakenham Hall, where she found Longford paying one of his flying visits and a whole tribe of merry, laughing children, Stewarts and Hamiltons. 'Lady Longford showed us a picture of Lady Wellington and her children; they are beautiful and she says very like – Lady Wellington is not like; it is absurd to attempt to draw Lady Wellington's face; she has no face, it is all countenance.'[4]

Kitty's 'steadiness' over the death of William was a family characteristic. Hercules, writing to his brother in February about William's death, told him: 'I was obliged, while stunned by the severity of the blow, to make arrangements of the duties for the siege [of Ciudad Rodrigo].... You see by the Gazette, my old friend, Mackinnon, was killed.... I was but a few paces behind him when the mine blew up and was, by the force of the explosion, staggered over a case of lighted hand grenades. I had just time to take up the mass of devilry and heave it down the rampart, when off they went without wounding any of us.'[5]

Later in the year, he was not to be so lucky. Kitty nursed Edward back to health, and by April the campaign in Spain was on the move again and final preparations in hand for the storming of Badajoz. Hercules had continued to distinguish himself and Kitty was with Colonel Torrens at the Horse Guards on 1 April 1812, arranging to despatch some boots to Arthur, when Torrens began to open the despatches from Wellington, dated 20 March. 'He opened but one', Kitty wrote to her brother,

> and that one gave me a feeling of delight that it is not in words to describe. The whole subject ... was the recommendation of a Major in his Army, who is, to use his own words, 'an excellent and exemplary officer'. My Hercules, if you know that Major, give my best and kindest love and let him know that those few words, which I came clattering home to repeat to my mother, have cured and charmed her, just at the moment when she was depressed by the information that Edward goes tomorrow. I am glad that he goes, though not

as strong as we wish him ... but he is becoming so anxious to join you all, now that you have been moving, that a longer delay in this country would vex and irritate his nerves and probably retard his recovery.

Hercules, writing to Longford on 3 April from Camp Badajoz, describes the situation. 'I have not written to Kate by this mail, being on the eve of a storming business in which our Division will most certainly be engaged; anything I said on this head must increase her anxiety and I never deceive her. I never saw Wellington look better ... I hope to write you next week from Badajoz.'

Edward left London for Spain on 14 April and arrived in Lisbon about ten days later. On 26 April he wrote to his mother about Hercules who 'has had two severe wounds.... One through the thigh, the other through the wrist.... It is necessary he should have a long confinement, even previous to his return to England.... The rapidity of my passage has so fatigued me, I have thought it well to stay a day or two here. I shall then set out for Hercules on my way to Headquarters. Adieu, my dear mother, be a stout old woman and support us by the belief that your suffering son has vastly distinguished himself.'[6]

Kitty's ability to withstand the horrors of war had once again been put to the test and it is not surprising, with all these anxieties, she had no time for her diary. Writing to Hercules on 29 April, she congratulated him on his promotion to lieutenant-colonel and promised to write 'by every mail. I have of late been idle and sad and will be so no more, Heaven bless you and your dear, excellent Chief. Most affectionately yours...'.

May 1812 brought a sensation to British politics and to the nation. The Prime Minister, Spencer Percival, was assassinated – shot and killed in the lobby of the House of Commons. Who would succeed him? London was full of gossip on the chances of Richard, Marquis Wellesley, much favoured by the Prince Regent; but his dissolute life was against him and past feuds not forgotten by his enemies. Many, including Arthur, considered his excesses might have impaired his intellect and, family loyalty notwithstanding, Arthur advised against the appointment. In any case, no one would agree to serve under Richard and eventually the Prince Regent abandoned the idea and sent for Kitty's good friend Lord Liverpool. Castlereagh would have the Foreign Office and Lord Bathurst, another of Arthur's friends, would be Minister for War.

The Liverpools had shown Kitty every kindness, but Arthur was doubtful of his ability and also annoyed that Richard, having been dropped from the main appointment, was given no place in the Cabinet. William Wellesley-Pole had refused the position offered to him and thus the Wellesley faction had practically disappeared from power under the new administration, which would add to Arthur's problems in bringing the war in the Peninsula to a successful conclusion.

The summer campaign was still in progress and, after the victory at Salamanca in July, Edward wrote to Hercules: 'The Peer was everywhere in the course of action and even surpassed himself in the clearness and energy of his instructions. There never lived such a warrior.'[7]

In June, Kitty returned to Tunbridge Wells with her children and took a house on Mount Ephraim, the hilly area above the town, which she chose as being a healthy situation for the boys. She stayed there until the autumn and, in November 1812, replied to a letter from Colonel John Malcolm, an old friend:

> You are quite right. My boys enjoy advantages here of which I should deprive them by removing to town and for which nothing in town could make amends, young as they are. The house which we occupy is on the top of Mount Ephraim and half an hour after violent and continued rain, the ground is perfectly dry, so that every fair moment my boys can be in the air. I wish you could see the delight, hear the shout of joy, with which they fly out of the house after the confinement of a day of rain. They are absolutely wild. Woe to the old lady who happens to be turning the corner as Charley dashes round it! After running about the Common as long as they like, they return to me glowing with exercise and health. They are beautiful and good and a thousand times happier than they would be confined to town. Another inducement to me to stay here is finding the air agrees so well with my brother, who is now so much recovered as to walk without the assistance of his crutch for an hour at a time without fatique.
>
> We have no society, but with the assistance of the children, who are very fond of Uncle Hercules, a little reading, a good deal of chatting, chess in the evening (which we play almost equally ill) and his admirable temper, we never feel even a moment of ennui.... My brother will allow me to write no more. Before I conclude, however, I must make you a request. I have lately received a letter from Mrs. Freese, by which I find that two letters of mine have miscarried. Perhaps you can tell me by what means I can convey mine safely to her?

Her letter also mentions Arthur's disappointment that in the autumn Madrid had fallen again 'into the hands of those merciless plunderers' (the French). At the beginning of August 1812, Arthur had made a dramatic entry into Madrid and Edward, in letters to Longford and to his mother, describes the splendour of the palaces in which they were quartered. Arthur was also impressed by the style of their surroundings and told Edward he had never seen anything like the elegance of the palace in which he was living.

*Homecoming*

Arthur was soon on the move again, leaving Madrid with his Staff on 31 August for the Douro and the disastrous siege of Burgos, having first installed Edward, still suffering from attacks of fever, in his own quarters at the royal palace for a few days, 'for a change of air'.[8]

During this successful interlude honours had again been heaped on Arthur. On 19 August, Prime Minister Liverpool wrote congratulating him on his victories and discribing the wild enthusiasm in London at the news of the fall of Madrid (which would soon be retaken by the French). The following day Bathurst informed Arthur that the Prince Regent had advanced him to the dignity of 'Marquis'. A few days later Bathurst wrote: 'The modest and retiring conduct of Lady Wellington during the exaltation of this city is universally commended.' A point of view in later years to be reversed. In addition to his new title, Arthur received a grant of £100,000 and an allowance of £25,000 per annum 'for your table'.[9]

With the end of summer, Kitty resumed her diary, reviewing the intervening period during which she had kept no record.

> September 9th. Once more and with what different feelings I begin my Journal, regretting, uninteresting as the events of my life are, that I have discontinued it so long. In the course of the last twelve months, what varied events have taken place; how different do I feel, although my situation exhibits no change – my husband still abroad, my children at home, my health nearly as it was: delicate, not positively unhealthy, but my mind is strengthened, my habits different.
>
> I can now occupy myself and look without terror at the future. Of the public events which have taken place, I will say nothing. My object is to compare in what I am engaged while he, the object of my thoughts, is engaged abroad. On 25th August, I took my children to town to visit my poor Hercules, whose wounds still confine him to his chair: the 27th, I went to the Portuguese Chapel, to hear the 'Te Deum' sung and to see the ceremony of High Mass. Colonel Malcolm had seen my boys the day before. I remained in town till Monday, 31st, when I began my journey home. My children in my carriage, Longford and I in his. As far as Bromley, all was well: from that time the children were so ill, we could get no further than Sevenoaks that night.
>
> On Tuesday 1st, we got home and they have gradually recovered.... A Reading Master attended on Wednesday at six in the evening, when Arthur took his first lesson from him in reading, spelling and arithmetic and his progress exceeds my expectations. He has each day taken two lessons and practised with me in the intermediate time. Charles and Gerald continue with me.
>
> This morning rose a little before eight to give Arthur his lesson.... At nine o'clock went to the Well; met Miss Godfrey; drank the water. Walked till ten. After breakfast, took my boys to their lessons. At one o'clock, went to the Poles: found Mr. Pole very angry with me for not having gone to the ball last night. It was given in honour of Lord Wellington's victory and taking posses-

sion of Madrid, the news of which arrived here on Saturday last, the 5th – I could not go. Met Sir Walter [Farquar] at Mr. Pole's, who showed me a very flattering letter to Lord Wellesley: I hate those kind of letters, of which copies are kept.... Walked from four to half past five with Mrs. Pole. Bought some flowers at Hervey's cottage. Brought home some raspberries for my boys. Mr. Fry came at six and gave Arthur his second lesson: very good. Dined at half past six. Told stories to the children: put them to bed at eight o'clock, The remainder of the evening unusually heavy. Wrote from ten to half past eleven.

The next day she heard that Hercules would be coming to stay with her, arriving the day after. 'Nothing ready and tomorrow I must go to the play.... Lord Bristol has made some excellent purchases for me ... at a very cheap book auction.' Kitty had attended auctions on several occasions and purchased books for her library. 'Spent the evening with the Poles and the Burghershes: they will not accompany me to the play, knowing that I must go alone, unless they do – no matter.' She went to the play anyway, 'with the little Bristols and felt quite grateful to Lord and Lady B. for allowing them to accompany me'.

On 29 September she was faced with another public engagement, this time sponsored by her friend Lady Liverpool: 'Being determined not to be held up "en spectacle" and finding myself totally unequal to attending the ceremony of putting up the Eagles, I thought my best plan was to leave Tunbridge Wells. I did so and wrote to Lady Liverpool from Sevenoaks to excuse myself. She must receive my letter tomorrow, before the ceremony commences.'

On her return, she found her brother was making a good recovery from his wounds and her children were well, but Lady Liverpool was furious at Kitty's desertion from the ceremony she had organized to celebrate raising the Eagles, the standards captured from the French by Wellington's troops. 'Lady L's displeasure is extreme', Kitty noted in her diary – she also recorded that the French were retreating from Moscow.

Kitty was an enthusiastic play-goer and often went to the theatre at Tunbridge Wells – on one occasion with Lady Boyne, a friend from County Meath, whom she described as 'extremely good-natured, but her vulgarity is truly shocking'. Attending the play with her was 'a matter of duty and most horribly disagreeable'. A few days later she saw *Hamlet* performed, with the famous actor 'Young Betty' in the leading part. 'I am not sure that I was disappointed or not.... The general impression was in his favour....'

Reading was usually a source of great pleasure but she found *The Princess of Beruth* 'full of disgusting slang'. Her boys were now 'reading uncommonly well' and in October had started one of Maria Edgeworth's books for children. Kitty was giving them geography lessons, putting the map of the World together from a number of jig-saw pieces. She was still nursing Hercules; he was now able to move about the room 'without the assistance of his servant'. 'October 31st. The evening as usual with my dear and excellent brother. My poor watch set a-floating in the bathing tub.' On 2 November she borrowed a drawing of a skull from Lady Donegal, to illustrate the poem by Robert Southey on the battle of Blenheim, which she had copied and kept among her papers, possibly for the amusement of the children.

Her diary entries for November are sparse notes on the progress of her children and her brother's recovery. They played chess most evenings and she played the harp to amuse him. After 1812, Kitty made no more personal notes. Almost the last entry is about her children. 'They are dear boys and my greatest comfort.'

The last volume of her diary is made up of copies of letters and extracts from newspaper reports. A long, unsigned communication, perhaps from one of her brothers, dated 4 August 1813, describes the action round San Sebastian in northern Spain. 'We have upwards of four thousand prisoners, beside the wounded that were left on the ground. Our loss has also been considerable; I should think at least five thousand five hundred men. Many, many very promising officers have fallen, but such is the fortune of war'.

Meanwhile, the beginning of 1813 found Kitty and her family back in Harley Street. She made no comment in her diary on Arthur's new title of marquis; she was not an ambitious woman and titles bestowed on Arthur she regarded as the nation's tribute, not as something to add to her own importance. She even extracted some amusement from her new style and shared the joke with her children. Laughter would have echoed round 11 Harley Street at her spoof invitation to her Irish friend Margaret Packer, one of the six daughters of the High Sheriff of Limerick and a frequent visitor.

> Catherine, Marchioness: Whereas our right and trusty Cousin and Counsellor, the Twopenny Postman, having this day laid before us a certain written document, touching the eating of Margaret Packer at Number 11, Harley Street, on Wednesday next, the 1st inst. We did, as the case appeared urgent, assemble our well-beloved Cousins and Councillors: Douro (the Lord, not the River), Charley, the Champion-General, Gerry, Worry of the House and Carlo, [the dog] Guardian of the Family and did command them to take said matter to their most serious consideration....
>
> We are happy to declare to Margaret Packer, that she is graciously commanded to be ready at half past eleven on Wednesday, a.m., at which hour We, the undersigned, will send Our carriage to convey Margaret to Number

11, Harley Street and will also convey said Margaret back again at night, on certain following conditions: Namely ... She shall not damage or deface the splendour of Our carriage. She shall not kick up a row in the streets by hooting out of the window, making faces or otherwise annoying His Majesty's subjects. She shall not stop in returning home at night, to mug herself at the Public house on the corner....

Honours were still falling on Arthur. On New Year's Day, 1813, he became colonel of the Horse Guards, and in March, a Garter knight. Kitty was still in London on their wedding anniversary, 10 April, and wrote to her sister Bess Stewart, in Dublin: 'My husband is blessed wherever his name is heard. He may possibly soon return to a wife who will no longer worry him because he, soft as well as strong, complying as well as firm, everything that is gentle and domestic; being obliged to live his soldier's hard and wandering life – I am grown wise, my Bess, and rejoice that I have lived to be seven years a wife.'

Her easily aroused emotions are reflected in her slightly incoherent letter. The wedding anniversary and the April days brought back so many memories. After all this time, she would 'no longer worry' Arthur when he returned home. She would accept that he must live his 'hard and wondering life', she had 'grown wise'. Kitty, in common with many of her countrymen, possessed an unending capacity for resilience and hope, often in the face of hopeless odds. She may have grown wise but had she overcome her capacity for obstinately holding to self-opinionated views when the strategy of marriage demanded flexibility? She had little experience of how to live amicably with her husband. Her desperate desire to make him happy was likely to be counterproductive and her chances of regaining his love and respect after the lapse of so much time were minimal. He did not trust her with money, and it is clear from the second part of her letter to Bess, that she did not have very much at her disposal.

She had heard from her mother that the Edgeworths were coming to London. 'I cannot express with what consternation I heard of the intended visit – particularly as my mother has written to desire me to be of use to them. What does that mean? I cannot, unless they desire me, introduce them to the very few people of high rank with whom I am acquainted; and strange to tell, I have no other society. I have no box at the Opera or Play, thinking that if I had it to spare, £250 a year may be spent in a more satisfactory way.... Lady Liverpool is well and enjoying the duties of her station.'

When Maria and her father reached London in May, Kitty rose to the occasion and Maria was delighted. 'Charming, amiable Lady Wellington! As she truly said herself, she is always Kitty Pakenham to her friends. After comparison with crowds of others – beaux esprit, fine ladies and fashionable scramblers for notoriety, her dignified, graceful simplicity rises in one's opinion and we feel it with more conviction of its superiority. She showed us her delightful children.'[10]

From Maria's lively account of her visit to London, she and her family had no need of Kitty's introductions – they were received by everyone. It is interesting to note how famous Maria was in literary circles. When Scott published *Waverley* in 1814, he wrote in a postscript to the novel that it has been his desire 'in some distant degree to emulate the admirable Irish portraits drawn by Miss Edgeworth' in the work.[11]

In June, Arthur was again the centre of national interest, and by the end of the month news reached England of his great victory at Vitoria in northern Spain, opening the way to France across the Pyrenees, perhaps the most decisive battle of the Peninsula War. Joseph Bonaparte's army was shattered and a vast quantity of equipment and treasure abandoned on the battlefield by the retreating French forces. Arthur was created Field Marshal and the end of the war in Europe was in sight, although hard fighting and privation in the mountains was still to come.

Kitty had returned to Tunbridge Wells for the summer of 1813 and from there she wrote to Sir John Malcolm on 30 July, telling him that little Gerald Wellesley had been very ill. The problem of her public appearances as wife of the national hero was becoming more acute. She had survived the criticism of her absence from the 'Eagles' ceremony but had compounded the offence by refusing to attend the fêtes to celebrate the latest victory. She had at least one ally, John Malcolm, who told her he approved of her non-attendance at such events.

In her letter to him, Kitty argued:

> If I did appear, I must be a conspicuous object. My feelings for Lord Wellington's victory cannot, I think, be doubted and surely need not be exhibited. Indeed, I believe that a woman can very seldom succeed in *exhibiting* without *exposing* herself. I know all this is unnecessary to *you*, but the displeasure of one or two of Lord Wellington's family on this subject by making me think more on the subject, induces me to mention it in writing. Did you ever hear of a really great man whose wife did not like keeping at home in the absence of her husband? I never did. Penelope herself had not half the husband that I have, yet she was right for staying quiet.

She justified her retirement from public events in this way, at least to herself, but in fact many public appearances would soon have revealed her lack of communication with Arthur. It was common knowledge that he had not once come home during the whole of the Peninsula campaign and this gave sufficient grounds for comment and speculation. It was not unknown for officers' wives to follow their husbands abroad and even to ride with them nearly to the scene of battle, while ordinary soldiers in such a protracted engagement often had the company of their wives and sometimes children. A great rabble of camp followers travelled to the rear of the armies as they marched and countermarched across the country. Between battles or in winter there were periods when the troops were in semi-permanent camps and enjoyed some domestic comforts, as did their officers in more luxurious quarters. Wellington disliked members of his staff asking for leave at home, but it was not uncommon. Sometimes they returned to England on official business and more often on sick leave; Arthur never did so, for more than five years.

Kitty wrote again to Malcolm from Tunbridge Wells on 19 August, after receiving reports of the campaign in the Pyrenees:

> I am not ambitious of titles for Lord W. Whether Marquis, Lord, Viscount or plain Arthur Wellesley, as when I first knew him, he is always the same, always the first of men and of soldiers, with this only difference, that every year of his life by giving opportunities of calling forth his talents, has made them better known to the world.
>
> Yet I do not myself at all like the thought that the battle of the Pyrenees should be undervalued, as I fear it will be in the public mind if it is followed by no distinguished mark of approbation, since it has become the custom to reward services by bestowing titles and promotions.... For the battles of the Pyrenees – the hardest fought, won by their most brilliant valour and most consumate skill, of the most essential consequence to the cause – for such a victory or rather series of victories – nothing at all! Is it possible this can be wise? Ten thousand Blenheims were nothing to this ...'

The letter ends on a domestic note: 'My boys are well and proud and good and beautiful. Believe me, dear Sir, your most truly obliged, C.D.S.Wellington.'

In September, she heard that Arthur had suffered from a most severe attack of rheumatism during the wet and cold conditions of the Pyrenees campaign. Kitty had asked Malcolm to obtain some Cazaputta oil, said to be a cure for rheumatics: 'Thank you, my dear Sir, for your efforts to get me the Cazaputta oil. I hope you may succeed, for though Lord W. is considerably better and will probably receive my offering with scorn, yet it may be of use to him,. as those who have once severely suffered from rheumatism are liable to a return.' She continues her letter with news of her brother Edward, 'Lord Wellington's pupil', who had been made a Knight of the Bath. 'He is a fine young man and you will like him very much indeed when you see him.... I cannot resist adding a nonsensical story which has amused me, relative to Lord Wellington and one of his Irish soldiers, who accidentally met him and said: 'Ah, God bless you, my darlin: we would rather see you than twenty whole Divisions, the Lord love your crooked nose ....'

Events were now moving quickly towards the end of the war. In October, Arthur's army crossed the Bidassoa into France and Napoleon's magic was broken at last. Fighting still continued, but now the countryside was rich and prosperous. The cold and hardship of the mountains was forgotten, although the rain continued relentlessly. There was fresh food for men and horses, this time from French farms; and time for rest. Everything was slowed down by the terrible weather.

At home, Kitty was arranging to move into a new London house – 4 Hamilton Place, at the beginning of Park Lane, looking across Hyde Park – a great improvement on Harley Street.

The war was now on French soil and the Allied officers had great difficulty in controlling the Spanish contingent, who had begun to loot and pillage the French villages, as the French had done in Spain. This lawlessness was put down by Arthur with the utmost severity. His trusted brother-in-law Edward Pakenham went about the countryside 'like a raging lion', forcing the Spanish allies to obey orders and respect the property of civilians. As soon as possible, the major part of the Spanish forces were sent home, leaving Wellington with a greatly reduced but more manageable army.

The winter months brought a lull in the fighting and Arthur was able to enjoy a little fox hunting, with hounds sent from England, in the hills above St Jean de Luz. By February, he was attacking Soult once again, and at the end of the month, during the engagement at Orthez, west of Bayonne, he was hit by a spent bullet. It struck the buckle of his sword-belt and severely cut and bruised his thigh, a painful injury which made riding difficult. Maria Edgeworth says of this incident that Arthur wrote to Kitty 'four times in one week ... without ever mentioning the wound'. This spate of letters may have been in connection with the move of his family to Hamilton Place.

Kitty heard of the incident before the end of March. She wrote to Malcolm: 'His contusion was, thank God, nothing of consequence, though more than enough to electrify me. I have always seen him in my mind protected by a transparent, impenetrable, adamantine Shield, and settled that he could not be *even touched*; so precious a life, so invaluable – surely the almighty hand of God will protect him.'

Her letter continues with a reference to the promised Dukedom, mentioned soon after the battle of Vitoria. 'With respect to our

Dukedom, I hardly know what to say. I recollect when my little Douro was quite an infant, his ambition was to have as large a nose as his father's and every day he used to feel his nose and that of the bust, to observe the growth of his own. At last, quite out of all patience and not perceiving any increase, he exclaimed with the strongest expression of impatience: "My nose is such a time a-growing...." I think I must say, like him – this Dukedom is such a time a-coming....' Kitty had to wait another month before the Dukedom was conferred, on 3 May, 1814.

In the interval, great events had taken place. On 6 April, Napoleon Bonaparte, Emperor of the French, had abdicated. The news reached the opposing armies in the south too late to prevent the last battle of the war, at Toulouse on 10 April, where allied casualties were very heavy. By the end of the month, Louis XVIII had returned to France and Napoleon had been sent to Elba; on 4 May, the newly created Duke was in Paris, for a review of the victorious armies by the King.

Kitty and her boys watched the celebration fireworks in Hyde Park from Hamilton Place and waited for a summons to Paris or news of Arthur's return. She did not know that Arthur had been offered the Paris Embassy by Castlereagh, Foreign Secretary, and Arthur had replied at once from Toulouse: 'I am very much obliged and flattered by your thinking of me for a situation for which I should never have thought myself qualified.... Although I have been so long absent from England, I should have remained so much longer, if it had been necessary; and I feel no objection to another absence in the public service.'[12]

On 30 April, Arthur wrote to Henry that he was going to Paris to see Lord Castelreagh regarding the new appointment: 'I must serve the public in some manner or other; and as under existing circumstances I could not well do so at home, I must do so abroad. Don't mention to anybody the intention that I should be the Ambassador at Paris.'

Arthur was in an awkward situation politically. He considered he could not accept an appointment in Lord Liverpool's administration, because of the slight to his brothers, in failing to include them in his ministry. Richard had expected to be Foreign Secretary, although William believed this to be impossible because of Richard's profligate life. Arthur's condemnation of Richard's behaviour was already well established. In 1810, writing to William on this subject, he remarked: 'I wish that Wellesley was castrated; or that he would, like other people, attend to his business and perform too. It is lamentable to see talent and character and advantages such as he possesses, thrown away upon whoring. Then the ruin of his private fortune, which at his time of life is irretrievable, is as certain as the loss of character and the misuse of his talents and the dereliction of his advantages; and the injury which the public and his Party must suffer from this folly. This really gives me the greatest concern.'[13]

William Wellesley-Pole had now broken with Richard and thought, as a result, he would be given a ministerial appointment. But Liverpool continued to ignore them both. Arthur, from family loyalty, decided he could not join the Government and service abroad was the best answer to this dilemma.

Kitty was not consulted or told of the new appointment until everything was settled. Arthur had decided on his policy towards her in Ireland and his mind had not changed. She was to be kept in ignorance of all important matters until the last moment to avoid unnecessary argument and possible indiscretion. He believed she talked too readily of his affairs to her friends and relations, that she was unreliable and covered her mistakes with 'lame excuses'. A harsh verdict from a man normally kind and good-natured, except when exposing deception or cowardice. He believed he had been deceived in his assessment of Kitty's character before he married her. He thought she was strong-minded, with strongly held principles – a view he had nurtured in India, based on his youthful admiration for the young and dominant Kitty and revealed in his letters to Olivia Sparrow. During their short years together he had found her a weak, argumentative creature, making demands on his valuable time, lacking intelligence, careless in paying household bills, and not above damaging his reputation by fearing to reveal debts to tradesmen incurred by misappropriating the housekeeping money to help a relative. This aspect of their relationship dominated his mind, when he had time to think about it, during the second long period of separation and hardened his determination not to give Kitty his confidence or affection on his return.

The fact that she had devoted herself to their children and brought them up alone for the last six years did not diminish his prejudice or allow him to consider the possibility that she might have gained strength of character from the experience. She was not to have a second chance.

In Paris, Arthur was experiencing the adulation of a French society newly loyal to the restored Bourbon. People flocked to the capital to see him, honours showered on him, beautiful women fainted with excitement when he entered the room. At last he was reaping the rewards of a conquering hero and very much enjoying the harvest.

Characteristically, he did not stay long in the delights of Paris, leaving after a few days on a mission to Madrid. He reached Toulouse on 14 May and left three days later, arriving in Madrid on 24 May. By 9 June he was in France again, at Bordeaux, arranging transports for his army to England.

In the meantime, Kitty had received a letter from Arthur, written in Madrid on 26 May, in which he asked her to decide if she wanted to join him in Paris in the autumn, as ambassadress. She replied at once from Hamilton Place on 13 June 1814.

> My dearest Arthur, I have received your letter of the 26th from Madrid, in which you permit me to decide for myself with respect to accompanying you to Paris or not. From the moment I heard of your acceptance of the appointment, I had no other thought than that of going with you and my wish would have been the same had your appointment been in any other part of the world to which you could, with safety, have permitted me to accompany you. I have no hesitation in deciding to go, no other wish than to go. I think, with you, that your task is a most arduous one, attended with what to many people would appear extreme difficulties; but to an Ambassador's wife there are no difficulties which I do not feel myself equal to overcome, no duties which I am not willing to perform and I may venture to add that you shall never have reason to regret having allowed me, on this subject, to decide for myself.'

Her new-found confidence had been put to the test the previous day, when she had attended an important diplomatic function given by Lady Salisbury in honour of the Allied monarchs and their families, visiting London for the victory celebrations. According to Lady Frances Shelley, describing the scene in her diary, the Prince Regent was present, 'covered in Orders', and the rest of the distinguished guests had used the occasion to display their most extravagant dresses and priceless jewels. The Emperor of Russia and the King of Prussia were there, with members of their entourage, but Frances was most impressed by the Grand Duchess of Russia, the Emperor's sister, 'in the most magnificent pearls I ever saw – scattered all over her head in large bunches and drops... and a necklace of egg-shaped pearls of enormous size.... All talked to the Duchess of Wellington, upon whom they had called in the morning. The Prussian French is very bad indeed.'[14]

Kitty was already playing her part as ambassadress, equal to the task of conversing with the crowned heads of Europe and understanding their ugly Prussian-French accents. They had all 'talked a great deal' to her and she had made a very favourable impression during their visit to Hamilton Place on the morning of the party. Her modest and disarming manner would have been a pleasant relief from the extravagance and vulgarity surrounding the visiting royals. During the lonely years, she had maintained her knowledge of French and her close contact with the Liverpools and the Edgeworths had kept her informed on international politics and on the leading writers, artists and musicians of the day. She no longer feared appearing in public in the absence of her husband, knowing she was soon to resume her place as his wife, at least in her official capacity as ambassadress. Gossiping tongues were silenced, for the time being.

Arthur was about to return to England. He had issued farewell orders to his troops at Bordeaux on 14 June, in his characteristic short, terse phrases, later criticized as lacking in warmth and grudging of praise. He told them, as their Commander-in-Chief, he had 'the warmest interest in their welfare and honour.... He will be at all times happy to be of any service to those to whose conduct, discipline and gallantry their Country is so much indebted ...'. With those words his great army dispersed, the close-knit community dividing into thousands of individuals returning to their homes, each one possessed of an indefinable sense of pride in having been part of a great enterprise, of enhanced manhood, of a capacity to endure; they had seen men and women rise to the heights of selfless sacrifice for others; they had seen unspeakable depths of depravity. The survivors were men apart, familiar with the inevitability of death: a few years more or less made little difference in the totality of human experience. To live could be as tragic as to die. The ultimate evil was the capitulation of the human spirit, forfeiting freedom in return for bodily survival. Soldiers had seen the aftermath of defeat and capitulation and knew that death in defence of liberty was a preferable alternative to life under a military dictatorship. As they returned to the towns and villages of Britain, they had cause for pride.

He landed at Dover on 23 June, cheered by crowds all the way to London. Kitty waited at Hamilton Place with the two boys – Arthur, aged seven, and Charley, six. Their father, forty-five, and Kitty, three years younger, had last seen each other five years before, after three years of a checkered marriage and frequent separation. Then he had been plain Sir Arthur Wellesley, today, the Great Duke, toast of Europe, friend of kings, a living legend.

His little wife, plumper now, hair touched with grey, stood at the long windows of the first floor salon looking over the park, over the restless crowds in Park Lane waiting impatiently for the hero's return. The children beside her were full of excitement and questions – Was he coming? Could she see him? Their small hands in hers may have felt her agitation, the agonizing prelude to tears, which she must not shed, for wasted years and prodigal hours spent in lonely depression. Tears not only of regret but joy at his homecoming and a hope, against all reason, that they might be reconciled.

The noise of the crowd suddenly increased with ragged cheers and a swaying press of bodies. A carriage and outriders had appeared in the distance. Pressing closer to the window, the little group strained their eyes to see what was happening. Behind them the door opened and a slim, upright figure was in the room. Plain blue coat, white cravat, hat in hand – suddenly the stern, brown face and penetrating blue eyes changed and softened with pleasure as the little boys turned in surprise from the window. Arthur had avoided the crowds by leaving his carriage and riding on ahead. He was home.

So ended the early years of Kitty and Arthur's marriage. What did the future hold for them? After the brief interlude in England and Paris came the trauma of Waterloo, a fitting climax to his military career and his last battle. For him, the future required painful efforts to adjust to a new situation, to civilian life at the centre of Court and Party intrigue, despising the process of compromise and appeasement, yet subject at all times to the importuning of place-seekers and beggars, worthy and unworthy – never losing his humanity yet intolerant of deceit.

From military hero he became a national symbol of moral strength – and, for a short time, Prime Minister – incorruptible in a corrupt age, uninfluenced by public opinion or personal popularity, his own man, under the Crown. Fearless in stating his opinions, contemptuous of blackmail, whether personal or political, yet in essence a kind and gentle man, sensitive to suffering, unfailing in loyalty and support for those with whom he served, but failing too often to understand or sympathize with the problems of his children and his wife. And yet he enjoyed female companionship. He found in Harriet Arbuthnot and her husband friendship, understanding and stimulating conversation and the peace and quiet of harmonious domesticity which to him was utterly enjoyable and relaxing. On Harriet's untimely death in 1834, the inconsolable widower shared Wellington's home for the rest of his life.

Arthur had no liking for deception. His brothers and their wives had demonstrated the misery which could be caused to others by broken marriages, elopements, desertions and promiscuity – misery he considered to be unnecessary and the product of their lack of principles. He was no Puritan – but his logical mind rejected self-destructive indulgence. He would try the favours of fashionable courtesans and generously help in their financial difficulties, but such relaxation played a minor role in a life he had dedicated to service to the nation.

He was always courteous, even when administering his sharp and unequivocal rebuffs to pretension and impertinence. Only in moments of intense provocation did his language become coarse and his temper out of control – outbursts which he sincerely regretted as soon as committed – his immediate family causing him to lose his temper more frequently than when in controversy with others. Once his fury passed, the matter was finished – he did not hold a grudge and would be on good terms with an offender as soon as a rebuke had been made and a fault acknowledged.

His most deeply held conviction was that the greatest evil that could be inflicted on a nation was civil strife. The first task of government was to ensure peace and security for the common people in their daily lives. In Ireland, in India and in Spain he had seen populations living in constant fear of their own kind, as well as of invaders – unable to understand the misery they suffered, victims of unscrupulous men who murdered, plundered and destroyed the social fabric of their existence, often in the spurious name of freedom and liberty. 'I would sacrifice my life', he once said, 'to avoid even one month of civil strife.'

He knew, as every solider knew only too well, the duality of human nature: evil and good being equally strong motives for individual behaviour; cruelty and greed, endemic in every personality, were restrained by moral decisions, based on principles inculcated most clearly in the Christian religion and the rule of law. Without these concepts and restraints, men were capable of the greatest cruelty, their atrocities calculated and deliberate. It was the release of these forces of evil on a defenceless population that he most feared and hated. For the remainder of his life he concentrated his diplomatic and political efforts on the preservation of peace, both at home and abroad. In this he was successful for nearly forty years, until his death in 1852.

For Kitty, the future held little tranquillity; a life devoted to her children combined with constant effort to please her husband or at least to avoid his criticism; a life of atonement for an error of judgement or a breach of trust connected with Ireland for which Arthur, usually so quick to forgive, never forgave her; a life of exile from the land of her birth which she had continued to love and he regarded with the deepest distrust.

She found consolation at Stratfield Saye, the house in Hampshire that became her home and where her happiest hours were spent with her children, although the later years were passed in periods of isolation and loneliness. She never learnt from her mistakes and remained impulsively generous to friends and relations in spite of the smallness of her allowance and occasional exploitation; the inevitable debts she concealed by borrowing, keeping the secret during her lifetime. Her greatest triumph was her devotion to children, bringing up not only her two boys, but the children of broken marriages in the Wellesley family, as well as an orphaned niece and the son of a woman she never met, Arthur's godson, whose family he had befriended in India.

Through all runs the theme of romantic love, a concept she obstinately refused to abandon in the face of every vicissitude. Not long before her death in 1831, she wrote to a friend, quoting an old French song

> which has been running in my head...

>> Oui, ma folie est de l'aimer
>> Je l'aimerai toute ma vie.
>> Gronde moi, si c'est ton envie
>> Mais ne crois pas me corriger
>> Car ma folie est de l'aimer
>> Je l'aimerai toute ma vie....

> So I will: I swore it.

# Appendix 1. Relationships

*The author is indebted to* Burke's Peerage *for much of the information in Appendix I.*

## KITTY PAKENHAM (FATHER'S SIDE): PAKENHAM/LONGFORD

THOMAS PAKENHAM (1718–66), 1st Baron LONGFORD (cr. 1756), married (1739/40) ELIZABETH, Countess of LONGFORD (cr. 1785), daughter and sole heiress of Michael Cuffe. She died 1794. Issue,
sons:
1 *Edward Michael* (*2nd Baron*) (*Kitty's father*)
2 Robert (died 1775)
3 William (1756–69)
4 Thomas (Sir) (1757–1836), Admiral. Married (1785) Louisa, daughter of John Staples by Henrietta, daughter of William Conolly of Castletown, with issue
daughters:
1 Frances, born 1744, married J.O. Vandeleur, with issue
2 Helena, born 1745, married William Sherlock, with issue
3 Mary, born 1749, married Thomas Fortescue, with issue

EDWARD MICHAEL PAKENHAM (1743–92), 2nd Baron LONGFORD, Post-Captain RN, married (1768) CATHERINE, daughter of Hercules Langford Rowley and Elizabeth, Viscountess Langford. Catherine died 1816. Issue,
sons:
1 Thomas (3rd Baron and 2nd Earl)
2 Edward Michael (Sir) (1778–1815), Major-General
3 Hercules Robert (Sir) (1781–1850), Lieutenant-General, married (1817) Emily Stapleton (Le Despencer), with issue
4 William, Captain RN (drowned, 1811)
5 Henry (Very Revd), Dean of St Patrick's (1787–1863), married (1822) Eliza Sand (Mountsandford), with issue
daughters:
1 Elizabeth (1770–1851), married (1793) Henry Stewart, with issue
2 *Catherine* (*Kitty*) (1772–1831), married (1806) Arthur Wellesley, 1st Duke of Wellington, with issue (see Mornington/Wesley/Wellesley)
3 Helen (died 1807), married James Hamilton (died 1805). Issue: sons, John, Edward; daughter, Catherine (born posthumously)

4 Caroline (died 1854), married (1808) Henry Hamilton

THOMAS PAKENHAM (1774–1835), 2nd Earl of LONGFORD and 3rd Baron, succeeded to the earldom on the death of his grandmother, Elizabeth, Countess of Longford (1794). Created Baron SILCHESTER, in Peerage of United Kingdom, (1821). Married (1817) GEORGIANA, daughter of 1st Earl Beauchamp. She died 1880. Issue,
sons:
1 Edward Michael, 3rd Earl
2 William Lygon, 4th Earl
3 Thomas
4 Francis
daughters:
1 Katherine
2 Georgiana

FRANCIS AUNGIER PAKENHAM, KG, PC, 7th and present Earl of LONGFORD. Created Baron Pakenham, 1945. Married (1931) ELIZABETH, CBE, daughter of N.B.Harman, FRCS, and Katherine (née Chamberlain) – with issue

## KITTY PAKENHAM (MOTHER'S SIDE): ROWLEY/LANGFORD/BECTIVE/HEADFORT/TAYLOUR

HERCULES LANGFORD ROWLEY, Rt Hon. (*c.*1712–94), married (1732) ELIZABETH ORMSBY, Viscountess LANGFORD, only daughter of Clotworthy Upton, elevated to Peerage of Ireland as Baroness SOMERHILL and Viscountess Langford (with remainder to her male issue) (1766). She died 1791, succceeded by her eldest son. Issue,
sons:
1 Hercules, 2nd Viscount (1737–96), died unmarried; the peerage expired and his niece, Frances Rowley, inherited the estates (see Clotworthy Taylour/Frances Rowley below)
2 Clotworthy, Major (died 1781), married (1775) Elizabeth, daughter of William Crosbie and Frances Wesley and granddaughter, maternally, of Richard Colley (Wesley), Baron Mornington. Issue, daughter, Frances.
3 Arthur
daughters:
1 Jane, married (1754) Thomas, Earl of Bective, and had with other issue (see Bective, below) a 4th son, Clotworthy Taylour, 1st Baron Langford, who married his cousin, Frances Rowley
2 *Catherine* (*Kitty's mother*) married (1768) Edward, Lord Longford (see Pakenham/Longford)

## Appendix 1

THOMAS, 1st EARL BECTIVE (1724–95) (Viscount Headfort), married (1754) JANE, daughter of Hercules Langford ROWLEY and Viscountess Langford (see above). Issue,
sons:
1 Thomas Taylour, 1st Marquis of Headfort
2 Hercules Langford (died unmarried)
3 Robert (died unmarried)
4 Clotworthy Taylour, 1st Baron Langford of Somerhill, married (1794) his cousin, Frances Rowley, with issue
5 Henry
daughters:
1 Marianne Jane
2 Louisa Catherine

## ARTHUR WELLESLEY (FATHER'S SIDE): MORNINGTON/WESLEY/WELLESLEY

RICHARD COLLEY (c.1690–1758), afterwards WESLEY, 1st Baron MORNINGTON married (1719) ELIZABETH (died 1738), daughter of John Sale. Issue,
son:
1 *Garret, 1st Earl* (*Arthur's father*)
daughters:
1 Elizabeth, married (1743) Chichester Fortescue, with issue
2 Frances, married (1750) William Francis Crosbie. Issue, daughter, Elizabeth, married (1775) Clotworthy Rowley.

GARRET, 1st EARL OF MORNINGTON (1735–81), created Viscount Wesley of Dangan Castle and Earl of Mornington (1760). Married (1759) ANNE HILL (1743–1831), daughter of 1st Viscount Dungannon. Issue,
sons:
1 Richard, 2nd Earl of Mornington (1760–1842), cr. Baron Wellesley of Wellesley, Somerset in Peerage of Great Britain (1797) and Marquis Wellesley in Peerage of Ireland (for services as Governor-General of India) (1799). Married (1) (1794) Hyacinthe Roland; (2) (1825) Marianne, widow of Robert Patterson, daughter of Richard Caton of Philadelphia, USA
2 William, 3rd Earl of Mornington and Baron Maryborough (1763–1845), assumed additional name, Pole (1778). Married (1784) Katherine, daughter of John Forbes. Issue,
son:
1 William Pole–Tylney–Long–Wellesley, 4th Earl, married (1812) Catherine, daughter and heiress of Sir James Tylney–Long
daughters:
1 Mary, married Sir Charles Bagot

    2 Emily, married 1st Baron Raglan
    3 Priscilla, married 11th Earl of Westmorland
3 *Arthur, 1st Duke of Wellington* (1769–1852). Married (1806) Catherine (died 1831), daugher of 2nd Baron Longford. Issue,
  sons:
    1 Arthur Richard (Lord Douro), 2nd Duke
    2 Charles, Major-General (1808–58), married (1844) Augusta Sophia (died 1893), daughter of Henry Manvers Pierrepont. Issue,
      sons:
        1 Arthur (died in infancy)
        2 Henry, 3rd Duke
        3 Arthur Charles, 4th Duke
      daughters:
        1 Victoria Alexandrina
        2 Mary Angela
        3 Georgiana
4 Gerald Valerian (Revd) (1770–1848), Prebendary of Durham. Married (1802) Emily, daughter of 1st Earl Cadogan (eloped 1819; died 1833). Issue,
  sons:
    1 Arthur
    2 William Henry Charles
    3 George Greville (Sir)
  daughters:
    1 Emily
    2 Georgiana
    3 Mary
    4 Cecil Elizabeth
5 Henry (1773–1847), created Baron Cowley of Wellesley, Somerset (1828). Married (1) (1803) Charlotte, daughter of 1st Earl Cadogan (divorced 1810. She married (2) Marquis of Anglesey). Issue,
  sons:
    1 Henry, 1st Earl
    2 William
    3 Gerald (Very Revd, Dean of Windsor), fostered by Duke and Duchess of Wellington
  daughter:
    1 Charlotte Arbuthnot
  Henry married (2) (1816) Georgiana, daughter of the Marquis of Salisbury.
daughters:
1 Anne, married (1) (1790) Henry Fitzroy, son of 1st Baron Southampton (he died 1794). Issue, daughters, Georgiana (died 1821), married (1814) Henry, Earl of Worcester (7th Duke of Beaufort), and Caroline. Anne married (2) (1799) Culling Charles Smith. Issue,
  daughter:

*Appendix 1*

    1 Emily Frances, married (1822) her stepsister's widower, Henry, 7th Duke of Beaufort
    NB   The name, Culling Charles Smith, is frequently recorded, in error, as 'Charles Culling Smith'
2 Mary (1772–94)

ARTHUR RICHARD, 2nd DUKE OF WELLINGTON (1807–84), Lieutenant-General. Married (1839) Lady Elizabeth Hay (died 1904), daughter of 8th Marquis of Tweeddale. Inherited dukedom and other British and foreign titles from his father in 1852 and Irish honours on the death of his cousin, the 5th Earl of Mornington, in 1863. Died without issue; succeeded by his nephew, Henry, 3rd Duke (see above)

ARTHUR VALERIAN WELLESLEY, 8th and present Duke of WELLINGTON, LVO, OBE, MC, DL. Married (1944) Diana Ruth, daughter of Major-General D.F.McConnel. Issue, four sons, one daughter

## ARTHUR WELLESLEY (MOTHER'S SIDE): HILL/ HILL-TREVOR/DUNGANNON

JOHN TREVOR, Sir (1637–1717), of Brynkinalt, Denbighshire. Master of the Rolls (UK), Speaker of the House of Commons. Married Jane (died 1704), daughter of Sir Roger Mostyn of Flint. Issue: four sons (died without issue) and a daughter, Anne, married (1) Michael Hill of Hillsborough, Co. Down. Issue,
    sons:
    1 Trevor (1693–1742), created Viscount Hill of Hillsborough, married Mary Rowe (died 1742). Issue: Wills Hill, 1st Marquis of Downshire (1718–93); and Anne, married 1st Earl Moira
    2 Arthur, assumed name Hill-Trevor, Viscount Dungannon and Baron Hill
Anne married (2) Alan Brodrick, Viscount Midleton

ARTHUR HILL-TREVOR, Viscount DUNGANNON (died 1771), of Belvoir, Co. Down, and Brynkinalt, Denbighshire. Chancellor, Irish Exchequer (1754–5). Married (secondly 1737) Anne (died 1799), daughter of Edmund Francis Stafford of Brownstown, Co. Meath, and Portglenone, Co. Antrim. Issue: two sons and a daughter, not recorded, and
son:
1 Arthur, married Letitia, daughter of Hervey, 1st Viscount Mountmorres. Issue, Arthur Trevor-Hill (1763–1837), 2nd Viscount Dungannon
daughter:
1 *Anne (died 1831), married (1759) Garret, 1st Earl of Mornington* (see Mornington/Wesley/Wellesley)

*Appendix 2. Family Trees*

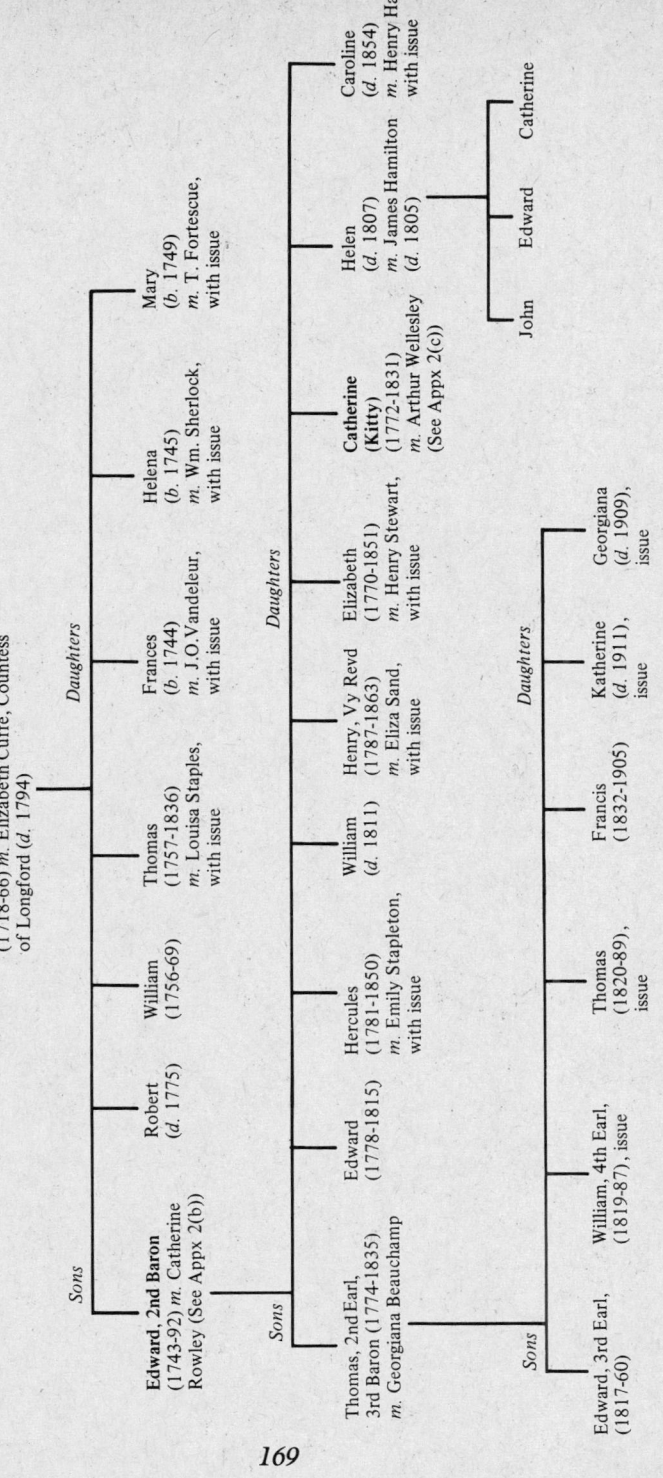

## (b) ROWLEY/LANGFORD/HEADFORT/BECTIVE/TAYLOUR (KITTY – MOTHER'S SIDE)

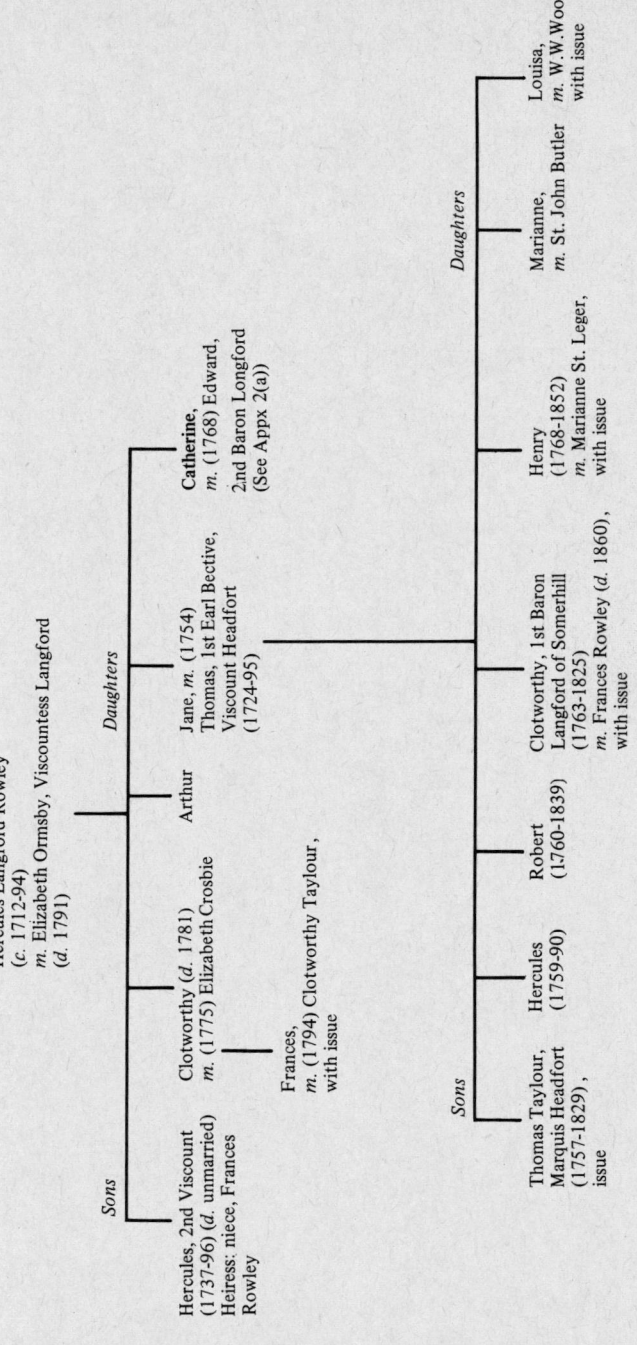

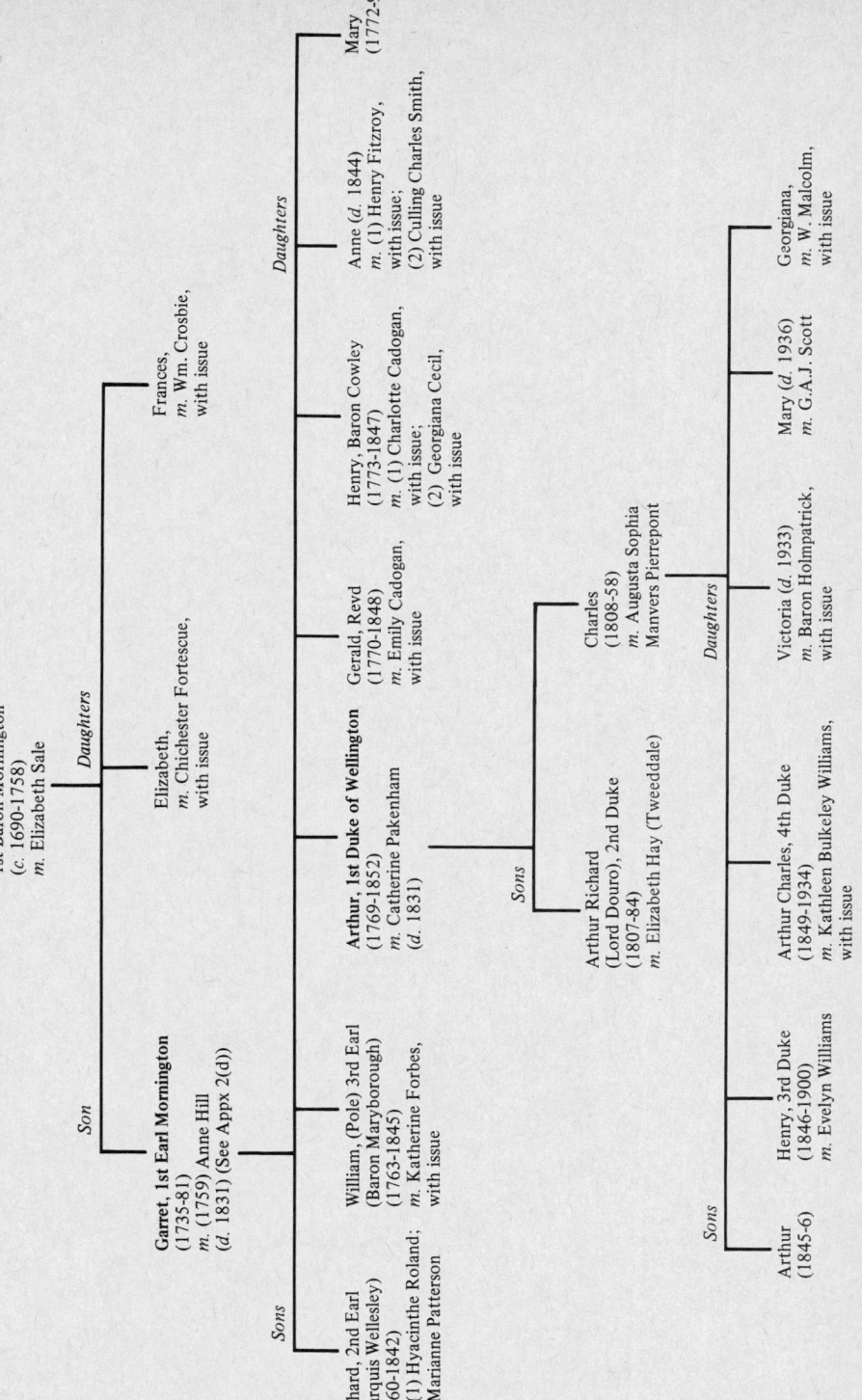

## (d) HILL/HILL-TREVOR/DUNGANNON (ARTHUR – MOTHER'S SIDE)

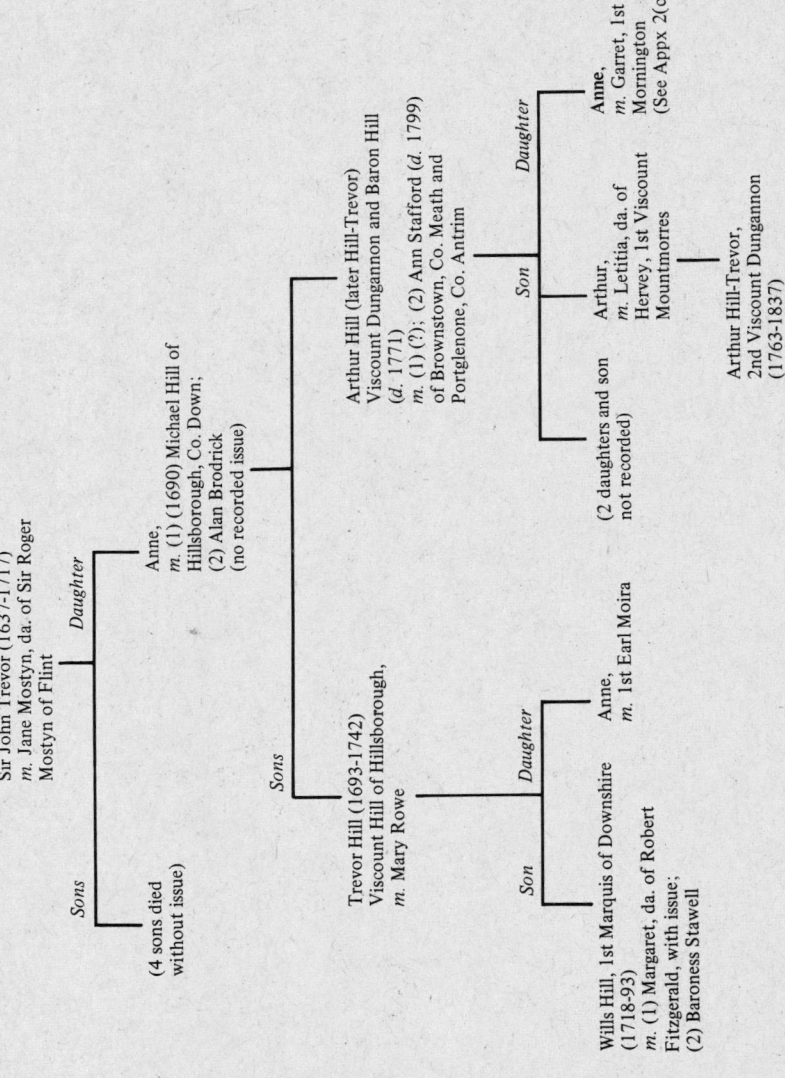

# Appendix 3. Wellington's Career (Summary)

1769 Birth of Hon. Arthur Wesley
    (Birth of Napoleon Bonaparte)
1787 Ensign
1790 MP for Trim, Co. Meath
1793 (France declares war on Britain)
1796 Colonel – sails for India
1798 Name changed to Wellesley
1799 Battle of Seringapatam
1803 Battle of Assaye
1804 Order of the Bath
1805 Returns to England
    (Battle of Trafalgar)
    Expedition to the Elbe
1806 Colonel of the 33rd Regiment
    MP for Rye, Sussex (later for other constituencies)
    Marries Catherine Pakenham
    Defends brother Richard in House of Commons
1807 Birth of Arthur Richard Wellesley (son, later Lord Douro)
    Chief Secretary of Ireland
    Commands Copenhagen expedition and returns to Ireland
1808 Birth of Charles (second son)
    Lieutenant-General, commands expedition to Portugal
    Battle of Vimeiro and Convention of Cintra
    Returns of Ireland
1809     (Death of Sir John Moore at Corunna, Spain)
    Resigns as Chief Secretary
    Commands expeditionary force to Portugal
    Enters Spain, Battle of Talavera
    Created Viscount Wellington of Talavera
    Retreat to Portugal, begins construction of Lines of Torres Vedras
1810 Battles of Ciudad Rodrigo (Spain), Almeida and Bussaco (Portugal)

|      | Enters Lines of Torres Vedras |
|------|-------------------------------|
| 1811 | Sieges of Badajoz, battle of Albuera (Spain), etc. |
| 1812 | Storming of Ciudad Rodrigo |

      Created Earl Wellington, Grandee of Spain, Ducque de Ciudad Rodrigo
      Battle of Salamanca, enters Madrid
      Created Marquis Wellington
      Siege of Burgos, retreat to Portugal
      Created Duque da Victoria (Portugal)
        (French retreat from Moscow)

1813  Knight of the Garter
      Battle of Vitoria, defeat of Joseph Bonaparte
      Becomes Field-Marshal
      Battles of the Pyrenees and San Sebastian
      Crosses Bidassoa into France

1814  Investment of Bayonne, battle of Orthez
      Allies enter Paris, abdication of Napoleon
      Battle of Toulouse
        (Louis XVIII returns to France. Napoleon exiled to Elba)
      Created Duke of Wellington; ambassador to France
      Returns to England for victory celebrations and reunion with family

1815  (Napoleon escapes from Elba and lands in France)
      Battle of Waterloo. Created Prince of Waterloo (by Prince of Orange)
        (Napoleon exiled to St Helena)

Wellington in civil life served as Master-General of the Ordnance, Commander-in-Chief, Prime Minister (1828–9), Lord Warden of the Cinque Ports, Foreign Secretary, etc.

Death of Duchess of Wellington, 1831; Death of Duke of Wellington at Walmer Castle, Kent, 1852.

# *Manuscript and Published Sources*

Quotations, letters and other source material used in this book are mainly from the Personal Papers of the 1st Duke and Duchess of Wellington in the archives at Stratfield Saye, unless otherwise indicated. These are the property of the present Duke and may not be reproduced without his authority. Among other published and unpublished sources consulted are those listed below. The Official Papers of the 1st Duke – military, parliamentary, etc. – are in Southampton University Library.

## CHAPTER 1. PATRIMONY AND POLITICS

1 Edgeworth, Richard Lovell, *Memoirs*, 2 vols (London, 1820).
2 Edgeworth, Maria, *Life and Letters*, 2 vols, ed. Hare (London, 1894).
3 Longford, Elizabeth, *Wellington*, 2 vols. I. *Years of the Sword* (London, 1969). (Hamwood Papers.)
4 Young, Arthur, *A Tour in Ireland* (Dublin, 1780).
5 Froude, James Anthony, *The English in Ireland in the 18th Century*, 3 vols (London, 1881), vol. III.
6 The original spelling of Somerhill is retained in the family title; Summerhill is used when referring to the estate.

## CHAPTER 2. LORD LONGFORD'S 'DETERMINATION'

1 Guedalla, Philip, *The Duke* (London, 1964).
2 Longford, I.
3 Barrington, Sir Jonah, *Selections from his Personal Sketches*, ed. Hugh Staples (London, 1968).
4 Guinness, Desmond, and Ryan, William, *Irish Houses and Castles* (London, 1971).
5 Pakenham, Thomas, *The Year of Liberty: The Great Irish Rebellion of 1798* (London, 1969).
6 Maxwell, Sir Herbert, *Life of Wellington*, 2 vols (London, 1899), vol. I.

## CHAPTER 3. THE STORM

1 Maxwell, I.
2 Guedalla.
3 Longford, I.
4 Guedalla.

## CHAPTER 4. REBELLION

1 Guedalla.
2 Pakenham, Thomas.
3 Cole, Sir Galbraith Lowry, *Memoirs*, ed. Maud Lowry Cole and Stephen Gwynn (London, 1934).
4 Froude, III.
5 Froude, III.
6 MacDermot, Frank, *Tone and his Times* (revised edn, Ireland, 1969).
7 Froude, III (Cornwallis to Portland, June 1798).
8 Pakenham, Thomas.
9 Froude, III.
10 Pakenham, Thomas.
11 Edgeworth, Maria.
12 Pakenham, Thomas.
13 Pakenham, Thomas.
14 Froude, III (Cornwallis to Ross, 1799).
15 Hickey, William, *Memoirs*, 4 vols, ed. Alfred Spencer (London, 1925).
16 Moore, Thomas, 'Pro Patria Mori', *The Golden Treasury*, ed. F.T.Palgrave.
17 Moore, Thomas, 'The Journey Onwards', *The Golden Treasury*.
18 Cole, *Memoirs*.
19 Maxwell, Constantia, *Dublin Under the Georges, 1718–1830* (London, 1956).
20 Guinness and Ryan.
21 Pakenham Letters, 1800–1815, ed. Thomas, 5th Earl of Longford (killed in action, 1915) (privately printed, 1914).
22 *Pakenham Letters*.
23 Cole, *Memoirs*.

## CHAPTER 5. LETTER TO INDIA

1 Bryant, Sir Arthur, *The Great Duke* (London, 1971).
2 Bryant.
3 Cole, *Memoirs*.
4 Longford, I.
5 *Pakenham Letters*.

## CHAPTER 6. MATRIMONIAL DILEMMA

1 Cole, *Memoirs*.
2 Wellington, *The Despatches of Field Marshal the Duke of Wellington*, 12 vols, ed. Lt-Col. Gurwood, (India, 1803; London, 1834–8).
3 Maxwell, Sir Herbert, 1.
4 Longford, 1.

## CHAPTER 7. 'CHANCE OF HER FAVOUR ...'

1 Longford, 1.
2 Wellington, *Supplementary Despatches, Correspondence and Memoranda of Field Marshal Arthur, Duke of Wellington*, 11 vols, ed. 2nd Duke of Wellington (India, 1803; London, 1858–64).
3 Longford, 1.
4 Guedalla.

## CHAPTER 8. BUSINESS AT HOME

1 Wellesley, Muriel, *The Man Wellington* (London, 1937).
2 Edgeworth, Maria.
3 Calvert, Frances, *An Irish Beauty of the Regency*, Journals, ed. Mrs Warrene Blake (London, 1911).
4 Calvert, Frances.
5 Stanhope, Philip Henry, 5th Earl, *Life of Pitt* (London, 1879), quoted Longford 1.
6 Guedalla.
7 Wellesley, Muriel.
8 Pakenham/Balfour, ms letter, March 1806. National Library of Ireland, Dublin.

## CHAPTER 9. FIVE DUBLIN DAYS

1 Longford, 1.
2 Edgeworth, Maria.
3 Wellington, *Speeches of the Duke of Wellington in Parliament*, ed. Lt-Col. Gurwood (London, 1854).
4 Longford, 1.
5 Edgeworth, Maria.
6 *Saunders's News-Letter and Daily Advertiser*, Dublin, 10 June, 1806; National Library of Ireland, Dublin.
7 *Freeman's Journal*, Dublin, 12 June 1806; National Library of Ireland, Dublin.
8 British Museum Additional Manuscripts (Wellesley Papers) 37415.

9 BM Add Mss 37415.

## CHAPTER 10. AN ENEMY'S COUNTRY

1 Calvert, Frances.
2 *Despatches* (1807).
3 Longford, I.
4 Wellington, *Civil Correspondence and Memoranda of Field Marshal Arthur, Duke of Wellington, Ireland, 1807–9*, ed. 2nd Duke of Wellington (London, 1860).
5 *Civil Correspondence*.
6 *Civil Correspondence*.
7 *Civil Correspondence*.

## CHAPTER 11. THE HOUSE IN THE PARK

1 *Pakenham Letters*.
2 *Camden Miscellany*, 'Some Letters of the Duke of Wellington to his Brother William Wellesley-Pole', ed. Sir Charles Webster, vol. XVIII (September 1807), Royal Historical Society.
3 *Civil Correspondence* (Ireland).
4 *Despatches*, 1807.
5 Hamilton, John, *Sixty Years an Irish Landlord* (London, 1894).
6 Longford, I.
7 Edgeworth, Maria.
8 *Civil Correspondence* (Ireland).
9 *Pakenham Letters*.
10 Swinton, Mrs J.R. *A Sketch of the Life of Georgiana, Lady de Ros*, by her daughter (London, 1893).
11 *Civil Correspondence* (Ireland).
12 Croker, John Wilson, *The Croker Papers*, 3 vols (London, 1884), vol. I.
13 BM Add Mss 37415.
14 *Supp. Despatches*, 1808.
15 *Civil Correspondence*, (Ireland).
16 Edgeworth, Maria.
17 Longford, I.

## CHAPTER 12. 'TILL MY HUSBAND RETURNS'

1 Calvert, Frances.

## CHAPTER 13. THE PUBLIC GAZE

1 *Supp. Despatches*, 1810.
2 *Pakenham Letters*.
3 *Supp. Despatches*, 1811.

## CHAPTER 14. HOMECOMING

1 *Pakenham Letters.*
2 BM Add Mss 37415.
3 *Pakenham Letters.*
4 Edgeworth, Maria.
5 *Pakenham Letters.*
6 *Pakenham Letters.*
7 *Pakenham Letters.*
8 *Pakenham Letters.*
9 *Supp. Despatches*, 1812.
10 Edgeworth, Maria.
11 Edgeworth, Maria.
12 *Despatches*, 1814.
13 *Camden Misc.*, vol. XVIII.
14 Shelley, Frances, *The Diary of Frances, Lady Shelley, 1787–1817*, ed. Richard Edgcumbe (London, 1912).

# Index

Abercorn, Marquis, 27
Acheson, Lady Olivia (*see* Sparrow)
Addington, Henry, 1st Viscount Sidmouth (Prime Minister), 39, 48, 139
Alice, kitchen maid, 136, 142–3
Amelia, Princess, 136
Antrim, Anne Catherine, Countess of, 15
Antrim, Letitia, Marchioness of, 15
Arbuthnot, Charles, 129, 160
Arbuthnot, Harriet, 68, 160
Astley's Amphitheatre (Assembly Rooms), 139
Aston, Colonel, 57
Athlone, Countess of, 85
Augustein, Mr, 85

Baird, General Sir David, 44
Balfour, Sir Blayney, 26
Balfour, Lady Florence (Cole), 26–7, 36, 76
Barfield's Library, 120, 125
Barrymore, Countess of, 85
Barrington, Sir Jonah, 12
Bathurst, Henry, 3rd Earl, 147, 149
Baxter (*see* Martha)
Bentinck, Lady William, 134
Beresford, Lady Isabella, 15
Beresford, Colonel M., 44, 46–8, 58
Beresford, William de la Poer, Lord Decies, 17, 83
Birchall, Robert (music shop), 65
Blakeney, Miss, 125
Bonaparte, Joseph, King of Spain, 110, 117, 153
Bonaparte, Napoleon (*see* Napoleon)
Braganza, dynasty of, 110

Bristol, Frederick 1st Marquis of, 150
Brodrick Mrs, 118, 139
Boyne, Lady, 150
Buckingham, George Nugent-Temple-Grenville, 1st Marquis of, 4, 66, 68–9, 75
Burgh, Captain (later General Sir) Ulysses (Lord Downes), 135
Burghersh, John Fane, (11th Earl of Westmorland), 143, 150
Burton, Miss, 125
Butler, Lady Eleanor, 5

Calvert, Hon. Mrs Frances, 70, 90, 116, 118, 127
Cambridge, H.R.H. Adolphus Frederick, 1st Duke of, 84
Camden, Sir John Jeffreys Pratt, 2nd Earl of, 17–19, 22, 26, 30
Campbell, Sir Colin, 42, 57, 105
Campbell, Sir John, 42
Canning, George (Prime Minister), 105
Carhampton, Lord, 27–8
Castlereagh, Robert Stewart, Viscount (2nd Marquis of Londonderry), 9, 12, 35–6, 38–9, 75, 91, 94, 104, 113, 124, 139, 147, 156
Cecil, Lady, 90
Charles IV of Spain, 110
Charlotte, Queen, 83, 85
Charleville, Lady, 85
Chatham, John Pitt, 2nd Earl of, 119, 127
Chester, Mary (later Lady Liverpool), 131–3
Clancarty, Richard, 2nd Earl and 1st Viscount, 139

## Index

Clarence, H.R.H. William Henry, Duke of (later William IV),, 142
Clare, Lord Chancellor Fitzgibbon, Earl of, 17–18, 28, 44–5
Clive, Edward, Lord, 43, 47
Cloncurry, Lord, 39
Cole, Florence (*see* Balfour)
Cole, General Sir Galbraith Lowry, 13, 25–8, 30–1, 34, 36, 38, 43–4, 46, 52, 54, 58, 71, 76, 81, 118, 144
Conolly, Louisa, 7
Conolly, Speaker, 7
Cooke, Lieutenant-General Sir George, 17, 45
Cornwallis, Charles, 1st Marquis of, 27, 30, 33, 34, 36, 39, 74
Craufurd, Colonel Sir Charles, 118
Cremorne, Lady, 'Philadelphia Hannah', 136
Croker, John Wilson, 109
Cuesta, General, 117
Cuffe, Michael, 1
Cumberland, H.R.H. Ernest, Duke of, 84, 109

Dalrymple, General Sir Hew, 26
Darnley, Lady Elizabeth, 142
Dashwood, Miss Anna Maria (Lady Ely), 125
De Ros, Lady Georgiana (*see* Lennox)
Dhoondiah Waugh, 43–4, 63
'Diomed', 57
Donegal, Lady Anna, 85, 151
Dorset, Arabella, Duchess of, 132–3
Douro, Arthur Richard Wellesley, Lord (2nd Duke of Wellington), 96, 101, 103, 105, 109–10, 118, 120, 124, 128, 130, 133–4, 137–8, 149, 151, 155–6, 159
Downshire, Lady, 85
Drummond, Mrs John, 129
Dungannon, Lady (Hill-Trevor), 5, 15

East India Company, 22, 41, 52, 57, 61, 65, 82
Edgeworth, Maria, 3, 6, 13, 18–19, 32–4, 46, 54, 61, 70, 77, 81, 83, 92, 106, 113, 146, 150, 152–3, 155, 158
Edgeworth, Richard Lovell, 3, 8, 13, 18–20, 33

Elers, Captain George, 23, 61
Elliot Mr, 98–9
Ely, Lady, 85
Emmet, Robert, 55
Enniskillen, William Willoughby, 1st Earl of, 13, 25, 27, 43
Enniskillen, Lady, 38

Fanshawe, Miss, 21
Farquar, Sir Walter (physician), 118, 129, 150
*Faulkner's Journal*, 8
Ferdinand VII, King of Spain, 110
Fitzgerald, Lord Edward, 7, 13, 29
Fitzgerald, Lady (*see* Genlis, Pamela de)
Fitzgibbon, Earl of Clare (*see* Clare)
Fitzroy, Anne Caroline, 103
Fitzroy, Georgiana, 103
Fitzwilliam, William Wentworth, 2nd Earl of, 16–17
Flight and Barr, Worcester china shop, 65
Fortescue, Sir Chichester, 21
Forsyth, Mr and Mrs, 125
Franklin, Benjamin, 9
Freame, Thomas, 136
*Freeman's Journal*, 85
Freese, Arthur, 62, 101, 118–20, 129–31, 137–40, 161
Freese, Captain John William, 61
Freese, Mrs, 61–2, 101, 137, 139, 148
Freese, Jesse, 139

Genlis Pamela de (Lady Edward Fitzgerald), 13
George III, 5, 17, 22, 38, 91, 123, 127–8, 136–7
George IV (*see* Wales, Prince of and Regent)
Gloucester, H.R.H. William Frederick, 2nd Duke of, 84
Gordon, Captain, 62
Gordon, Mrs, 62
Gosford, Lady, 129
Granard, George, 6th Earl of, 8, 18
Grattan, Henry, 9, 11, 16–18
Grenville, William Wyndham, Baron (Prime Minister), 75, 87
Greville, Charles, 131, 134

*182*

# Index

Hamilton, Mrs Henry (Caroline Pakenham), 46, 80, 86, 110, 113, 121
Hamilton: (Helen Pakenham's children), 66, 93, 95, 97, 99, 105, 146; Catherine, 14–15, 21, 161; Edward, 'race' in Phoenix Park, 78
Hamilton, Henry, 110
Hamilton, Mrs James (Helen Pakenham), 36, 46, 51, 66, 78, 80, 95
Hamilton, James, 66
Hamilton, Sir William, 83
Hardwicke, Philip, 3rd Earl of, 39
Hardwicke, Lady, 39–40
Harrington, Earl of, 110
Harrington, Lady, 118
Harris, General George, 38, 43
Hawkesbury, Robert Bankes, Lord (see Liverpool, Earl of)
Headfort, Marquis of, 97
Headfort, Lady, 85–6
Hertford, Francis, 2nd Marquis of, 104
Hickey, William, 36
Hill-Trevor (see Dungannon)
Hoche, General Lazare, 25–6
Hood, Lady, 124, 139
Hope, Thomas, 84
Hope, Mrs, 83, 140
Humbert, General, 31–4
Hume, Surgeon, 136, 138

Johnston, Francis, 12, 39

Kenmore, Lady, 85
Keogh, John, 8–9
Kilwarden, Lord Chief Justice, 55

Lake, General, 27–9, 33–4
Langford, Viscountess, 6, 9
Langford, Lady Elizabeth (see Rowley)
Lawrence, Sir Thomas, 134
Lee (Spithead mutineer), 28
Legge, Revd and Hon. Augustus George, 132–3
Legge, Mrs Honora, 132–3
Leinster, Amelia, Duchess of, 7, 85
Lennox, Lady Charlotte, 112, 137
Lennox, Lady Georgiana (later de Ros), 108
Lennox, Lady Louisa, 112, 137

Lennox, Lady Louisa (see Conolly)
Limerick, Lord Bishop of, 109
Liverpool, Robert Bankes (Hawkesbury), 2nd Earl of (Prime Minister), 93–4, 104–5, 109, 118, 124, 129–30, 135–7, 147, 149, 156–8
Liverpool, Lady Louisa Theodosia, 121, 137–9, 141, 143, 150, 152
Longford, Lady Catherine, 1, 3, 10–11, 15, 39, 45–6, 49–50, 60, 66, 69, 71, 75, 77, 81, 85, 89–90, 93, 95, 97, 100, 102, 109–10, 131, 133–6, 139, 145–8, 152
Longford, Lord Edward Pakenham, 2nd Baron, 1, 6, 8, 10–11
Longford, Elizabeth, Countess of, 1, 10–11, 13
Longford, Thomas, 2nd Earl, 3rd Baron, 11–15, 31, 34, 39, 47, 49, 54, 60, 69, 71, 80, 94, 100, 110–12, 117–21, 123, 125, 136, 139, 142–5, 147–9
Louis XVI, 12–13
Louis XVIII, 156

Mackinnon, Colonel, 146
McKenzie, Lady, 141
Malcolm, Sir John, 61, 74, 91, 148–9, 153–5
Manchester, Duchess of, 127
Manners, Lord, 106
Mansfield, Lady, 90
Marie Antoinette, Queen of France, 13
Martha (Baxter), 119, 126, 128, 133
Massena, Marshal André, 131, 135
Mayo, Dr John, 134, 136, 142–3
Mirabeau, 9
Molyneux, 9
Moore, General Sir John, 31, 35, 111, 113
Moore, Thomas, 37
Mornington, Anne Hill, Countess of, 4, 110, 119, 128, 130, 135, 137, 140
Mornington, Garret Wesley, 1st Earl and 2nd Baron of, 4
Mornington, Richard Colley Wesley, 2nd Earl of (see Wellesley, R.C.W., Marquis)
Murphy, Father John, 31
Muckle, Mr, 120
Mulgrave, Lady, 118, 143
Munster, Count of, 133
Mysore, Rajah of, 42–3

# Index

Napoleon Bonaparte, Emperor of the French, 23, 25, 31, 41, 48, 55, 64, 73–4, 95, 102, 110, 117–18, 155–6
Nelson, Admiral Lord Horatio, 73
Nelson, Lady Sarah, 124–5
Nelson, William (succeeded brother as Baron of the Nile, Viscount Merton, Earl of Trafalgar), 125
Nelson, Charlotte (Lady Bridport), 125
Newcastle, Anna Maria, Dowager Duchess of, 118
Newport, Lady, 85
Nollekens, Joseph, 118, 138

Ormonde, Walter, Marquis and 18th Earl of, 45

Packer, Margaret, 151
Page, John, 10
Paget, Lady Charlotte (*see* Wellesley, Charlotte)
Paget, Lord Henry, Earl of Uxbridge, Marquis of Anglesey, 140–2
Pakenham, Caroline (*see* Hamilton, Mrs Henry)
Pakenham, Catherine (Kitty), Duchess of Wellington (*see* Wellington, 1st Duchess of)
Pakenham, General Sir Edward, 13, 35, 39, 46–7, 76, 80–1, 92, 95, 100, 102–3, 106, 108, 122–3, 125, 129, 131, 144–9, 154–5
Pakenham, Elizabeth (Bess) (*see* Stewart, Mrs Henry)
Pakenham, Helen, (*see* Hamilton, Mrs James)
Pakenham, Henry, Dean of St Patrick's, 46, 105–7, 113, 133, 136
Pakenham, General Sir Hercules, 39, 46, 100, 102–3, 106, 108, 111, 123, 144–51
Pakenham, Louisa (Staples), 6–7, 29, 74, 76–8, 80
Pakenham, Admiral Thomas, 6, 19, 30, 34, 45–6, 52, 56, 92, 99–100, 102, 119
Pakenham, Thomas (*see* Longford, 2nd Earl of)
Pakenham, Tom (son of Admiral Pakenham), 7–8, 52, 56–7, 80

Pakenham, Captain William, R.N., 46, 130, 143, 145–6
Paull, James, 82–3
Penn, William, 136
Percival, Spencer (Prime Minister), 147
Pius VII, Pope, 55
Pitt, William (Prime Minister), 6, 9, 16–17, 30, 39, 44–5, 55, 64, 73–5
Pole (*see* Wellesley-Pole)
Portland, William Bentinck, 3rd Duke of (Prime Minister), 30, 91, 109
Prussia, Frederick William III, King of, 158

Quin, Major Wyndham, 118

Rawdon, Mrs Frances, 125
Regent, Prince (*see* Wales, Prince of)
Richmond, Charles Lennox, 4th Duke of, 91–3, 95–6, 106–14, 137
Richmond, Charlotte, Duchess of, 106, 121
Richmond, children (*see* Lennox)
Rivers, George, 2nd Baron, 139
Roland, Hyacinthe (*see* Wellesley, Lady)
Ross, David, 57
Rowley, Lady Elizabeth (Crosbie), 30, 49, 80–1, 83, 93
Rowley, Rt Hon. Hercules Langford, 1
Rowley, Hercules, 2nd Viscount Langford, 9
Russia, Alexander I, Emperor of, 158

Salisbury, Emily Mary, Marchioness of, 89–90, 113, 158
Saltoun, Lady, 127
St Helens, Alleyne Fitzherbert, Baron, 139
*Saunders's News-Letter*, 84
Scott, Sir Walter, 3, 134, 153
Seymour, Lady Robert, 132
Shawe, Colonel Meyrick, 56, 132
Shelley, Lady Frances, 158
Sherlock, Mr, 94
Scindiah, Prince of Gwalior, 56–7, 61
Slater, Josiah, 134, 138, 141
Smith, Adam, 22
Smith, Lady Anne (Wellesley, Fitzroy), 94
Smith, Culling Charles, 99
Smith, Henrietta, 23

*184*

## Index

Sneyd, Mary (Edgeworth), 146
Somerset, Fitzroy, 1st Lord Raglan, 119
Soult, Marhsal, 155
Southey, Robert, 151
Sparrow, General Robert Bernard, 26
Sparrow, Lady Olivia (Acheson), 26, 44–50, 52–3, 55–6, 58–9, 61, 64, 66, 68–73, 81–2, 138–40, 143, 157
Staples, Grace, 6–7
Staples, Louisa Anne (see Pakenham, Louisa)
Stewart, Mrs Henry (Elizabeth, 'Bess', Pakenham), 12, 19, 46, 69, 80, 93, 151
Stewart, Henry, 12, 80, 93
Steward, Miss, 138
Stewart, Lord Robert (see Castlereagh)
Stewart, Lady Selina, 142
Swift, Dean, 22

Taylour, General Sir Robert, 131, 138
Taylour, Lady Catherine, 97
Teeling, Barclay, 32
Templetown, Lady Mary, 85, 118
Tierney, George, 30
Thomond, Lady, 85–6
Tipoo Sultan, 38
Toler, John, 1st Earl of Norbury, 17
Tone, Theobald Wolfe, 9, 11, 25–6, 28–32, 35
Tone, Mathew, 32, 34
Torrens, Colonel Henry, 119, 121, 136, 139, 146
Tyrone, Lord, 27

Villiers, John Charles, 3rd Earl of Clarendon, 113, 139

Wales, George, Prince of (and Regent), 84–5, 133–4, 147, 149, 158
Warren, Admiral Sir John, 35
Washington, George, 5, 9
Waterford, Lady, 85–6
Webbe, Josiah, 43
Wellesley, Anne (see Smith)
Wellesley, Arthur (see Wellington, 1st Duke of)
Wellesley, Arthur (Gerald's son), 101
Wellesley, Arthur Richard (see Douro, Marquis of)

Wellesley, Charles, 108–10, 120, 133–4, 137, 148–9, 151, 159
Wellesley, Lady Charlotte (Paget), 122, 138, 140–2
Wellesley, Charlotte (Henry's daughter), 122
Wellesley, Gabrielle Hyacinthe, Lady (Roland), 15, 65
Wellesley, Gerald Valerian, Prebendary of Durham, 76, 78–81, 101, 140–2
Wellesley, Gerald (Henry's son, later Dean of Windsor) 122, 140, 143, 149, 151, 153
Wellesley, Henry (Lord Cowley), 37, 43–4, 80, 91, 101, 122–6, 140–2, 156
Wellesley, Richard Colley, Marquis of (Mornington, 2nd Earl of), 4–6, 10, 12, 15, 18–19, 21–2, 27, 37–8, 41, 43, 52, 60–1, 64–5, 75–6, 80, 82–3, 87, 91, 110–11, 128–9, 135, 145, 147, 150, 156–7
Wellesley-Pole, Mrs William, 68, 123, 139, 142
Wellesley-Pole, William (Mornington, 3rd Earl of and Baron Maryborough), 5, 35, 68, 71, 80, 82, 87, 91, 104, 121, 124, 129, 139–40, 147, 149–50, 156–7
Wellesley-Pole, William (Tylney-Long, Mornington, 4th Earl of) 128, 132, 145
Wellington, Arthur, 1st Duke of: ADC, 3–4; MP for Trim, 5, 21; Flanders campaign, 14, 18; sails for India, 22–3; attitude to India, 22, 41–4, 61; Seringapatam, 38; Assaye, 56–7; sails for home, 61; MP for Rye, 76; Chief Secretary, Ireland, 91–4; attitude to Ireland, 73, 93, 101–2, 106–7, 116; Danish expedition, 95–6, 100, 103–4; Portuguese expedition, 110–12; Cintra enquiry, 112–13; command in Portugal, 113; takes Oporto, 116; Peninsula war, background, 110–11, 117–18; Viscount Wellington, 124; Vitoria, Field Marshal, 153; battles in France, 155; Dukedom, in Paris, 156; appointed Ambassador, 156–7; returns home, 159–60; family, 3–6, 15; character and appearance, 4–6, 10–11, 13–14, 23, 64–5, 77, 79, 109, 154–6, 160–1;

*185*

# Index

Wellington, Arthur, 1st Duke of (*contd.*) letters about Kitty; 44–8, 52, 55–61, 66, 68–9; marriage proposal, 10–11, 14; second proposal, 68–72; marriage settlement, 75–6; marriage, 79–81; domestic fantasy, 67–8; desire for active service, 87, 94, 105, 113; visits Cheltenham, 68–75; hunting, 79, 89–91, 113, 155; homes in London, 22, 65, 73, 81–2, 87, 114; gossip, 23, 52–3, 59–62, 83; views on morality, 42, 52, 56–7, 59–60, 127, 156–7, 159, 160–1; bravery, 42, 57, 148; music, 4, 13–14, 62, 65, 79; shopping, 65–6; books, 10, 18, 22, 43, 62; health, 21, 44, 61, 74, 94, 107, 154; homesickness, 37, 45; views on service, 80, 94–5, 156, 160–1; fond of children, 62–3, 95, 105–6, 112, 116; will, 101–3; Kitty's 'deception', 114–16; wounded, 155; political problems, 64–5, 67, 74–6, 82–3, 91, 156–7; Richmond's friendship, 109, 112, 114, 137

Wellington, Catherine, 1st Duchess of (Kitty Pakenham): family, 1–3, 6–7, 9, 11, 20, 36, 66–7; character and appearance, 3–4, 6, 10, 19, 22, 29, 53–4, 70, 77, 79, 113–4, 121, 126, 139, 142, 152–3, 158, 161–2; friends in Ireland, 3, 6–7, 13, 25–8, 31, 36, 40, 44, 52, 89; courtship, 6, 10, 28, 34, 44, 49–50, 53, 59, 67–74, 76–8; marriage proposal refused, 10–11; second proposal, 69–72; communication embargo, 15, 18, 22, 44, 48, 55, 70, 83; Lowry Cole affair, 25–8, 30–1, 36, 38, 44, 46, 54, 58; Cheltenham, 54; marriage, 76–81; marriage settlement, 75–6; pregnancies, 82, 87–8, 95–6, 104–7; childbirth, 90, 107; baptisms, 109–10; health, 20–1, 54, 74, 77, 134, 137, 149; religious conviction, 29, 51–3, 122, 125–6, 132; housekeeping, 89, 97, 107, 114, 126–7, 136, 138; London homes, 81–2, 87, 92–3, 114, 135–6, 151, 155; Secretary's Lodge, 93, 100, 103, 105–9, 111, 113–14; leaves Ireland, 113–14; unpaid bills, 97–8, 114; Helen's death, 95; maid's suicide, 96–8; poetry, 7–8, 20–1, 51–2, 162; music, 6, 10, 19, 121, 125, 132–3, 140, 143; painting, 19, 138, 141; shoe-making, 118–19, 129, 135; libraries, 119–20, 122, 125, 127–8, 132; sea-bathing, 119–20, 125, 127–8; children's education, 118, 128–9, 131, 135–6, 149–51; portraits, 134, 137–8, 146; begins journal, 118; dislike of public appearances, 133–4, 137, 139, 149–50, 153–4, 158; Wellington's attitude to, 'neglect', 82–3, 98, 108, 111, 114, 116, 135, 157, 160–1; Broadstairs, 119, 145; Tunbridge Wells, 131, 148; Ramsgate, 119–22, 127–8; fosters Arthur Freese, 118, 129–31, 137, 139–40; fosters Gerald Wellesley, 122–3, 126, 140–3; William's death, 145–6; Hercules wounded, 147, 149; entertainments: Antrim ball, 15, Hopes' reception, 83–5, presented at Court, 83, Queen's Drawing-room, 85–7, Salisbury reception, 158–9; titles, 123–5, 149, 151–2, 154–6; Wellington's invitation, 'ambassadress', 158; receives Allied monarchs, 158; reunion with Wellington, 160

Wesley (see Wellesley), change of spelling, 27

Westmorland, John Fane, 10th Earl of, 4, 9, 15–16, 18, 91

Whitworth, Lord, 132

William, Lady, 52, 59, 60

Wyatt, Benjamin Dean, 100

York, H.R.H. Frederick Augustus, Duke of and Albany, 14

Young, Arthur, 6

'Young Betty', 150